Communications in Computer and Information Science   **798**

Commenced Publication in 2007
Founding and Former Series Editors:
Alfredo Cuzzocrea, Xiaoyong Du, Orhun Kara, Ting Liu, Dominik Ślęzak,
and Xiaokang Yang

More information about this series at http://www.springer.com/series/7899

Miguel Botto-Tobar · Nelly Esparza-Cruz
Joffre León-Acurio · Narcisa Crespo-Torres
Marola Beltrán-Mora (Eds.)

Technology Trends

Third International Conference, CITT 2017
Babahoyo, Ecuador, November 8–10, 2017
Proceedings

 Springer

Editors

Miguel Botto-Tobar (iD)
Eindhoven University of Technology
Eindhoven
The Netherlands

Nelly Esparza-Cruz (iD)
Universidad Técnica de Babahoyo
Babahoyo
Ecuador

Joffre León-Acurio (iD)
Universidad Técnica de Babahoyo
Babahoyo
Ecuador

Narcisa Crespo-Torres
Universidad Técnica de Babahoyo
Babahoyo
Ecuador

Marola Beltrán-Mora
Universidad Técnica de Babahoyo
Babahoyo
Ecuador

ISSN 1865-0929   ISSN 1865-0937   (electronic)
Communications in Computer and Information Science
ISBN 978-3-319-72726-4   ISBN 978-3-319-72727-1   (eBook)
https://doi.org/10.1007/978-3-319-72727-1

Library of Congress Control Number: 2017962875

Printed on acid-free paper

This Springer imprint is published by Springer Nature
The registered company is Springer International Publishing AG
The registered company address is: Gewerbestrasse 11, 6330 Cham, Switzerland

Preface

The Third International Conference on Technology Trends (CITT 2017) was held on the main campus of Universidad Técnica de Babahoyo (UTB), Ecuador, during November 8–10 2017. The CITT series of conferences aims to become the premier venue for research on technology trends. It brings together top researchers and practitioners working in different domains in the field of computer science and information systems to exchange their expertise, and to discuss the perspectives of development and collaboration in these areas. The purpose of CITT was to facilitate technology and knowledge exchange among researchers, academics, and industry to obtain benefits from advances in computing technologies. The content of this volume is related to the following subjects:

1. Communications

   a. Internet of Things
   b. Mobile and Wireless Networks

2. Computer and Software Engineering

   a. Security and Privacy
   b. Computational Intelligence
   c. Data Engineering and Data Science
   d. Human–Computer Interaction
   e. Software Engineering
   f. Software Design

CITT 2017 received 71 submissions, both English and Spanish, from 187 authors coming from nine different countries. All these papers were peer-reviewed by the CITT 2017 Program Committee consisting of 59 accomplished researchers coming from 14 different countries. To assure a high-quality and thoughtful review process, we assigned each paper at least three reviewers. Based on the results of the peer reviews, 16 full papers were accepted (they were written in English), resulting in a 23% acceptance rate, which was within our goal of less than 40%.

We would like to express our sincere gratitude to the invited speakers for their inspirational talks, to the authors for submitting their work to this conference, and the reviewers for sharing their experience during the selection process.

November 2017

Miguel Botto-Tobar
Nelly Esparza-Cruz
Joffre León-Acurio
Narcisa Crespo-Torres
Marola Beltrán-Mora

Organization

Honorary Committee

Rafael Falconí Montalván	Universidad Técnica de Babahoyo, Ecuador
Pedro Rodríguez Vargas	Universidad Técnica de Babahoyo, Ecuador
Adelita Pinto Yerovi	Universidad Técnica de Babahoyo, Ecuador
Teodoro Flores Carpio	Universidad Técnica de Babahoyo, Ecuador
José Sandoya Villafuerte	Universidad Técnica de Babahoyo, Ecuador

Organizing Committee

Miguel Botto-Tobar	Eindhoven University of Technology, The Netherlands
Nelly Esparza-Cruz	Universidad Técnica de Babahoyo, Ecuador
Joffre León-Acurio	Universidad Técnica de Babahoyo, Ecuador
Narcisa Crespo-Torres	Universidad Técnica de Babahoyo, Ecuador
Marola Beltrán-Mora	Universidad Técnica de Babahoyo, Ecuador

Program Committee

Julio Albuja Sánchez	James Cook University, Australia
Gustavo Andrade Miranda	Universidad Politécnica de Madrid, Spain
Guilherme Avelino	Federal University of Piauí, Brazil
Allan Avendano Sudario	Università degli Studi di Roma La Sapienza, Italy
Monica Baquerizo Anastacio	Universidad de Guayaquil, Ecuador
Ronald Barriga Diaz	Universidad de Guayaquil, Ecuador
Gabriel Barros Gavilanes	INP Toulouse, France
Miguel Botto-Tobar	Eindhoven University of Technology, The Netherlands
Andres Carrera Rivera	The University of Melbourne, Australia
Priscila Cedillo	Universidad de Cuenca, Ecuador
Lorenzo Cevallos Torres	Universidad de Guayaquil, Ecuador
Andrés Efraín Chango Macas	Universidad Politécnica de Madrid, Spain
Jorge Charco Aguirre	Universitat Politècnica de València, Spain
Erick Cuenca	Université de Montpellier, France
Angel Cuenca-Ortega	Universitat Politècnica de València, Spain
Andres Cueva Costales	The University of Melbourne, Australia
Felipe Ebert	Federal University of Pernambuco, Brazil
Maria Escalante Guevara	University of Michigan, USA
Nelly Esparza Cruz	Universidad Técnica de Babahoyo, Ecuador

Cristian Zambrano-Vega   Universidad de Malaga, Spain
Miguel Zuñiga-Prieto   Universitat Politècnica de València, Spain
       Universidad de Cuenca, Ecuador

Local Organizing Committee

Miguel Zuñiga Sánchez   Universidad Técnica de Babahoyo, Ecuador
Gladys Guevara Albán   Universidad Técnica de Babahoyo, Ecuador
Ana Fernández Torres   Universidad Técnica de Babahoyo, Ecuador
Fredy Jordán Cordones   Universidad Técnica de Babahoyo, Ecuador
María Isabel Gonzales   Universidad Técnica de Babahoyo, Ecuador
   Valero
José Mejía Viteri   Universidad Técnica de Babahoyo, Ecuador
Geovanny Vega Villacis   Universidad Técnica de Babahoyo, Ecuador

Sponsoring Institutions

Universidad Técnica de Babahoyo
http://www.utb.edu.ec

Contents

Communications

Optimization of Recommendation ITU-R P.1812-3 for the Propagation Losses Prediction in Digital Terrestrial Television System

Enrique Ismael Delgado Cuadro$^{(\boxtimes)}$ ⓘ and Joffre León-Acurio ⓘ

Universidad Técnica de Babahoyo, Babahoyo 120102, Ecuador
{edelgado,jvleon}@utb.edu.ec

Abstract. This work was developed for the propagation characteristics of outdoor environments in the cities of Quito-Ecuador and Caracas-Venezuela, using one of the most innovating propagation models used in the planning and dimensioning (PyD) of Digital Terrestrial Television (DTT), specifically Recommendation ITU-R P.1812-3. For this, measurements of the received electric field level (Quito) and power level received (Caracas) made for conditions of fixed reception, with DTT standards, were used during the processes followed in both countries for the selection of the DTT standard base. For the development of four versions, the Particle Swarm Optimization (PSO) and genetic algorithm (GA) techniques were applied individually to the measurements mentioned above, which were part of the intelligence computational techniques family. The performance of these versions, in terms of RMSE (Root Mean Square Error), in the prediction of propagation losses in the environments where the measurements were carried out, were compared with the performance of the unmodified version of the recommendation ITU-R P.1812-3, resulting all versions of the developed model here with better performance.

Keywords: Optimization · Recommendation ITU-R P.1812-3
Particle Swarm Optimization · Genetic algorithm · Digital Terrestrial Television

1 Introduction

Digital Terrestrial Television system (DTT) is today one of the main technological alternatives for the real social inclusion and democratization of the information. This is because the TV, the DTT receiver equipment, is the electronic device with the highest worldwide penetration percentage (number of analogue televisions per 100 inhabitants), according to the records from the ITU (International Telecommunication Union) [1].

In order for a user to have all the advantages offered by DTT systems, it is necessary to guarantee an adequate planning and dimensioning (PyD) of them, which is a step before the process of physical implementation of the system. The process of PyD allows estimating requirements, such as the distance of coverage for a certain transmitter, the interference level that may be present in the system, antennas that can be used, among others.

© Springer International Publishing AG 2018
M. Botto-Tobar et al. (Eds.): CITT 2017, CCIS 798, pp. 3–17, 2018.
https://doi.org/10.1007/978-3-319-72727-1_1

One of the most important requirements is the prediction of coverage, which in the specific case of wireless telecommunications systems, like the DTT system, focuses its precision mainly on the successful selection of the propagation model.

A propagation model that does not comply with this requirement will produce an oversizing or undersizing in the estimation of system propagation losses.

In the particular case of DTT systems, in the literature there are some propagation models for the estimation of propagation losses in these systems, being perhaps the most important the Okumura-Hata model [3] and the models contained in the Recommendations ITU-R P.1546-5 [4] and ITU-R P.1812-3 [5].

Since none of the mentioned models were developed in places with their own propagation characteristics, for example, from Ecuador and Venezuela (South American countries), the main purpose of this work is to optimize the Recommendation ITU-R P. 1812-3, based on measurements made in Quito (Ecuador) [6] and Caracas (Venezuela) [7], using two (2) known computational intelligence (CI) techniques, such as optimization by PSO, Particle Swarm Optimization [8–11] and genetic algorithm [10–12].

2 Propagation Models Used for Digital Terrestrial Television Systems

There are several models in the literature that can be used for the estimation of propagation losses in Digital Terrestrial Television system (DTT). However, the most commonly used are Okumura-Hata and Recommendations ITU-R P.1546-5 and ITU-R P.1812-3.

2.1 Okumura-Hata Model

The Okumura-Hata model [2, 3] allows predicting the propagation loss value for the following conditions:

- Frequency range (f): 150 MHz to 1500 MHz.
- Height of the transmitting antenna (h1): 30 m to 200 m.
- Receiver antenna height (h2): 1 m to 10 m.
- Transmitter-receiver distance (d): 1 km to 20 km.

On the other hand, the surroundings or environments of application of the model Okumura-Hata are:

- Urban areas:
  - Big cities
  - Small or medium-sized cities
- Suburban areas
- Rural areas

It should be noted that a version of the Okumura-Hata model valid for distances greater than 20 km is described in Annex 8 to ITU-R P.1546-5 [4].

2.2 Recommendation ITU-R P.1546-6

It is a method for the electric field strength prediction in point-area systems, especially in maritime mobile terrestrial and mobile broadcasting services, as well as certain fixed services (for example, those using point-to-multipoint systems) in the frequency band 30 MHz to 3000 MHz and for distances between transmitter and receiver between 1 km and 1000 km [2, 4].

The complete procedure or algorithm for the estimation of the electric field at a certain point located at some distance from the transmitter is quite meticulous and appears in Recommendation ITU-R P.1546-5 [4]. A summary of the details of this algorithm is found in the work of Uzcátegui [2].

2.3 Recommendation ITU-R P.1812-3

The model allows to predict the electric field strength exceeded during a certain percentage of time (p%) of an average year, in the range of $1\% \leq p \leq 50\%$ and a percentage of the locations (pL%), in the range of $1\% \leq pL \leq 99\%$. It applies to terrestrial point-area communications systems, operating in the frequency range of 30 MHz to 3000 MHz, with paths from 250 m to 3000 km and with receivers located up to 3 km above the earth's surface [2, 5].

Recommendation ITU-R P.1812-3, which is actually considered as a complement to ITU-R P.1546-5, implies, in general terms [2, 5]:

- Calculation of basic transmission losses not exceeded during p (%) of the time.
- Calculation of the effects of receiver location variability and penetration in buildings.
- Conversion of electric field strength to apparent radiated power (a.r.p.).

The procedure for the estimation of the electric field strength described in Recommendation ITU-R P.1812-3 is done in a specific path; therefore, the point-area prediction consists of a set of point-to-point predictions in the area of interest. Therefore, from a practical point of view, the application of the model under consideration requires a digital database of terrain elevations in the area of interest, which suggests that the model is a more accurate method for the prediction of propagation losses than that of Recommendation ITU-R P.1546-5.

The factors or elements considered by the model for the estimation of electric field strength are [2, 5]:

- Direct visibility or LOS (Line of Sight).
- Diffraction.
- Tropospheric dispersion.
- Pipeline propagation, reflection, etc.
- Variation by land occupation and location of the receiver.
- Penetration in buildings.

Finally, if required, the value of the electric field strength E (dBμV/m) for an apparent radiated power (a.r.p) of 1 kW can be determined from the loss value Lb according to:

$$E\left(\frac{dB\mu V}{m}\right) = 199,36 + 20\log(f) - L_b \qquad (1)$$

3 Overview of PSO and Genetic Algorithm

In this section, we will briefly address the general fundamentals and philosophy of algorithms for techniques of computational intelligence (CI), particle swarm optimization (PSO) and genetic algorithm.

3.1 PSO (Particle Swarm Optimization)

PSO is a bioinspired technique in the behavior exhibited by certain living beings to search for food, such as flocks of birds, shoal of fish, swarm of bees and even some social behavior of humans. This technique consists of a number of particles that move together in a search space, to find the global optimum (solution).

3.1.1 Mathematical Model of PSO

The strategy of solving a PSO optimization problem is based on the position of each cluster particle, which is determined by three (3) distinct fractions of displacement, as illustrated in Fig. 1 [10].

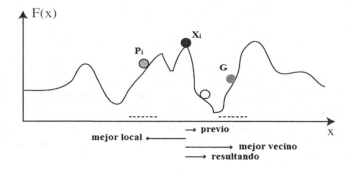

Fig. 1. Update of the position of a particle in PSO.

Each particle has a velocity vector $Vi = (vi1, vi2, \ldots, vin)$, which stores the velocity of the particle "i". The vector "Vi" directs the movement of the particle and is generally composed of one component related to the current movement and another component that supplies the search direction at the next iteration.

In short, the new position of each particle is determined by considering the vectors velocity (Xi) and position (Vi) [13, 14]:

$$V_i^{k+1} = \omega V_i^k + C_1 R_1 \left(P_i - X_i^k\right) + C_2 R_2 \left(G_i - x_i^k\right) \qquad (2)$$

$$X_i^{k+1} = X_i^k + V_i^{k+1} \qquad (3)$$

Where:

ω: Inertia or moment (consider the effect of the previous velocity, to avoid that the particle moves drastically from one iteration to another).

C1: Cognitive parameter (quantifies the particle's own experience and refers to the tendency of the particle to return to the best position found).

C2: Social parameter (represents the cooperation of the particle with the rest of the group).

R1 and R2: Numbers generated randomly uniformly, in the interval (0, 1).

3.1.2 Basic PSO Algorithm

The main steps of the PSO algorithm are [8]:

1. Initially (first iteration), the experience of each particle is its current position. After that, the next position and velocity are determined according to the equations in (2) and (3).
2. We proceed to quantify the performance of the particle, which specifically refers to the fitness of each particle "i" concerning its best position within the search space.
3. The search for the particle is performed with the best presentation. This particle will be the leader that will guide the rest of the group or swarm, that is, it becomes the "best overall".
4. A new generation is created (new conformation of the group) adjusting the speed and position. The process is repeated until it meets the algorithm's stop criteria, which can be compliance with a maximum number of iterations set or the achievement of an acceptable error value.
5. If in one of the generations there is a particle that presents a better aptitude than the current leader, this particle will become the new leader that will guide the rest of the swarm.

At the end of the execution of the algorithm, the solution that throws the method corresponds to the best previous position found by one of the particles of the cluster, that is, the leader.

3.2 Genetic Algorithm

The genetic algorithm (GA) is an artificial intelligence technique that has the structure of an evolutionary algorithm and consists of an iterative procedure on a population made up of individuals of different genetics. It is a method that uses mechanisms of evolution of nature, simulating the behavior of individuals in a population in which the fittest or strongest are those who survive by adapting more easily to the changes that occur in their environment.

The basic principle of the genetic algorithm, therefore, refers to the "survival of the fittest" among individuals of a generation, to solve a problem.

3.2.1   Functioning of a Genetic Algorithm

The genetic algorithm is implemented by studying the performance or quality of all individuals in the population. Once the fitness or quality function is evaluated, a new population is generated through genetic operators, selection, recombination (crossover) and/or mutation (optional), reproduction and selection of surviving individuals. Each iteration, a new generation of individuals is created, product of the combination of good characteristics coming from different ancestors and exclusion of the unfit individuals of the old generation. Then, species and individuals, as they evolve, acquire characteristics increasingly adapted to the environment in which they live and these will be the best individuals created by the algorithm so far.

In the initial or zero (0) generation of the procedure, the population is randomly generated with elements of the domain of the cost or performance function. From this, the genetic operators are responsible for improvising on the new generation of the population and the process is repeated until an individual with the desired performance is met or a condition of stopping the algorithm is fulfilled [10].

The flowchart describing the development of the genetic algorithm is seen in Fig. 2 [15].

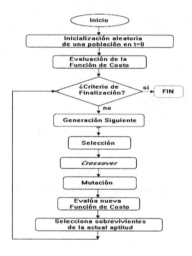

Fig. 2. Flowchart of genetic algorithm.

4   Measurements of Losses of Propagation in DTT Systems in Quito-Ecuador and Caracas-Venezuela

The measurements made in Quito and Caracas, which will be used in this work to optimize the model of Recommendation ITU-R P.1812-3, correspond to the technical evaluation campaigns made in the field in 2008 (Venezuela) and 2010 (Ecuador), for the selection of the base standard of their respective DTT systems, which eventually proved to be the ISDB-Tb (Integrated Services Digital Broadcasting - Terrestrial Built-in), the ISDB-T of Japanese origin, but with the modifications introduced by Brazil.

In the case of Quito, the measurements being considered were coordinated by the Superintendency of Telecommunications (SUPERTEL) of Ecuador and corresponded to the electric field level received, using the ISDB-T and ISDB-Tb standards [6].

The measurements carried out in Caracas, under the coordination of the National Telecommunications Commission (CONATEL) of Venezuela and which included the ISDB-T, DVB-T/H (Digital Video Broadcasting - Terrestrial/Handheld) and DTMB Digital Terrestrial Multimedia Broadcast), consisted of the power level received [7].

4.1 Experimental Configuration Used in the Measurements Made in Quito-Ecuador

For the three (3) models considered in the selected dimensions, the technical specifications of the transmission-level equipment, summarized in Table 1, were the same (even, the same radiant system was used) [6].

Table 1. Transmission parameters (measurements made in Quito-Ecuador)

Parameters	Values
Frequency of operation, f (MHz)	641 (Channel 47 UHF)
Transmission power, PT (W)	500
Gain of transmitting antenna, GT (dBd/dBi)	11 dBd/13, 15 dBi
Height of the radiation center above ground level (m)	30
Loss of feeder/connectors, LT (dB)	1, 5

From the parameters in Table 1, the equivalent isotropic radiated power (EIRP) is determined, as follows [16]:

$$EIRP(dBm) = P_T(dBm) + G_T(dBi) - L_T(dB) \qquad (4)$$

EIRP equal to 68.64 dBm.

Next, the apparent radiated power (a.r.p) is determined by [17]:

$$a.r.p(dBm) = PIRE - 2,15 \qquad (5)$$

That is, a.r.p is equal to 66.49 dBm.

The EIRP will be used in the present work to decide the propagation losses measured for each measurement point considered in both Quito and Caracas, while a.r.p. will be used to estimate the propagation losses in the measurement points of both cities, applying the model of Recommendation ITU-R P.1546.5.

The transmitter was installed in Pichincha hill, at the geographical coordinates 0,1673° South latitude and 78.5228 West longitude and at a height above sea level of 3,776 meters. As antenna of transmission, an array of antennas was used, with a gain of 11 dBd, composed of four (4) panels [6].

On the other hand, an 8-element Yagi antenna, gain of 14 dBi (11.85 dBi), with narrow beam width [6] was used at the reception. This antenna was placed on a mast of the vehicle used for the measurements, at a height of 10 m. The power losses in the receiver system were 2.2 dB.

4.1.1   Points of Measurement in Quito

The measuring points were approximated by the intersection of twenty (20) radials drawn from the transmitter room, spaced 10° from each other, with arches at 2, 5 km to 20 km (at 2.5 km intervals) from the transmitter site, with this as the center.

4.2   Experimental Configuration Used in the Measurements Made in Caracas-Venezuela

The technical specifications of the transmission-level equipment, which are summarized in Table 2, were the same (even, the same radiant system was used) [6].

Table 2. Transmission parameters (measurements made in Caracas-Venezuela)

Parameters	Values
Frequency of operation, f (MHz)	677 (Channel 48 UHF)
Transmission power, PT (W)	500
Gain of transmitting antenna, GT (dBd/dBi)	11,4 dBd/13,55 dBi
Height of the radiation center above ground level (m)	35
Loss of feeder/connectors, LT (dB)	2
EIRP (dBm), in the direction of maximum radiation of the transmitting antenna	67,34
a.r.p (dBm), in the direction of maximum radiation of the transmitting antenna	65,19

The transmitter was installed at the Mecedores Station, in the El Ávila National Park, at the geographic coordinates 10.5284° north latitude and 66.8776° West longitude, at a height above sea level of 1,773.6 m [2, 7] (Table 3).

Table 3. Reception parameters (measurements made in Caracas-Venezuela)

Parameters	Values
Frequency of operation, f (MHz)	677 (Channel 48 UHF)
Gain of transmitting antenna, GT (dBd/dBi)	15,0 dBd/17,15 dBi
Height of the radiation center above ground level (m)	10
Loss of feeder/connectors, LT (dB)	0

The transmission antenna used was similar to that used 2 years later in the Quito measurements, while the receiving antenna consisted of an angular array of three (03) grid-connected log-periodic antennas and reflective electromagnetic mirrors on a central dipole [7].

It is worth pointing out that a system with variable power amplifier was implemented in the receiver side, between the antenna and the spectrum analyzer, in order to compensate the losses of connectors and feeders so that the power received in the spectrum analyzer coincided at all points with the input power at the receiving antenna [7].

4.2.1   Points of Measurement in Caracas

In this case, the measurement points, where the measurements were made, were roughly obtained at the intersection of ten (10) radiations drawn from the transmitter room, spaced 10° from each other and arcs of circumference with center at the transmitter. The receiver was located at intervals of 1 km apart. Finally, we considered those points where the measure for itself was feasible [9].

5   Measurements Results

In this section we calculate the propagation losses considered from the measurements of the received electric field level (Quito) and received power level (Caracas). These losses are compared with those estimated by the Okumura-Hata propagation models, ITU-R Recommendation P.1546-5 and ITU-R Recommendation P.1812-3.

The measured propagation losses, L, are given by the classical link budget equation of wireless communications systems [16]:

$$L(dB) = EIRP\ (dBm) - P_r(dBm) \tag{6}$$

Where Pr represents the power level received.

5.1   Loss of Propagation Measured in Quito

Since in this case the measurements correspond to the electric field level received, the power received from [18] must be calculated beforehand:

$$P_r(dBm) = E\left(\frac{dB\mu V}{m}\right) - 20\ \log\ f(GHz) - 137,25 \tag{7}$$

5.2   Loss of Propagation Measured in Caracas

Because measurements in the city of Caracas corresponded to the power level received, the propagation losses at each of the points considered are determined directly from Eq. (6), extracting the necessary information, power of transmission, transmission antenna gain, and transmitter transmission line losses, from Table 2.

6   Comparison of Results

Using the algorithms discussed in Sect. 2 for the calculation of propagation losses using the models considered there, as well as the information provided in Sect. 4 about the height of the transmitting and receiving antennas, height above sea level of the transmission and reception points, etc., for both cities, the results shown in Figs. 3 and 4 are obtained, in which the propagation losses calculated by the models and the measured losses are simultaneously shown for the cities of Quito and Caracas, respectively. Likewise, in both figures the tendency lines are seen for both the estimates and the measurements of propagation losses.

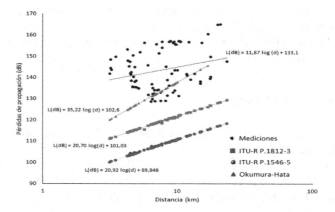

Fig. 3. Estimated and measured propagation losses in Quito

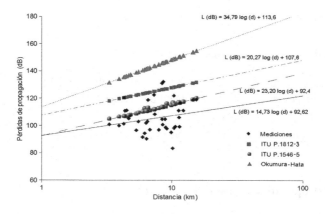

Fig. 4. Estimated and measured propagation losses in Caracas [9].

In order to have a more objective appreciation of the performance of each of the three (3) models of literature considered in this work for comparison with experimental values, we use the RMSE, Root Mean Square Error, given by [19]:

$$\text{RMSE} = \sqrt{\frac{\sum_{i=1}^{N} \left(V_{m,i} - V_{c,i} \right)^2}{N-1}} \tag{8}$$

Where:

Vm, i: Loss value measured at each point "i".
Vc, i: Estimated loss value, at each point "i", by the propagation model.
N: Number of measurement points considered.

In Tables 4 and 5, where OH refers to the Okumura-Hata model, the RMSE values obtained for the three (3) propagation models are shown for the cities of Quito and Caracas, respectively.

Table 4. RMSE values of literature models for Quito.

	ITU-R P.1812-3	ITU-R P.1546-5	OH
RMSE	25,99	36,36	14,42

Table 5. RMSE values of literature models for Caracas.

	ITU-R P.1812-3	ITU-R P.1546-5	OH
RMSE	22,65	23,29	40,63

In Table 4, it is observed that for the case of the city of Quito the model of propagation that smaller RMSE yields is that of Okumura-Hata, with 14.42 dB, whereas the model that presents the lowest performance in the estimation of the propagation values is that of ITU-R Recommendation P.1546-5.

For the case of Caracas, Table 5 shows that the propagation models of Recommendations ITU-R P.1812-3 and P.1546-5 are the ones with the best performance, with a slightly lower error (2.75%) for the first. Table 5 also shows that the Okumura-Hata model presents a highly significant error in its estimation of propagation losses in Caracas.

7   Optimization of the Model of Recommendation ITU-R P.1812-3

In general terms, the optimization of the propagation model of Recommendation ITU-R P.1812-3 by means of the swarm optimization of particles or PSO and genetic algorithm (GA), consists of defining, first, the objective functions, that is, the equations of said model that will be modified using such computational intelligence (CI) techniques.

In this paper the following four (4) objective functions are defined, all resulting from the model of Recommendation ITU-R 1812-3.

$$L_b = x_1 L_{bu} + A_{hr} \qquad (9)$$

$$L_b = x_2 L_{bu} + x_3 A_{hr} \qquad (10)$$

$$L_b = x_4 92,44 + 20 \log f + 20 \log d + L_{dp} + A_{hr} \qquad (11)$$

$$L_b = x_5 92,44 + 20 \log f + x_6 20 \log d + L_{dp} + A_{hr} \qquad (12)$$

Where:

Lb: Propagation losses given by the optimized model.
Lbu: Transmission losses (in dB), not exceeded during p% of the time and
                 50% of the locations, without considering the effects of the land occu-
                 pation in which the transmitter and the receiver are located.
Ahr: Additional losses, in dB, as a result of the environment in which the
                 receiver is located.
f: Operating frequency, in GHz.
d: Transceiver distance, in km.
Ldp: Diffraction losses not exceeded during p (%) of the time.
x1, x2, … x6:   Determined using PSO and GA.

In the case of the cities of Quito, Ecuador and Caracas, Venezuela, the implementation of Recommendation ITU-R P.1812-3 yielded an Aht value (additional losses, in dB, because of the environment in which the transmitter is located) equal to zero. Also, it was not necessary to add extra losses because in the application of said model a percentage of the locations, pL, of 50% and the environments surrounding the measurement points were considered external.

Once the objective functions to be optimized are defined, the cost functions are established, which will allow PSO and AG to generate x1, x2 … x6 values that improve the performance of the Recommendation ITU-R P.1812-3 model in the prediction of propagation losses, i.e. that RMSE decreases compared to the RMSE values thrown by the original version of the model.

Then, we proceed to implement the algorithms of the IC techniques considered for optimization in the Matlab computational tool, taking into account the particularities of each of these techniques.

For the PSO application, the following values are considered for the fixed parameters, as well as the following initial values for the variables:

- C1 = C2 = 2 [8].
- ω = 0,45 [8].
- Particle start position = Random value.
- Particle initial velocity = Random value.
- Number of variables to be optimized = 1 or 2, depending on the objective function).
- Number of particles = Between 5 and 100.
- Number of iterations = Between 10 and 300.

On the other hand, in the case of the genetic algorithm, as mentioned above, we chose the paired selection according to tournament, recombination by single point crossing and mutation by bit interchange.

In relation to the values of the fixed parameters and the initial values of the variables, selected for the GA application, they were:

- Number of individuals in the population = Between 5 and 20.
- Number of chromosome bits = 36 (objective functions of 2 terms) and 50 (objective function of 5 terms).

- Probability of mutation = 0.02.
- Number of iterations = Between 200 and 1000.

Table 6 summarizes the values of the variables x1, x2, ... x6, obtained through the PSO implementation, for the cities of Quito and Caracas. In said tables, V-1, V-2, V-3 and V-4 refer to the modified versions of the ITU-R Recommendation 1812-3 model, obtained from the objective functions (9), (10), (11) and (12), respectively.

Table 6. Values of the variables "x" obtained for the cases of Quito and Caracas, using PSO, with RMSE as cost function.

	x_1	x_2	x_3	x_4	x_5	x_6
Quito						
V-1	1,2107	–	–	–	–	–
V-2	–	1,1798	1,7928	–	–	–
V-3	–	–		1,2625	–	–
V-4	–	–	–	–	1,3457	0,5532
Caracas						
V-1	0,8594	–	–	–	–	–
V-2	–	0,8567	1,0885	–	–	–
V-3	–	–		0,8270	–	–
V-4	–	–	–	–	0,9332	0,3692

By replacing the values of x1, x2, ... x6 of Table 6 in the respective equations of the objective functions, the four modified versions of the model of Recommendation ITU-R P.1812-3 will be taken. The RMSE values for these versions, adjusted using the RMSE cost function, range from 9.39 dB (version No. 4) to 9.80 dB (version No. 1), for Quito, while for the case of Caracas, are between 10.40 dB (version No. 4) and 10.69 dB (version No. 3). Therefore, it is observed that for all versions the RMSE is significantly lower than that obtained with the application of the original model, which is 25.94 dB for Quito and 22.75 dB for Caracas (see Tables 4 and 5). It is also observed that the best fit for the measurements in both cities is obtained with the modified version No. 4.

Finally, the values of the variables x1, x2, ... x6 are shown in Table 7 when using genetic algorithm (GA) for the adjustment of the four modified versions of the Recommendation ITU-R P.1812-3.

With the modified versions of the model, based on the values of x1, x2, ... x6 in Table 7, the efficiency of GA in the optimization of the model in question is verified, since the RMSE values ranged from 9.56 dB (version No. 4) to 9.8 dB (version No. 1), for Quito and between 11.48 dB (version No. 4) and 11.81 dB (version No. 3), for Caracas.

Table 7. Values of the "x" variables obtained for the cases of Quito and Caracas, using GA, with RMSE as cost function

	x_1	x_2	x_3	x_4	x_5	x_6
QUITO						
V-1	1,2109	–	–	–	–	–
V-2	–	1,1523	2,4999	–	–	–
V-3	–	–	–	1,2625	–	–
V-4	–	–	–	–	1,4261	0,1245
CARACAS						
V-1	0,8178	–	–	–	–	–
V-2	–	0,1282	19,0626	–	–	–
V-3	–	–	–	0,7717	–	–
V-4	–	–	–	–	0,8938	0,2882

8   Conclusions

In this article, four optimized modified versions of the ITU-R Recommendation P. 1812-3 were developed for the prediction of propagation losses in the cities of Quito-Ecuador and Caracas-Venezuela in Digital Terrestrial Television. For this, measurements of the electric field level (case of Quito) and power level received (case of Caracas), as well as computational intelligence (CI) techniques were used, namely optimization by swarm of particles or PSO and genetic algorithm (GA), for the adjustment to propagation losses of the four modified versions under consideration.

The performance of the four modified versions, regarding RSME, in the estimation of propagation losses improved significantly compared to the performance shown by the original version of the model, demonstrating the efficiency of PSO and GA techniques in optimization of propagation models, always based on actual dimensions.

References

1. Unión Internacional de Telecomunicaciones (UIT). Medición de la Sociedad de la Información (Resumen Ejecutivo), Ginebra, Suiza (2013)
2. Uzcátegui, J.R.: Implementación de la Recomendación ITU-R P.1812-3 para la Estimación de las Pérdidas de Propagación en Televisión Digital Abierta (TDA). Tesis de Grado de Maestría en Telecomunicaciones, Universidad de Los Andes, Mérida, Venezuela (2015)
3. Molish, A.F.: Wireless Communications, 2nd edn. Wiley, Hoboken (2011)
4. International Telecommunications Union (ITU). Recommendation ITU-R P.1546-5: Method for Point-to-Area Predictions for Terrestrial Services in the Frequency Range 30 MHz to 3000 MHz, Ginebra, Suiza (2013)
5. International Telecommunications Union (ITU). Recommendation ITUR P.1812-3: A Path-specific Propagation Prediction Method for Point-to-area Terrestrial Services in the VHF and UHF Bands, Ginebra, Suiza (2013)

6. Páez-Vásquez, X.S.: Evaluación Técnica del Desempeño de los Estándares de Televisión Digital Terrestre en el Distrito Metropolitano de Quito. Tesis de Maestría, Redes de Información y Conectividad, Universidad de las Fuerzas Armadas - ESPE, Quito, Ecuador (2014)
7. Comisión Nacional de Telecomunicaciones (CONATEL). Informe Técnico sobre las Pruebas Comparativas de Desempeño en Campo de los Estándares para Televisión Digital Terrestre DVB-T, ISDB-T y DTMB. Caracas, Venezuela (2008)
8. Pérez, T.: Evaluación del Uso de PSO (Particle Swarm Optimization) para el Ajuste de Controladores PID, Aplicados al Proceso de Levantamiento de Petróleo Mediante Bombeo Centrífugo Sumergido. Trabajo de Grado, Ingeniería de Sistemas, Universidad de Los Andes, Venezuela (2015)
9. Pinto, Á.D., Torres, J.M., García Bello, A.S., Pérez, N.A., Uzcategui, J.R.: Modelo para estimación de pérdidas de propagación en sistemas de televisión digital abierta, RIELAC, vol. XXXVII 2/2016, pp. 67–81, Mayo–Agosto. ISSN: 1815-5928
10. Floreano, D., Mattiussi, C.: Bio-Inspired Artificial Intelligence: Theories, Methods, and Technologies. The MIT Press, Cambridge (2008)
11. Sumathi, S., Paneerselvam, S.: Computational Intelligence Paradigms: Theory & Applications using MATLAB. CRC Press, Boca Raton (2010)
12. Rondeau, T.W., Bostian, C.W.: Artificial Intelligence in Wireless Communications. Artech House, London (2009)
13. Franco, J.A.: Un Algoritmo Basado en Optimización por Enjambre de Partículas para el Problema de Asignación Axial 3-Dimensional. Tesis de Maestría, Sistemas Computacionales, Instituto Tecnológico de La Paz, Baja California Sur, México (2011)
14. Nieto, J.M.: Algoritmos Basados en Cúmulos de Partículas para la Resolución de Problemas Complejos [En línea]. Disponible en, Septiembre 2006. http://neo.lcc.uma.es/staff/jmgn/doc/Memoria_PFC_JMGN.pdf. consultada en junio 2015
15. Ortiz, S.: Sintonización de un Controlador PID basado en un Algoritmo Heurístico para el Control de un Ball and Beam. Tesis de Maestría, Instrumentación y Control Automático, Universidad Autónoma de Querétaro, México (2014)
16. Pérez-García, N.: Cálculo de Cobertura de Sistemas WLL e LMDS. Tesis de Maestría, Pontificia Universidad de Católica do Rio de Janeiro (PUC/Rio), Brasil (2000)
17. Seybold, J.S.: Introduction to RF Propagation. Wiley, Hoboken (2005)
18. International Telecommunications Union (ITU). Recommendation ITU-R P.525-2: Calculation of Free-Space Attenuation, Ginebra, Suiza (1994)
19. Wu, J., Yuan, D.: Propagation measurements and modeling in Jinan City. In: The Ninth IEEE International Symposium on Personal, Indoor and Mobile Radio Communications, Boston, MA, USA (1998)

IoT Android Gateway for Monitoring and Control a WSN

Dixys Hernandez-Rojas[1,2(✉)] 🆔, Bertha Mazon-Olivo[1,2] 🆔, Johnny Novillo-Vicuña[1,2] 🆔,
Carlos Escudero-Cascon[2] 🆔, Alberto Pan-Bermudez[2] 🆔,
and Gustavo Belduma-Vacacela[1] 🆔

[1] Universidad Técnica de Machala, 5.5 km Pan-American Av, Machala, El Oro, Ecuador
dhernandez@utmachala.edu.ec
[2] Department of Computer Science, Universidade da Coruña,
15071 A Coruña (03082), Spain

Abstract. Precision agriculture and the automation of agricultural processes such as irrigation with the use of current technologies, create the need to develop IoT gateways for WSN with Bluetooth Low Energy motes that demonstrate their functionality through a testbed. The challenge of developing both the testbed and an application for Android smart phones with gateway functionalities to package the sensor data into MQTT messages and send it to remote server or cloud computing and, in turn, be a tool for monitoring on-site of sensors and controlling the actuators present in the mote motivated the development of this work. We carried out tests on the proposed testbed, which denotes its functionality, and shows there is a fast and stable IoT gateway with low CPU and RAM usage, ready for IoT applications such as Precision Agriculture. The application design is extensible to other OS for smart phones and tablets.

Keywords: Android · Bluetooth Low Energy · Gateway · Internet of Things
Wireless sensor network

1 Introduction

Nowadays, not only people connect to the Internet; but also, millions of objects or things (smart objects) and this number is growing exponentially. The Internet of Things (IoT) is the Internet of physical objects with an intelligence that enables them to communicate with other objects and human beings, for controlling critical or relevant situations to a specific domain or application.

The devices (motes) integrate sensors and actuators; and, these are located geographically forming wireless sensor networks (WSN) [1]. For real-time monitoring and control of smart objects, software applications have increased focus on different IoT domains, some of them are Smart Cities, Smart Homes, Smart Buildings, Smart Healthcare, Precision Farming or Smart Agriculture and others [2, 3]. The desired characteristics of these types of applications according to [4] are automation of data management, data capture, communication, data processing and collaboration with other objects [5].

The domain IoT approached in this paper is Precision Agriculture (PA), known by some authors as Intelligent Agriculture and is defined as the use of Information and Communication Technologies (ICT) in the localized management of crops or

© Springer International Publishing AG 2018
M. Botto-Tobar et al. (Eds.): CITT 2017, CCIS 798, pp. 18–32, 2018.
https://doi.org/10.1007/978-3-319-72727-1_2

agricultural parcels [6, 7]. An example is drones that come equipped with global positioning systems (GPS), cameras and sensors, that are used to obtain images and geo-referenced data of a parcel or crop, with the purpose of generating maps of performance in Geographic Information Systems (GIS). It helps the farmer to make decisions that benefit the production process by integrating monitoring and controlling systems in real time based on IoT [8]. However, some of these technologies are still being developed and there are several challenges to be resolved. Some of these challenges include the optimization of data capture and communication between Smart objects and the Data Processing Center (DPC) or cloud computing, handling and integrating large volumes of data to generate information for a more accurate evaluation of the optimum sowing density, estimating fertilizers, more accurately predicting crop production, etc. [7, 9].

The purpose of this research work is communication between the wireless devices (motes) and the DPC, through the implementation of an IoT Gateway based on the Android operating system that allows automation of the following processes: (1) Discovering elements of WSN called motes (devices that integrate sensors and actuators); (2) connecting with the motes using Bluetooth Low Energy (BLE) technology; (3) gathering and monitoring of sensor data; (4) controlling of actuators; and (5) Internet connecting and communicating with the DPC or cloud computing that remotely stores, processes, controls and monitors devices installed in an agricultural parcel [10].

2 Background and Related Work

In this section, we make a small revision of the technological effects of the technological linkage and of the gateway system, as well as, similar researches in different IoT gateways.

2.1 Wireless Sensor Network (WSN)

The advances and advantages of modern wireless technologies, such as Wifi, Zigbee, Bluetooth Low Energy, Z-Wave, Lora, Sigfox and LTE, among others, have found their main niche on the Internet. That is why smart sensors [11], also known as motes, incorporate these wireless communication modules that allow them to group and intercommunicate in WSN networks. Currently, we can cite the most popular commercial open-mote hardware: Arduino, Raspberry Pi [12, 13] and RedbearLab [14]. In this paper, we use the hardware RedbearLab nRF51822.

One of the variables most used in IoT applications is temperature [15–19], either to measure the ambient temperature, soil, water or other material or process. The Resistance Temperature Devices (RTD) are devices that vary the metal resistance (mainly Platinum) as a function of the temperature variation, typically characterized by the Callendar-Van Dusen equation [20]. In this paper, we use Platinum RTD PT1000.

2.2 Bluetooth Low Energy (BLE)

Bluetooth Low Energy (BLE) is a short-range wireless technology, also known as Bluetooth Smart. Unlike the classic Bluetooth present in computers, keyboards and mice; this technology is low-power, small size, low cost, robust, efficient and allows interoperability between different manufacturers. Nokia created this technology and they called Wibree [21], to be later adopted by Bluetooth SIG [22]. The dizzying development of BLE is due to the fact that the main smartphone manufacturers have incorporated it into their computers with iOS, Android, Apple OS or Windows operating systems.

We establish the communication between BLE devices through a star network topology, where these devices adopt peripherals and central roles. The peripherals are small devices with low power (motes) and the central roles are mainly occupied by smartphones, which acts as a master device for communicating and scanning, while the peripherals act as slaves doing the advertisement. When a central device is connected to peripheral, they make use of the GATT (Generic Attribute Profile) services and characteristics to communicate. For this, we use the popular UART service with two characteristics: one to transmit (Tx) and one to receive data (Rx).

The physical layer of BLE uses the free 2.4 GHz frequency band, shared with other technologies like Zigbee and Wi-Fi. This is the reason, we use the technique of frequency to avoid or reduce interference.

2.3 Android Evolution

Android is a Linux-based operating system, developed by Google. It leads the market with approximately an 82.2% share compared to its immediate follower iOS that has 14.6% [23]. Android controls more than one billion mobile touch devices of different makes and models such as Smartphones, tablets, televisions, car radios, hand watches, etc. [24]. To develop Android applications, we need a software development kit (SDK) known as the Application programming interface (API).

2.4 Related Works

Given the heterogeneity of the sensors used in different IoT application domains, we can find three types of gateways in the scientific literature, which allows us to discover the motes present in the WSN, to gather the data of its sensors and to transmit it in another technology to a server or the cloud. These three gateways are: gateways based on raspberry pi, gateways based on smart phones (using Android mainly) and custom gateways for ZigBee or BLE networks and/or Ethernet or cellular data communication ports (4G or LTE) that access a server or the cloud. This is the case of [25] which develops an efficient IoT Gateway over 5G Wireless. While in [26], an Android App is used as a proxy to connect a BLE sensor from a medical device that does not meet the standard through an MQTT broker within the gateway or middleware developed with the standard IEEE 11073 software stack so that, other applications can access the patient's medical information. In [27], they developed a custom gateway using an IT ZigBee module as a coordinating node and a GSM/GPRS module to send SMS with the data acquired by the sensors. In [28], they use the raspberry pi as (IoMTaaS) Platform of a WSN based on ZigBee motes. In [29], they also use a raspberry pi as a gateway, in which they implement a docker for ARM to detect BLE motes in their environment.

3   Methodology

This section describes the hardware used in the implementation of the WSN, the programming of the mote, the development process of the mobile application and the communication protocol used between the mote and the mobile application.

3.1   BLE Mote

For the demonstration of our testbed of a WSN, we chose RedbearLab because it is a commercial kit that allows a quick introduction to IoT, since it has connectors with a compatible Arduino pinout (Fig. 1). It allows two methods to burn your firmware either through the J-Link SWD interface or the mbed platform. This kit is based on the Nordic chip nRF51822, in which Nordic is the leading manufacturer of chips for Bluetooth Low Energy.

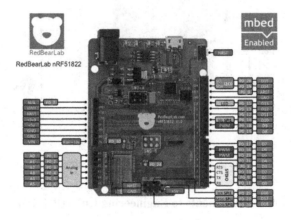

Fig. 1. Mote RedBearLab nRF51822

An important feature of this card is the mbed programming mode is enabled [30]. Enabled mbed mode means that the board has been validated by the enabled mbed program, which guarantees compliance with the criteria and technical requirements for interoperability with other enabled mbed products (Arm community). Some of the benefits of belonging to this program are: the developed code can be downloaded to any hardware with enabled mbed without making any changes; and the availability of an online development tool that allows us to edit, compile and download your application to our PC desktop and drag it onto a development board. Mbed has a large community of programmers, so it has a lot of reusable code. It also includes an OS that allows the programmer to control the hardware and connection with the cloud in a transparent way.

3.2 Testbed

With the chosen hardware, it is possible to evaluate the operation of a gateway based on Android. For this reason, we implement a testbed that allows us to monitor and to control the WSN motes. To test analogue sensor monitoring, an RTD (PT1000) temperature sensor (DIN EN 60751) may be used within a resistance divider as shown in Fig. 2. We measure the proportional voltage by the AC/DC of the kit and analyze the interpretation of the measurements in the next section. Digital sensors are tested with the use of a simple pushbutton. To check the control on actuators, the use of LEDs is sufficient, as these can be easily replaced by relay to control motors and valves for irrigation control. We added a PWM output to the testbed to demonstrate its functionality in the case of using controllable motors or actuators with PWM signals. In this case, the light intensity of the LED varies depending on the PWM signal sent.

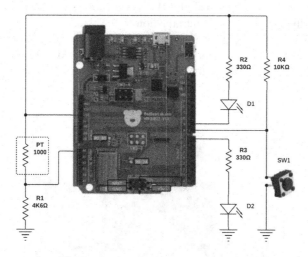

Fig. 2. Testbed for precision agriculture

3.3 Conversion of Measurements to Engineering Units (Pt1000)

In this section we analyze the logic followed for the interpretation of the digital measurements obtained from the Analog Digital Converter (ADC) to bring them to engineering units. In this case, the variable is temperature and the output is given in degrees Celsius (°C).

The above-mentioned processor uses a 10-bit A/D converter and 3.3 VDC reference voltage (V_{ref}) for analog measurements, so a least significant bit value (LSB) is equal to:

$$LSB = \frac{Vref}{2^{10\,bits}} = \frac{3.3\,V}{1024} = 3,22265625\,mV \qquad (1)$$

$$Vtemp = LSB * Pd \qquad (2)$$

On the other hand, V_{temp} can be calculated by means of a voltage divider formed by the resistor of R4600 and the RTD (Pt1000), see (Fig. 3). So:

$$V_{temp} = \frac{Vref * R4600}{R4600 + RTD} \tag{3}$$

$$RTD = \frac{15180}{V_{temp}} - 4600 \tag{4}$$

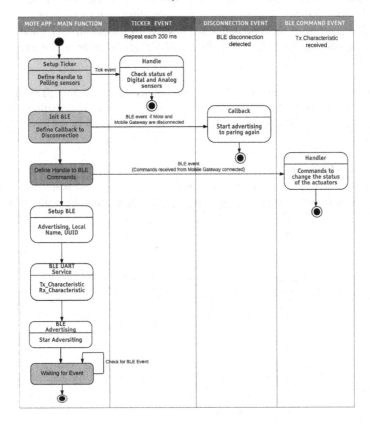

Fig. 3. Activity diagram of the mote firmware

Once the RTD value is known, we can then determine the temperature value using the following approximation:

$$RTD = R_0\left(1+ \propto \left(T_f - Ti\right)\right) \tag{5}$$

where R_0 is the resistance at 0 °C, $\propto$ *is* temperature coefficient of PT1000 at *0,00385055*, T_f y T_i are final and initial temperature, respectively.

$$T_f = \frac{RTD - 1000}{3,85055}[°C] \tag{6}$$

3.4 Mote Programming

The BLE uses UART Service and we program the mote application in "C" language using the BLE UART service. The main function has several parameters of BLE and the application is initialized and configured by itself. The rest of the functions of the mote are for attending to events such as sampling polling of the sensors and the sending of data, disconnecting of the mote with some low energy Bluetooth device and execution of the commands sent from the paired device BLE with the mote, as we can see in the Fig. 3.

Main Function. In this function, we configure the necessary parameters for the correct operation of the testbed, such as sample time for measurements, the creation of handlers and callbacks for each event of the application. After this, the rest of the mote operations are by events.

Disconnection Function. This function attends the disconnect event, when the device that was paired with the mote is disconnected for any reason and restarts the "Advertising" process. Figure 4(a) shows the diagram of the programming logic of the class.

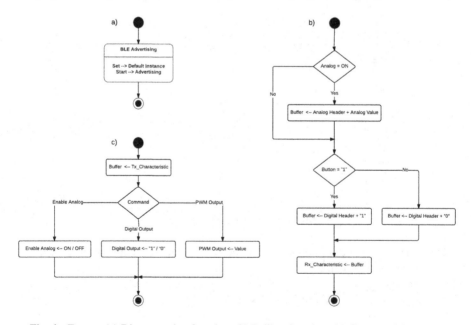

Fig. 4. Events: (a) Disconnection function, (b) Polling function, (c) Command functions

Polling Function. This function records the Tick event of the operating system, so every time a tick occurs, this function is executed. It uses this execution to read the corresponding analog and digital inputs, as shown in Fig. 4(b).

Command Functions. These functions handle the event when the paired device sends data or commands via BLE. First, it extracts commands and data from the "tx_characteristic" according to the established communication protocol.

The operation is then performed by modifying the output variable of the corresponding mote, either as a digital output by turning on or off an LED, or a PWM (Pulse Width Modulation) output with the value defined in the user interface of the smart phone. See Fig. 4(c).

3.5 Communication Protocol Used

As mentioned the mote firmware should be as light as possible, so the communications protocol is light too. In Fig. 5, we can see the protocol used, where the first byte corresponds to the command or action to be executed on one of the mote outputs, if it is digital or analog. Then, there is another byte that indicates which output variable is modified and finally, two bytes indicate the desired value to obtain at the output variable. For the testbed, we use three types of commands, however different types of commands in a byte, are sent up to 256, enough for almost any IoT application.

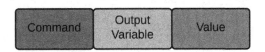

Fig. 5. Communication protocol

3.6 Implementation of the Android Application

In Fig. 6, we show the workflow of the developed telemetry system, which has three main components: mote, gateway and server. The mote or "thing" is in charge of interacting with the specific process. It acts as peripheral advertising every 100 ms in the application, and it waits for a central device to pair. Once a central device discovers it, the central device connects to it, so, both the central and peripheral switch to a state called paired. At that moment, the communication is done through the generic profile UART, with a characteristic (Tx) to send data from the mote to the gateway, and another characteristic (Rx) to receive the commands.

The application on Android (App) has dual functionality, monitoring and controlling the WSN as a gateway. To do this, it verifies that the BLE service on your smartphone is active; otherwise the application is terminated. Then, there are several screens or interfaces for authentication on the server, for interacting in real time with the motes of a WSN and for plotting the sensor data in real time. All these functions are accessible through functional buttons. It then lists all the discovered tags for the user to select who to connect to. Once the smartphone enters a paired state, the application allows it to

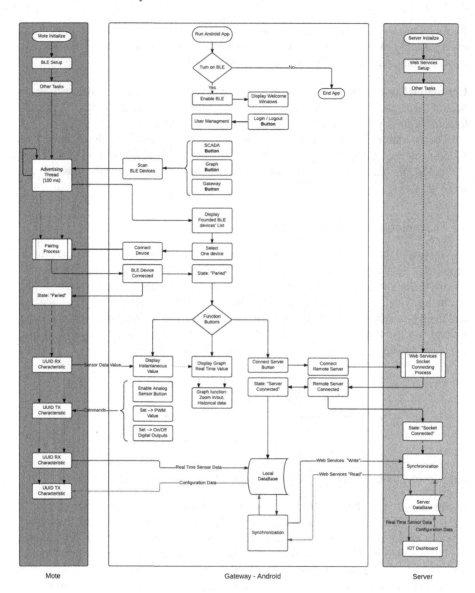

Fig. 6. Telemetry workflow

interact directly with the mote; and as a gateway, to establish a data gateway from the mote to the server and vice versa through a mechanism of synchronization of both ends with data persistence and commands in the local database. Finally, we have the server, where an end user through a dashboard from a traditional browser can remotely monitor the variables of a process in real time, as well as remotely send commands to open or close a solenoid valve, turn on an LED, etc. This is possible in the system thanks to the synchronization mechanisms implemented in the server.

4   Results and Discussion

Following the flow diagram described in the previous section in Fig. 6, we implement a telemetry system by developing firmware for a Mote BLE, IoT gateway and cloud computing. The implementation results are shown in this section.

4.1   Android Application Functionality

We implement the Android application with two requirements: monitoring and controlling in situ a WSN and acting as a gateway between the BLE motes with cloud computing, that allows users to access the data acquired of the IoT application domain (Agriculture) from the web and to send a remote command, for example to turn on or off a water pump or solenoid valve. Figure 7 shows several screenshots of the Android application that demonstrate the fulfillment of the stated objectives. In (a) the initial screen of the application, with a menu of options based on buttons. In (b) an interface that allows the configuration of the necessary parameters to make a connection with a remote server in the cloud. In (c) the first screen that appears when the SCADA option is pressed, where all discovered motes appear. Clicking on one of them, establishes a connection between the mote and the smartphone that permits visualization of instantaneous values of variables that are measuring the mote, as well as the controls necessary to send commands to the actuators, as seen in (d).

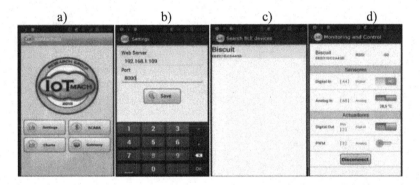

Fig. 7. Mobile gateway screenshots for IoT. (a) Starting screen, (b) Server connection parameters, (c) BLE devices found, (d) Monitoring and control.

4.2   Evaluations

Similar to the functionality demonstration of the application, these are according to the design requirements. Tests are also performed to measure the response rate of the proposed testbed for both local solutions and a complete IoT solution, i.e. the response time from the sensor to the cloud. The performance of the gateway was also measured in terms of the use of CPU and memory of the smart phone with different messenger loads.

The proposed test scenario consisted of three components: Mote, Mobile Application and IOTMACH Server. We used the following tools for gathering the measurements: Software Tera Term to capture the time when the mote packs a new sensor reading and to send it to the gateway. The Tera Term runs on the PC where the mote (RedbearLab) is connected via a USB serial port. Android Studio 2.3.3 was also used on a PC to take the logs sent by the Smart phone (Samsung J500 M, Version of android: 6.0.1) connected via USB to the PC. To capture the arrival time of messages from the Gateway on the server, we used the MQTT SPY, connected to the same MQTT Broker where the Gateway connects to send its messages. The connection between the Gateway and the mote is via Bluetooth Low Energy and via Wi-Fi for connection with the cloud (IoTMACH sever). An overview of this scenario is shown in Fig. 8(a).

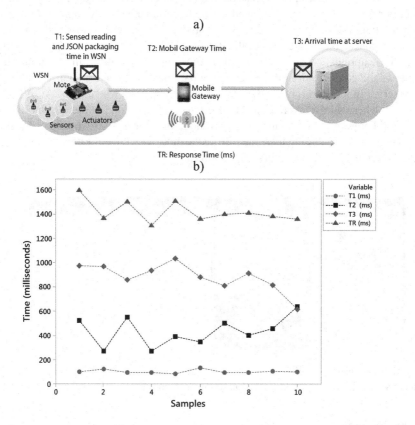

Fig. 8. Response time evaluation. (a) Test scenario, (b) Response time per connections and overall.

The experiment results, sending ten messages from the mote to the cloud can be observed in Fig. 8(b), where T1 represents the delay introduced by the mote to pack the data of the sensor. T2 represents the media delay (BLE) for sending the data between the mote and the gateway. T3 is the delay between the Gateway and the server. These times can vary depending on the medium used, whether Wi-Fi or GPS, 4G or LTE and depending on the data plan and smart phone used. TR represents the overall time of a sensor reading until it reaches the cloud. In Table 1 you can find more statistical details of the experiment, where we can highlight the speed of our testbed, with an average response time of only 1.4 s. This is excellent for precision agriculture applications where variables like temperature, humidity, etc. vary slowly over time.

Table 1. Response time statistics.

Variable	Average	Standard deviation	Min	Q1	Q3	Max
T1 (ms)	101,5	14,93	80	93,5	111	130
T2 (ms)	435,1	121,3	269	329,8	529	640
T3 (ms)	880,9	118,3	616	812,3	972	1036
TR = T1 + T2 + T3 (ms)	1417,5	88,8	1304	1357,8	1503	1594

In the second experiment, we measured the performance of the Gateway. The Android application was modified to increase the messaging load between the Gateway and the server, which would allow a total of 30 separate observations in three series with 10 iterations for each one. In the first series, 10 messages were sent, in the second series, 100 messages and in the third series, 1000 messages. Using the internal functions of Android Studio, it is possible to obtain the use of CPU and memory for each one of the mentioned series. The results are shown in Fig. 9 and statistical details in Table 2, where we can highlight that the CPU usage is practically constant regardless of the number of messages handled, with a small average variation between 11.79% and 13.30%. The use of the RAM shows a logical behavior proportional to the number of messages transmitted, which has to be processed in the Gateway.

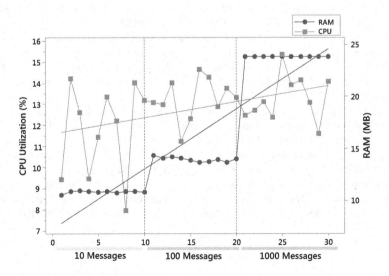

Fig. 9. Performance of the gateway, CPU and RAM utilization

Table 2. Smart phone performance statistics.

#Messages	CPU utilization AVG %	CPU utilization stan. dev.	RAM (MB) AVG	RAM stan. dev.
10	11,79	2,161	10,80	0,102
100	13,27	1,000	13,94	1,104
1000	13,30	1,097	23,87	1,414

5   Conclusions

We develop an Android application in this paper, which discovers BLE tags in the environment and when establishes connections with motes. The application allows the monitoring and controlling in situ of the sensors and actuators connected to the mote. Also, it works as an IoT gateway by receiving the messages coming from the WSN and by encapsulating them to be transmitted via MQTT to the cloud. This allows users of different application domains, as is the case of Precision Agriculture, to remotely, via the web, manage their processes by monitoring variables such as temperature and humidity; or by manipulating electro valves and water pumps to control irrigation. The results of our experiments demonstrate that a fast gateway is available, with low latency and excellent performance in commercial smart phones. The low CPU usage allows the smart phone to perform other functions and operations without affecting the gateway operation. The proportional cost of RAM offers the possibility of handling high rates of messaging or several motes. Following the workflow of the telemetry system shown in this work, this testbed can be implemented on other smartphone operating systems.

References

1. Atzori, L., Lera, A., Morabito, G.: The internet of things: a survey. Comput. Netw. **54**(15), 2787–2805 (2010). https://doi.org/10.1016/j.comnet.2010.05.010
2. Botta, A., et al.: Integration of cloud computing and internet of things: a survey. Future Gener. Comput. Syst. **56**, 684–700 (2015). https://doi.org/10.1016/j.future.2015.09.021
3. Chen, S., et al.: A vision of IoT: applications, challenges, and opportunities with China perspective. IEEE Internet Things J. **1**(4), 349–359 (2014). https://doi.org/10.1109/JIOT. 2014.2337336
4. Sarkar, C., et al.: A scalable distributed architecture towards unifying IoT applications. In: 2014 IEEE World Forum on Internet of Things (WF-IoT), pp. 508–513. IEEE, Seoul (2014). https://doi.org/10.1109/WF-IoT.2014.6803220
5. Campoverde, A., Hernández, D., Mazón, B.: Cloud computing con herramientas open-source para Internet de las cosas. Maskana **6**(No. Especial), 173–182 (2015)
6. Mat, I., Kassim, M., Harun, A.: Precision irrigation performance measurement using wireless sensor network. In: 2014 Sixth International Conference on Ubiquitous and Future Networks (ICUFN), pp. 154–157. IEEE, Shanghai (2014). https://doi.org/10.1109/ICUFN. 2014.6876771

7. Bendre, M.R., Thool, R.C., Thool, V.R.: Big data in precision agriculture: weather forecasting for future farming. In: 2015 1st International Conference on Next Generation Computing Technologies (NGCT), pp. 4–5. IEEE, Dehradun (2015). https://doi.org/10.1109/NGCT. 2015.7375220
8. Zhang, Q.: Precision Agriculture Technology for Crop Farming, 1st edn. CRC Press Taylor & Francis Group, Washington (2016)
9. Ivanov, S., Bhargava, K., Donnelly, W.: Precision farming: sensor analytics. IEEE Intell. Syst. **30**(4), 76–80 (2015)
10. Gartner Newsroom: Gartner Says Worldwide Smartphone Sales Recorded Slowest Growth Rate Since 2013. http://www.gartner.com/newsroom/id/3115517. Accessed 27 July 2017
11. Islam, T., Mukhopadhyay, S., Suryadevara, N.: Smart sensors and internet of things: a postgraduate paper. IEEE Sens. J. **17**(3), 577–584 (2017). https://doi.org/10.1109/JSEN. 2016.2630124
12. Raspberry Pi 3 Model B Homepage. https://www.raspberrypi.org/products/raspberry-pi-3-model-b/. Accessed 27 July 2017
13. Novillo, J., Redrován, F., Espinoza, F., Molina, J.: Raspberry analysis in the teaching of computer sciences. Int. J. Appl. Eng. Res. **12**(7), 1182–1189 (2017)
14. RedBearLab nRF51822 Homepage. http://redbearlab.com/redbearlab-nrf51822/. Accessed 27 July 2017
15. Sreekantha, D., Kavya, A.: Agricultural crop monitoring using IOT - a study. In: 2017 11th International Conference on Intelligent Systems and Control (ISCO), pp. 134–139. IEEE, Coimbatore (2017). https://doi.org/10.1109/ISCO.2017.7855968
16. Alahi, M., et al.: A temperature compensated smart nitrate-sensor for agricultural industry. IEEE Trans. Ind. Electron. **64**, 7333–7341 (2016). https://doi.org/10.1109/TIE.2017.2696508
17. Shailaja, M., Nikkam, G., Pawar, V.: Water parameter analysis for industrial application using IoT. In: 2016 2nd International Conference on Applied and Theoretical Computing and Communication Technology (iCATccT), pp. 703–707. IEEE, Bangalore (2016). https:// doi.org/10.1109/ICATCCT.2016.7912090
18. Maddikatla, S., Jandhyala, S.: An accurate all CMOS temperature sensor for IoT applications. In: 2016 IEEE Computer Society Annual Symposium on VLSI (ISVLSI), pp. 349–354. IEEE, Pittsburgh (2016). https://doi.org/10.1109/ISVLSI.2016.113
19. Russell, L., et al.: Sensor modality shifting in IoT deployment: measuring non-temperature data using temperature sensors. In: 2017 IEEE Sensors Applications Symposium (SAS), pp. 1–6. IEEE, Glassboro (2017). https://doi.org/10.1109/SAS.2017.7894057
20. Sinclair, I.: Sensors and Transducers, 3rd edn. Newnes, Great Britain (2001)
21. Agarwal, K., Sharma, D.: Wireless communication wibree (bluetooth low energy technology). EEC J. **2**(2), 1–4 (2017). https://doi.org/10.24001/eec.2.2.1
22. Bluetooth Working Groups Homepage. https://www.bluetooth.com/membership-working-groups/working-groups. Accessed 27 July 2017
23. Android Homepage. https://www.android.com. Accessed 27 July 2017
24. Platform versions. https://developer.android.com/about/dashboards/index.html#Platform. Accessed 27 July 2017
25. Saxena, N., et al.: Efficient IoT gateway over 5G wireless: a new design with prototype and implementation results. IEEE Commun. Mag. **55**(2), 97–105 (2017)
26. Schmidt, M., Obermaisser, R.: Middleware for the integration of Bluetooth LE devices based on MQTT and ISO/IEEE 11073. In: 2017 IEEE 30th Canadian Conference on Electrical and Computer Engineering (CCECE). IEEE (2017)
27. Dener, M.: A new gateway node for wireless sensor network applications. Sci. Res. Essays **11**(20), 213–220 (2016)

28. Maiti, P., et al.: Sensors data collection architecture in the internet of mobile things as a service (IoMTaaS) platform. In: IEEE International Conference on I-SMAC (IoT in Social, Mobile, Analytics and Cloud) (I-SMAC 2017), SCAD Institute of Technology, Coimbatore, India, 10–11 February 2017

29. Dupont, C., Raffaele, G., Luca, C.: Edge computing in IoT context: horizontal and vertical Linux container migration. In: Global Internet of Things Summit (GIoTS). IEEE (2017)

30. mbed IoT Platform Homepage. https://www.mbed.com/en/platform. Accessed 27 July 2017

Smart Mobile Application for the Prediction of the Loss of Signal in Telecommunication Networks Basing on Meteorological Variables

Kenya Anmarit Guerrero Goyes⬛,
Angie Sthepanie Aguilar Zambrano⬛⬛,
Gabriel Fernando Nuñez Villalba⬛,
and Eduardo Amable Samaniego Mena

Universidad Técnica Estatal de Quevedo, Quevedo, Ecuador
kenanmarl@gmail.com, angie_sthepanie@hotmail.com,
gabymakoto@gmail.com, esamaniego@uteq.edu.ec

Abstract. The objective of the research project was developing a mobile app to allow the signal loss prediction. The prediction is based on meteorological characteristic, because it is looking to support the decision-making by the telecommunication specialists. A data Pre-processing realized by the outlier's deletion and variables correlations resulted in a new Dataset. Different data mining classification techniques were analyzed using an optimization approach. The result of this analysis allows to determinate that, the algorithm based on Artificial Neural Networks was the one who has the better accuracy index. It was almost the 100% of accuracy. The project Aim to take advantage of an obtained model, it was represented in the Predictive Model Markup Language (PMML) and processed with JAVA technologies in a mobile app development. The app name is SignalPred; this app predicts signal loss through the signal reading of meteorological variables.

Keywords: Signal loss · Datamining · Artificial Neural Networks
Predictive Model Markup Language · Mobile application

1 Introduction

Today is essential to keep a solid communication in wireless telecommunications networks for the transfer of information because it is necessary to know the problems that can cause the loss of the sign. In the article [1] the meteorological variables have a good effect in the signal quality, but there is a doubt about with variables have possibilities to influence the signal loss.

To understand the meteorological variables effects is necessary to apply Knowledge Discovery in Databases (KDD), this process thru datamining Techniques will generate a mathematical model able to predict the signal loss. This model must be capable of being applied on a development language, because that a mobile app has been developed for Android named SignalPred (Signal Prediction). The objective of the

© Springer International Publishing AG 2018
M. Botto-Tobar et al. (Eds.): CITT 2017, CCIS 798, pp. 33–42, 2018.
https://doi.org/10.1007/978-3-319-72727-1_3

application gets meteorological information based on the localization and monitoring the results of a mathematical model for the signal prediction at that moment.

The application is expected to generate high acceptance by telecommunication specialists and be accessible to all users because it will work with the meteorological variables available according to their GPS location and this form will generate the prediction.

2 Literature Review

Among the reviews of different studies conducted between the periods, 2013 to 2016 were several articles related to the study of data mining using several techniques to obtain a model or prediction of the precipitation and about the loss of signal from meteorological variables.

The master's thesis on connectivity and computer networks [2], performs research to obtain a model of data mining that characterizes the quality of the wireless signal in function of the meteorological variations. This work used two data mining tools: Weka for the pre-processing of the data and Keel for applying the extensive rules; the FURIA-C algorithm based on fuzzy logic obtained an accuracy of 0.8774 with an amount of 8 rules and a standard deviation of 0.0199.

In the year 2015, the authors Anochi and Campos Velho [3], made a study to predict the seasonal climatic precipitation variable in the Central-West region of Brazil. A method based on the Artificial Neural Network was used, that method was applied to the seasonal precipitation of climate prediction using the method of Data Reduction by the Rough Set Theory, and the results obtained show the effectiveness of the proposed methodology.

The author [4], in collaboration with his coauthors, proposes a service of indexation of urban climatic disasters which: detect, predicts and analyzes the tendency of several risks such as disasters and safety accidents. This service is used for decision-making in the management of climatic disasters and aims to determine the risks based on natural disasters caused by man.

In the year 2016 the authors [5] presented a study on obtaining a data mining model, using the Global System for Mobile Communications and Global Positioning System to collect the meteorological data, in order to evaluate the ability to monitor rainfall, several sorting algorithms such: k-Nearest Neighbors, Support Vector Machine and Decision Tree used to identify precipitation types (rain, light rain, heavy rain), that in order to verify the feasibility of a system for rain alerts.

It observed that the topics based on the study of data mining using different techniques for the obtaining of a model or the prediction of the climatic precipitation. In the study [2], the signal loss prediction performed, but it does not have a mobile application. For this reason, the development of the research project is favorable, because there is no research that develops a mobile application based on a data mining study aimed at the signal loss.

3   Materials and Methods

For the investigative study, the research data used [2], in which 16 meteorological variables identified: day, month, year, min temperature, average temperature, max temperature, oscillation temperature, min humidity, average humidity, humidity maximum, vapor pressure, dew point, heliophania, evaporation, rain, signal loss.

For the data mining study were used the RapidMiner data mining tool where performed a pre-processing to eliminate Outliers, correlation and identify the class variable; through an optimization process, several predictive algorithms analyzed, and an optimized model obtained as a result.

Making use of the IDE Android Studio developed a mobile application on the platform Android 4.0 (Ice-Cream Sandwich) aimed at predicting loss of signal in wireless networks. This application makes use of a weather service to obtain the meteorological variables.

4   Architecture

The mobile application is based on a three-tier architecture: Presentation, Business, and Data

- Presentation level: The mobile application is responsible for collecting the data and visualizing the result.
- Business Level: The desktop application loads, processes, and evaluates the model.
- Data Level: The remote database agglomerates all transactions between the two applications: Mobile and Desktop.

Lifecycle: The implementation based on the methodology of Extreme Programming (XP), this worked on a light development methodology that is subject to frequent changes throughout the life cycle of the project. The following are phases of the methodology to be used (Fig. 1):

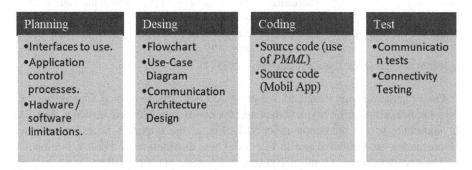

Planning	Desing	Coding	Test
•Interfaces to use. •Application control processes. •Hadware / software limitations.	•Flowchart •Use-Case Diagram •Communication Architecture Design	•Source code (use of *PMML*) •Source code (Mobil App)	•Communication tests •Connectivity Testing

Fig. 1. Phases of Extreme Programming methodology –XP.

5 Results

5.1 Data Mining Results

For the investigative study, we used the data of the investigation [2], in which 16 meteorological variables identified. Table 1 shows the meteorological variables of the original data set to be analyzed, the alias, measures and their descriptions observed.

Table 1. Variable Analysis

Variables	Alias	Measure	Description
Min temperature	TMIN	Celsius	It is the lowest temperature recorded on the day. It registers from 7:00 pm and 7:00 am
Med temperature	TMED	Celsius	It is the average temperature between the maximum and minimum temperature
Max temperature	TMAX	Celsius	It is the highest temperature recorded in a day. It registers from 7:00 am and 7:00 pm
Thermal oscillation	TOCS	Celsius	It is the difference between the highest and lowest temperature recorded in the day
Min relative humidity	HMIN	Percent	It is the minimum percentage of relative humidity during the day
Average relative humidity	HMED	Percent	It is the max amount of water vapor that can contain saturated air
Max relative humidity	HMAX	Percent	It is the maximum percentage of relative humidity during the day
Water vapor pressure	TENVA	Celsius	Pressure would have the water vapor if it occupied only the volume of moist air
Dew point	PUROC	Celsius	Temperature where the air reaches saturation
Heliophania	HELIO	Hours	Number of hours solar brightness in the day
Evaporation	EVA	Millimeter	It is the change of liquid state to gaseous state without considering the temperature
Rain	LLUV	Millimeter	It is produced by condensation of the water vapor contained in the clouds
Signal loss	PESE	Boolean	It is produced by the decrease of power per unit area

Source: Master Thesis of Telecommunications -2015 [2]

Once the dataset was identified, the pre-processing was performed, identifying the class variable, eliminating atypical data and the correlation between variables that did not contribute to the prediction process. In Fig. 2, the operators necessary for the pre-processing are presented and in Fig. 3 the new distribution of the data is shown.

The new dataset has a total of 200 cases: 126 cases of Signal (Blue Color) and 74 cases of Interference (Red Color) with a total of 10 Attributes including type "Loss of Signal" type. As you can see, the Signal surpasses the Interference with 63%.

This dataset has an inclination toward cases where there is a signal, which will cause over-learning when constructing a model. In order to avoid this kind of

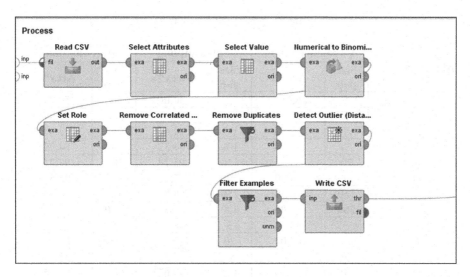

Fig. 2. Pre-processing RapidMiner

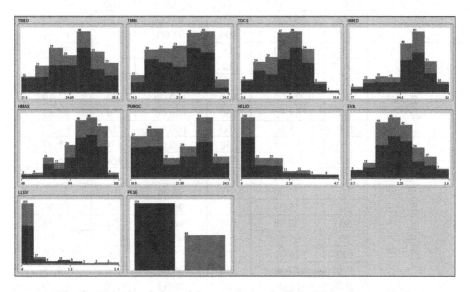

Fig. 3. Main description of the new dataset in Weka (Color figure online)

inconvenience were necessary proceeded to perform an Over-sampling and Sub-sampling process to balance the class attribute and avoid over-learning.

The next algorithms were used: Tree Decision and Tree Random belonging to Decision Tree, Red Learning and Neural Net pertaining to the Neural Networks, finally the Regularized Discriminant Analysis of the Discriminant Analysis. These were optimized with different population sizes to obtain a high accuracy index, as is shown in Table 2.

Table 2. Optimization results

Algorithm	Unbalanced Data		Sub-sampling		Over-sampling	
	Size pop	Accy%	Size pop	Accy%	Size pop	Accy%
Random Forest	5	65.50	5	50.00	5	53.47
	10	65.50	20	80.67	10	53.47
	20	72.50	50	91.63	20	53.47
	50	73.00	100	94.33	50	84.72
	70	73.50	150	95.14	**70**	**97.22**
	100	75.00	200	97.22	100	96.53
	150	78.50	**250**	**98.05**	130	96.53
	200	**79.00**	300	96.33	150	95.14
Decision Tree	5	65.50	5	88.67	5	53.47
	10	69.00	20	93.00	10	63.89
	20	69.00	50	95.33	20	61.81
	50	69.00	**100**	**99.67**	**50**	**68.75**
	70	69.00	150	93.00	*70*	68.75
	100	**72.50**	200	93.00	100	68.75
	150	69.00	250	93.00	130	68.75
	200	69.00	300	93.00	150	68.75
Neural Net	5	72.00	*5**	*100.00**	5	53.47
	10	73.50	20	100.00	10	55.56
	20	74.00	50	100.00	20	61.81
	50	74.00	100	100.00	50	63.19
	70	68.50	150	100.00	*70*	**66.67**
	100	75.50	200	100.00	100	64.58
	150	**77.50**	250	100.00	130	65.97
	200	74.50	300	100.00	150	65.97
Deep Learning	5	65.50	5	80.67	5	65.97
	10	77.50	20	94.00	10	54.86
	20	75.00	50	96.00	20	68.06
	50	**78.00**	**100**	**96.33**	50	65.28
	70	65.50	150	96.33	*70*	61.81
	100	76.00	200	96.33	100	67.36
	150	77.50	250	96.00	130	**68.75**
	200	76.00	300	96.33	150	63.89
RAD	**5**	**34.50**	5	**50.00**	5	**53.47**
	10	34.50	20	50.00	10	53.47
	20	34.50	50	50.00	20	53.47
	50	34.50	100	50.00	50	53.47
	70	34.50	150	50.00	*70*	53.47
	100	34.50	200	50.00	100	53.47
	150	34.50	250	50.00	130	53.47
	200	34.50	300	50.00	150	53.47

The result with the highest accuracy is in the over-sampling, where the Neural Net algorithm obtained an accuracy index of 100% with a population size of 5, working with a total of 300 cases. This result is repeated for different population sizes greater than 5, in the rest of the algorithms the result varies depending on the size of the population. Table 3 shows the parameters necessary for the overall model.

Table 3. Optimized parameters of the Neural Net Model

Parameters	Values
training_cycles	63
learning_rate	0.7628774515705214
momentum	0.681461325038434
error_epsilon	0.0
local_random_seed	74

5.2   Results of the Mobile Application Development

Once the optimized model was obtained, proceeded to export it to the PMML modeling standard, with the purpose of practically executing a signal loss prediction taking into account the values of the meteorological variables.

The PMML documentation were studied and tested by the different methods that the language provides, finding certain limitations between the platforms: Mobile and Web. For this reason, the PMML libraries were incorporated into the desktop platform that is used as a JAVA developing language.

The research is targeted at Android 4.0 (Ice Cream Sandwich) devices or higher, that for the prediction of signal loss in wireless networks based on weather conditions. The data collection is either manually or automatically, where the data will be entered or generated by the GPS location.

It was developed in JAVA a desktop application, which aims to build and evaluate the model of data mining with the values that the mobile application will deliver.

Once the two applications were developed, was obtained as a result an effective communication, as shown in Fig. 4, the remote database is in charge of communication by agglomerating all transactions between the two applications.

The model evaluation within the mobile application is achieved by entering a record of the meteorological variables in the database; the desktop application makes in a period of time certain queries to the database in search of new values to process the model.

The desktop application downloads the information and evaluates the model; the results are re-entered into the database and the mobile application displays the generated result.

As a result, an application was developed that consists of three modules: Values Entry, Generate List and Help, a series of interfaces were designed to interact with the user. Once inside the application will be shown the main screen where the

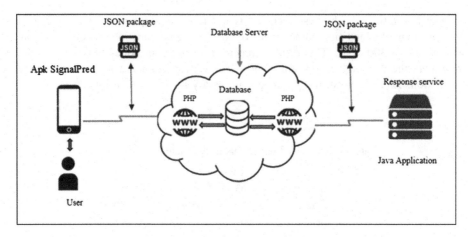

Fig. 4. Communication between apps: Mobile and Desktop

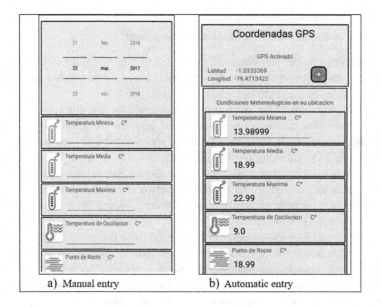

Fig. 5. Data insertion

meteorological data of the GPS location is observed as long as it is available, the sidebar shows the available modules. The operation of the application is detailed below.

In Fig. 5 can see the two ways of entering data, in (a) it is observed the data entry manually, a list of the variables that the model needs to generate the result is seen, (b) the data is entered automatically, once the GPS is activated, the GPS coordinates will be displayed at zero until the new GPS location is obtained, then the data of the variables will be visualized and the result will be generated.

Figure 6 shows the results and feedback. Once the prediction function has already been executed, either by manual or automatic input, the result obtained will be displayed; generating a result that is expressed in numbers, graphs and a question is asked to feed back the model. In case of selecting NO in feedback question will be presented a window where all the data of the available variables will be displayed and also the possible results options.

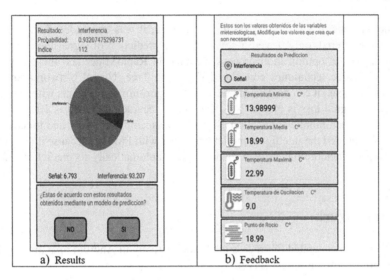

Fig. 6. Results and feedback

5.3 Results and Discussion

The results of the development are discussed below:

This research so far is unique, because there are many investigations that use data mining, but few are intended to predict signal loss, except for the thesis [2], which conducts a study, but not implements its model in a practical way as this one does.

In relation to the previously mentioned investigation, it is observed that the FURIA-C algorithm based on Fuzzy Logic obtained an accuracy of 87.74% with an amount of 8 rules. In contrast, in the present investigation the Neural Net model based on Neural Networks obtained an accuracy of 100% taking into account 9 meteorological variables and applied to a publication size of 5. It would be ideal to perform the data mining process again with a new data set that has a greater amount of information and is up to date.

During the tests with the PMML standard, the intelligent data analysis model was executed in a desktop application. For communication between the Mobile platform and the Desktop platform, a form of communication was needed, taking into account that free information access services were used, communication was done with a remote database.

The SignalPred mobile application predicts signal loss based on weather variables. The application is considered friendly and intuitive since the user can identify the actions to be performed within it, serving in this way as a support tool for decision making.

6 Conclusions

With the analysis of the pre-processing of the data, it was concluded that, of the 15 variables considered, only 9 were relevant for the prediction of signal loss.

Starting at the optimization process included in RapidMiner and the comparison between the three techniques considered (Decision Tree, Neural Networks and Discriminant Analysis) it can be determined that the algorithm that predicts with the mayor accuracy the signal loss is Neural Net. The better accuracy obtained is 100%.

The developed mobile application, SignalPred, is simple, friendly and functional. It is not only included the intelligent model generated with PMML, because it also allows the reading of meteorological data manually and automatically to predict signal loss effectively.

7 Future Work

As future work is intended to process the model natively in Android operating systems in order not to rely on a data server.

References

1. Bri, D., Fernandez-Diego, M., Garcia, M., Ramos, F., Lloret, J.: How the weather impacts on the performance of an outdoor WLAN. IEEE Commun. Lett. 16(8), 1184–1187 (2012)
2. Najarro, I.R.: La calidad de la conexión inalámbrica y su relación con las condiciones meteorológicas, Universidad Técnica Estatal De Quevedo (2015)
3. Anochia1, J.A., de Campos Velho, H.F.: Meteorological data mining for climate precipitation prediction using neural networks. J. Comp. Int. Sci. 6(2), 71–78 (2015)
4. Kim, J.-C., Jung, H., Chung, K.: Mining based urban climate disaster index service according to potential risk. Wirel. Pers. Commun. 89(3), 1009–1025 (2016)
5. Brito, L.F.A., Albertini, M.K.: Data mining of meteorological-related attributes from smartphone data. INFOCOMP J. Comput. Sci. 15(2), 1–9 (2016)

Open Source IoT Technology to Connect Environment Monitoring System

Andrés Efraín Chango Macas(✉)

Escuela Técnica Superior de Ingeniería de Sistemas Informáticos, Universidad Politécnica de Madrid, Campus Vallecas, Calle Alan Turing s/n, 28031 Madrid, Spain
ae.chango@alumnos.upm.es

Abstract. Internet of Things (IoT) is transforming people lives in recent years, because of this concept has been developed in new technologies that people use in their homes, public transportation and their jobs. Furthermore, the need for people to be connected and interact with the different situations that occur around them, through the use of sensors, low cost embedded systems, and actuators. The new devices should be connected and require a reliable communication between each other. This paper describes the implementation of an environmental monitoring system based on a wireless sensors network and IoT open source gateway that allows scalability and integration with different IoT services in the cloud like AWS IoT. Additionally, this paper shows the new technologies to connect a complete IoT system using low-cost hardware and open source gateway platforms based on Linux System.

Keywords: IoT · Embedded systems · Gateway

1 Introduction

Nowadays the growth of IoT applications is transforming the way in which people perform their daily activities, how organizations communicate with their consumers, distributors, and suppliers. The use of interconnected sensors has allowed that generated information be analyzed and it could be used by simple people or organizations [1]. Also, the low cost of embedded devices and their easy configuration has diminished the time of introduction and acceptance of this concept in homes and industries.

Innovation in hardware like the Raspberry Pi [2], Intel Edision [3] and Beagle-Bone [4], has made the development of new acquisition devices possible, besides the different communication interfaces that Raspberry Pi presents, allows integration with microcontrollers. These interfaces can be used to integrate wired or wireless communication protocols.

Some software platforms also provided configuration and monitoring IoT tools. The use of open source platforms has allowed the growth and decoupling of proprietary monitoring systems linked to industrial systems (SCADA) [5], providing community access to tools with greater exploitation in both the industrial, medical and environmental applications along with others linked to the comfort and safety of users.

© Springer International Publishing AG 2018
M. Botto-Tobar et al. (Eds.): CITT 2017, CCIS 798, pp. 43–54, 2018.
https://doi.org/10.1007/978-3-319-72727-1_4

The use of a gateway as an intermediary between data acquisition devices and data processing, visualization and analysis systems has taken on a significant importance since the miniaturization of the data acquisition terminal devices. On the other hand, this terminal device needs a long battery life. For this reason, the devices cannot communicate directly with Internet services over Wi-Fi networks. So the systems must be capable of communicating and acquiring the data without the highest energy consumption, for which there are protocols such as those contemplated under the standard 802.15.4, for example, Lora, Xbee, Zigbee, etc.

The use of these protocols allows a reliable and real-time communication. However, the communication to the rest of the monitoring system cannot be interpreted and must use proprietary devices that carry out the transformation of the protocol to its different web platforms.

The use of open source gateway allows decoupling the dependency of proprietary transformation and visualization platforms without losing the possibility of using these low-power protocols as a first level architecture.

The present paper describes a system based on the IoT architecture, using a network of wireless sensors capable of measuring environmental variables such as luminosity, temperature, humidity and CO_2 level, which constitute the device level. The open source Kura IoT framework as a gateway, which is responsible for the interaction of data obtained and services in the cloud.

2   Related Work

Some companies have developed IoT platforms for device management such as Euro-Tech. This company uses a gateway based on free software for the connection of the physical devices with its platform. In its publication, Everyware Software Framework [6], details the use of OSGi [7] and its usefulness in the connection of the platform with the devices and their portability. Also, Eclipse-IoT makes progress in the use of systems based on open software for the integration of low-cost IoT systems. Kura IoT is an open source de gateway based on Linux System. Related works like ConnectOpen – Automatic Integration of IoT Devices [8], use Kura IoT as a gateway and presents a configurable and modular communication agent, which separates concerns at Gateway level, like protocol interpretation, data parsing, data transmission and it was implemented as an OSGi bundle.

Kura is an open source gateway that allows communication between terminal devices or sensors through different protocols, such as RS232, RS485, Modbus, CAN. Kura also allows IPV4 monitoring and processing system using the MQTT protocol for Publish/Subscribe architecture. This protocol permits a fluid communication and only communicating the events associated with each device.

They also provide a foundation for IoT solutions based on OSGi, therefore it has a component-oriented execution environment for dynamic maintenance, manage and control devices or applications remotely. OSGi provides a programming model for applications and services in many industries. The Kura components expose a service

API, most of the Kura components are written in JAVA, and others are invoked through JNI and have a dependency on the Linux operating system.

3   Research Method

The IoT system presented in this article bases its architecture on the ITU-T Recommendation Y.2060 (06/2012) as a global infrastructure for the information society [9]. The ITU-T recommendation divides the structure of an IoT project into four layers. These layers cover implementation and security levels. The application layer, service support and application support layer, network layer and the device layer. The system has three fundamental parts. The first part is the Environmental Variables Acquisition System. It has the device layer, the second part is gateway its represent the network layer and Storage, and Data Processing has application layer and service support and application support layer. The system is shown in Fig. 1.

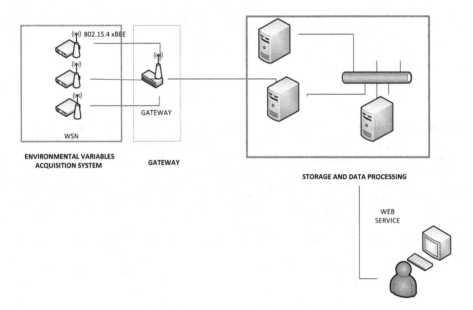

Fig. 1. System architecture.

3.1   Environmental Variables Acquisition System

The wireless terminal devices formed the environmental variables Acquisition System. The function of terminal devices is collecting environmental variables, such as temperature, light intensity, humidity, CO_2 levels and transmit this values wirelessly to the gateway. For the analysis of the design, is necessary to consider the Remote Sensing Acquisition Terminal (RSAT), as an entity that has a power supply, and environmental variables. The main function of RSTA is to obtain the environmental variables and transmit it as shown in Fig. 2:

Fig. 2. Remote sensor acquisition terminal.

The design of RSAT is decomposed into three subsystems as shown in Fig. 3. The separation in subsystems gives modularity to the design, which facilitates the selection of the electronic components that form the System.

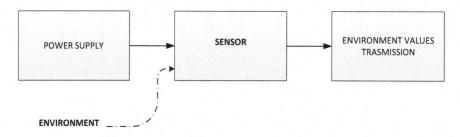

Fig. 3. RSAT subsystems.

Modules Identification. The RSAT has three modules that contain the general structure of the system. The separation of the system into modules allows the identification of functionalities. The modules are considered as an isolated subsystem, as seen in Fig. 4:

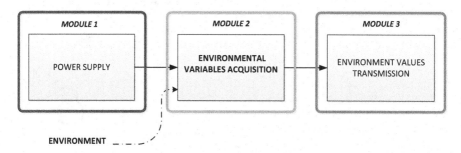

Fig. 4. Functional RSAT modules.

- Module 1: Power Supply.
- Module 2: Environmental Variables Acquisition.
- Module 3: Environment Values Transmission.

Module 1: This module has to supply energy to the terminal device RSAT. This project uses a rechargeable 5-V battery that powers the sensors and the wireless transmission plate.

Module 2: This module has four sensors that were connected to the data acquisition system of the XBee plate using signal conditioning systems to decrease the voltage from 5 V to 3.3 V. The entrances of the XBee plate accept a 3.3 V maximum input signal, so the sensors were calibrated to deliver the maximum value of 3.3 V as output.

Module 3: Environmental Values Transmission is responsible for receiving the analog signals from the data acquisition module using a digital converter (ADC) and sending that information wirelessly to the gateway. For this module, it analyzes each of the tasks that must fulfill and makes a comparison of the electronic elements that satisfy the requirements of each task. Finally, the selected module is a XBee Transmitter from Digi International. The XBee modules integrate a ZigBee transceiver and a microcontroller into the same device, allowing the user to develop operational prototypes quickly and easily using the user-programmed programming functions [10].

XBee modules are inexpensive, powerful and easy to use. There are two series, the series S1 and the series S2. XBee series 1 and series 2 have the same pin-out, however, none are compatible with each other, and they use a different chipset and protocols [11].

Series 1 uses point and multiple points 802.15.4 protocol. However, the Series 2 modules are used in applications with repeaters. In this project, the XBee series 1 was selected because the architecture proposed is multipoint. The transmitter devices will receive the data and send it to a single receiver that will connect directly to the gateway. For this reason, the series 1 is the cheapest option and fits the resolution of the problem. The final RSAT device is shown in Fig. 5.

Fig. 5. Remote sensor acquisition terminal module.

3.2 Kura IoT Gateway

Existing IoT platforms provide a connection between end devices and the platform using Ethernet, limiting the communication protocols of the end devices. Due to these limitations, additional hardware must be used to implement communication with the IoT platform. The project uses a framework as a communication gateway between the end devices and the platforms for visualization and data processing for the Internet of the

Existing Things. There are different options for using frameworks to implement a communication gateway with Kura IoT, Mahini, and IoTivity.

Kura IoT due to its ease of installation and the use of Java as a programming language. Kura IoT is a project developed by Eclipse IoT, which seeks to develop different Internet applications of things, using an easy-to-use Gateway; Kura runs under the Java virtual machine (JVM) providing APIs for connection to the Platform hardware, USB, GPIOs, Serial, I2C, etc. and connectivity with IoT visualization platforms using Cloud Services or MQTT [12].

IoT gateway is responsible for coordinating the connectivity between the sensors and actuators with the systems that are in the external network. A gateway must be a physical piece of hardware or a functional part in a system. The typical gateway architecture may be used to connect sensors to the network (see Fig. 6).

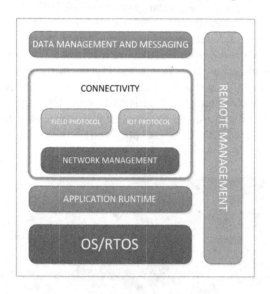

Fig. 6. IoT gateway architecture.

The first layer refers to the typically Linux operating system. The second layer contains the Runtime Application to execute code in Java, Phyton, etc. languages. The next layer allows communication with the terminal devices; these can be sensors or actuators. Open protocols, like Zigbee, RS232, Ethernet, and Bluetooth provide the communication. The network management layer handles the communication latency control, and the last layer handles the tester remote control access for Gateway administration [13].

Figure 7 shows the architecture on which the Kura IoT gateway is formed. It runs on a Linux operating system so it can be implemented on low-cost hardware, like raspberry pi. It also has an OSGi Application Runtime that allows modular programming and support for native java libraries.

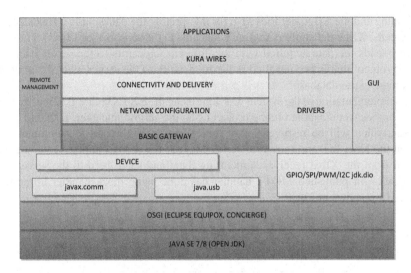

Fig. 7. Kura IoT architecture [13].

The connectivity layer presents several drivers for both GPIO management of raspberry Pi and industrial modules based on RS232, RS 485. The Network layer is based on IPV4 communications via Ethernet or Wi-Fi. Data and Messaging management is done through the native implementation of MQTT, which allows transparent communication with the Cloud Platform, without having to deal with the availability of the network interfaces, or how to represent IoT data.

Support for additional messaging protocols is available through the built-in Apache Camel message routing engine. For the implementation of the project the values are sent to the Gateway Kura IoT through serial port, that is connected to the Raspberry Pi from the receiver XBee module, for which you must use the libraries of RXTXJava for the

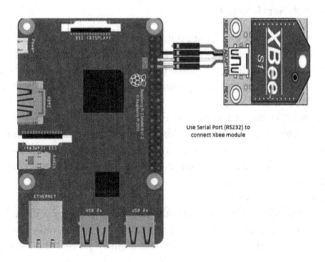

Fig. 8. Serial communication raspberry pi.

port reading and the XBee libraries Java for interpreting the data sent in a Hexadecimal way from the XBee transmitters that are connected to the sensors (see Fig. 8). The Kura Gateway sends the data acquired with the different indicators to the server using the MQTT protocol that is pre-installed in the framework to the server with Mosquito for later storage in the database.

The implementation of the system was done using the RXTXJava and XBee libraries. These libraries were installed in the project using the eclipse manager. It should define a bundle which will be responsible for the execution of the call to communication between the Kura IoT and mosquito server MQTT; the second bundle reads the data received from the XBee receiver, structuring them and send them to the server. The configuration of published MQTT handler has done using block handler libraries of Eclipse-ID; it shows in Fig. 9.

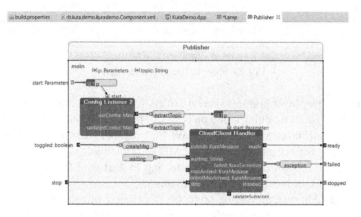

Fig. 9. MQTT publisher handler

3.3   Amazon Web Services IoT

AWS IoT provides bi-directional communication between devices such as sensors, actuators, or smart appliances and the AWS cloud. AWS receives data from multiple devices, store and analyze the data. Also, provides a secure communication channel using SSL certificates that ensure communication between the devices by exchanging the public keys [14].

AWS IoT has different components like Device gateway, Message Broker, Rules Engine, Security and Identity services, thing register, thing shadow, thing Shadows service. The device gateway allows a secure and efficient communication with AWS IoT. The message broker ensures communication between to publish and receive messages from AWS IoT to devices. Also, the MQTT protocol can be used directly or MQTT protocol over Web Socket.

Rules Engine provides the integration with AWS services using SQL-based language to select data from pipe load and process it with other AWS tools like: AWS Lambda, Amazon Dynamo, Amazon S3. The security and Identity service shared responsibility for AWS cloud security. The message broker and rules engine use AWS security. Thing register referred to as device registry; thing shadow is a JSON document.

IoT Devices report their state using the topic in an MQTT messages; each topic has a name that identifies the device and their state. After that, the message is sent to the AWS IoT MQTT message broker. This broker is responsible for sending all messages to all clients that have subscribed to specific topics. The Communication between the gateway and AWS IoT is protected through the use of X.509 certificates. AWS can generate the certificate or you can use yours owns. The architecture is shown in Fig. 10.

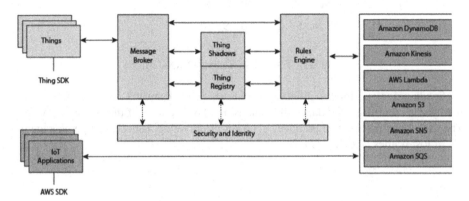

Fig. 10. AWS IoT functionality [14].

For connecting Kura IoT to the Amazon server, you must create SSL certificates. After, the registration in the Amazon account chose a certificate for embedded C devices because Kura uses a JNI system that encapsulates C code for the implementation of communication libraries and messaging management. The certificates will allow identification between the server and the Raspberry Pi device for messaging exchange.

After generating the certificates, a PCK8 file must be exported copy the public and private keys for mutual authentication between the server and the gateway. This process can be done using the graphical interface of Kura IoT.

Finally, the connection between the broker and the AWS IoT platform must establish communication with the gateway and allow the exchange of information using MQTT messages only by defining the headers and topics.

4   Results

Connectivity tests were performed between the Gateway and the XBee environmental data collection system. The data was transmitted directly using the Raspberry Pi UART port and the XBee receiver using the API mode. The use of this mechanism did not produce good results; the frames are lost or overlap each other. The lost frames were about 61% (see Fig. 11).

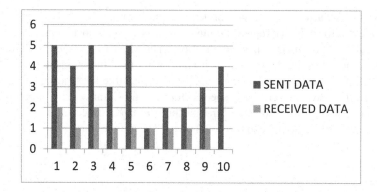

Fig. 11. Transmission using TXRX-Java

Sending and receiving configuration was changed. Kura-IoT uses the XBee Java library and controlling the data collection using MAC address of the terminal devices. The use of this mechanism produces good result obtaining a successful percentage of 4% of lost frames (see Fig. 12).

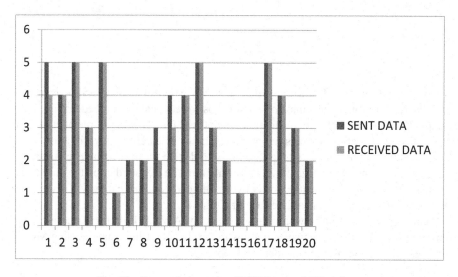

Fig. 12. Transmission using TXRXJava and XBee-Java

Connection tests were performed between AWS IoT and Kura, the frames sent and received through the topics of the MQTT protocol delivered positive results. However, some frames were affected by the latency of the test network. The messages percentage received in AWS IoT were 93.75% (see Fig. 13).

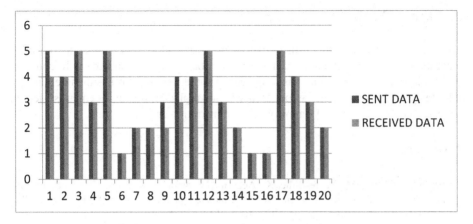

Fig. 13. Transmission between Kura-IoT and AWS-IoT

5 Conclusions

IoT solutions require software and hardware technologies to facilitate integration with existing components in today's markets. These solutions will allow a coupling of different proprietary and free technologies. For this reason is necessary to design independent equipment of proprietary platforms that limit the integration of the systems. The use of communication framework with Kura IoT allows a simplified integration into the data acquisition and data management systems.

The use of 802.15.4 networks allows sensors to communicate with the gateway reliably and ensuring low power consumption. In addition to allowing the use of various topologies to improve network coverage.

The motivation of this paper was fulfilled because using the Kura IoT gateway allowed the integration of devices based on technologies of low power consumption and without a direct connection to the Internet as XBee towards a management platform in the cloud. The use of this gateway facilitates the integration of different communication protocols into a single device. Kura IoT gateway was able to integrate serial communication and data collection management of XBee devices with the AWS Platform through the use of MQTT protocol. MQTT messaging allows the possibility of integration with other management platforms of IoT devices such as Carriots and Node-Red.

The integration of the library TXRX Java and XBee Java allowed the reading of the data sent from the terminal devices. However, the control of the low-power modes of the XBee transmitters was not handled from the libraries. This problem causes a processing consumption in the gateway because it is necessary to perform a loop for each device by collecting the data and using the MAC addresses of the XBee transmitters to form the MQTT messaging themes to determine each device.

6 Future Work

About the experience in this project can be proposed future case studies as the full integration of the management system with the sensors, using a dashboard for the control and monitoring the state of the sensor devices. Another relation work is the integration of security systems and home automation systems replacing the management systems that each has and uses an IoT gateway for administration and monitoring.

References

1. Pazos, N., Müller, M., Favre-Bulle, K., Aeberli M., Ouerhani. N.: Dynamic street-parking optimisation, Advanced Information Networking and Applications (AINA). In: 2016 IEEE 30th International Conference, pp. 1020–1026. IEEE (2016)
2. Wallace, M., Richardson, S.: Getting started with Raspberry Pi. O´Reilly, Sebastopol (2013)
3. Intel Software Developer Zone. https://software.intel.com/en-us
4. BeagleBoard Homepage. http://beagleboard.org/bone
5. Hwaiyu, G.: Internet of Things and Data Analytics Handbook, 1st edn. Wiley, Hoboken (2016)
6. Eurotech White Papers. https://www.eurotech.com/en/library/white+papers
7. OSGI Alliance. https://www.osgi.org/developer/white-papers
8. Pazos, N., Müller, M., Favre-Bulle, K., Aeberli, M., Ouerhani, N.: ConnectOpen - automatic integration of IoT devices. In: 2015 IEEE 2nd World Forum on Internet of Things (WF-IoT), pp. 640–644. IEEE (2015)
9. Recommendation ITU-T Y.2060. http://www.itu.int/en/ITU-T/gsi/iot/Pages/default.aspx
10. Digi. XBee® 802.15.4. http://www.digi.com/products/xbee-rf-solutions/modules/xbee-series1-module
11. DIGI. XCTU. http://www.digi.com/products/xbee-rf-solutions/xctu-software/xctu
12. Kura IoT. http://eclipse.github.io/kura/intro/intro.html
13. IoTEclipse. https://iot.eclipse.org/gateways
14. AWS IoT Developer Guide. http://docs.amazon.com/iot/latest/developerguide/what-is-aws-iot.html

Computer and Software Engineering

Development of Prototype Suit for Modeling of Lower Limbs Using NodeMcu and Matlab

Javier J. Gavilanes(✉) ⓘ, Henry Lema ⓘ, Jairo R. Jácome ⓘ,
Alexandra O. Pazmiño ⓘ, and Luis Zabala ⓘ

Facultad de Mecánica, Escuela Superior Politécnica de Chimborazo,
Panamericana Sur km 1 ½, Riobamba, Ecuador
{javier.gavilanes,giebi,jjacome,apazmino_a,
luis.zabala}@espoch.edu.ec

Abstract. In the present project a prototype was developed, that models the lower limbs movement, unlike other commercial devices, this prototype seeks to obtain data through low-cost electronics in order to be replicated by the scientific community interested in this research line, it integrates electronic boards and programming software such as Arduino, NodeMCU, Accelerometers and Matlab. The sensors have been placed on a shield that facilitates their connection. The connection through a bus of all the sensors is presented in a NodeMCU board, through Wi-Fi sends a table of all this data for processed in Matlab. Data shows the main articular positions of the lower limbs of a person, using the homogeneous transformation matrices we obtain a seven-bar model that shows positions and accelerations produced by individual joints, the data obtained by the suit can be contrast with simulations performed in previous works, providing good results, and allowing future developments in topics such as gait analysis, teleoperation and modeling of physical therapies to ensure their effectiveness.

Keywords: Client · Server · NodeMcu · Gyroscope · Wireless network
Sensory suit

1 Introduction

The process of reading and simulating the movements of the human body employs different technologies, of which the most employed are based on a sensory suit or a camera system. These systems are used in medical, sports, entertainment, robotics, among others, with the aim of improving the efficiency of the methods used in the different activities performed by the human being.

The sensory suit consists mainly by inertial sensors with which, measure the angular position of the members, the values obtained are sent to a main card which processes and sends the manipulated data to a computer where the user is digitally reconstructed. The best-known existing commercial systems are the Xsen MVN Biomech system suit [1] and the Nexonar sensory modules. Their advantage is that they are easy to use, because the user must wear them with tapes in the extremities, but the problem that presents is the noise due to environmental interferences.

© Springer International Publishing AG 2018
M. Botto-Tobar et al. (Eds.): CITT 2017, CCIS 798, pp. 57–70, 2018.
https://doi.org/10.1007/978-3-319-72727-1_5

The camera-based system uses artificial vision together with a cloth suit which has stamped designs of specific figures or a reflective system such as the Vicon system [2], which allows to capture gestures not recognized by the sensory suit as is the case of a person lying down, the disadvantage of using this technology is their sensitivity to external light, for that reason it requires a conditioned place, with a controlled lighting system and a background suitable for the scenes. Another limitation is in terms of computer technology, because of high features that are required by the computer to process quickly and accurately.

A more complex procedure is to merge the two techniques described above with the purpose of constructing a more robust system [3], this system achieves greater precision in the reconstruction of the models, due to the comparison between the two devices, obtaining excellent results, however, the system greatly increases the complexity in operation and implementation, as well as the price grows to a large extent.

The system that was designed here had to meet two requirements to be implemented, the first of which is to have a low-cost in materials and implementation and the second is the simplicity in construction for the future to allow improvements or reproductions of it without drawbacks. Due to the previously explained points, it is opted to develop a system based on inertial sensors, taking as a starting point the device Pedalvatar [4] and sensor model for step analysis [5].

2 Related Works

There are systems focused on the tracking of human body movement, generally fusing inertial sensors, electronic compass and computer vision [3]; others use inertial sensors and Kinects to capture the body movement data [6], that systems are limited to operating within a controlled light environment. An independent system of a controlled environment is a sensorial suit [2], although it delivers accurate data, is an expensive system, it does not accept hardware modifications and works with specific software. Less complex system limited to obtain the angular position of a single joint [7] in the sagittal plane, have been successfully implemented. In terms of wireless data transmission through Wi-Fi [5], presents an economic device which allows communication with internet networks, but requires a rotational model to properly reconstruct the movement in the computer.

This project is focused on obtaining the angular position of the lower limbs, through of a network of accelerometers interconnected to each other, linked to a NodeMcu development board that acts as a reception center for bit-packets and as a server for transmission of data to the Matlab graphical interface.

Due to the above, it is necessary to adequately measure the rotation angle of a link with respect to its origin, which results in the searching for sensors available to the local market. The sensor modules used are: gy-521 and gy-85, subjecting them to tests to choose the one with the best performance.

3   Methodology

For the present project, tests were carried out on the different components used in the design of the suit, such as the choice of the sensors with the best performance for our needs, as well as, test boards or modules to be employed were tested, focusing in: minimizing the error level, increasing the performance of the sensors and mainly improving response times between the hardware and the interface developed for visualizing the movements of the individual's joints.

3.1   Boards

Arduino Pro-Micro: It is a microcontroller board based on the ATmega32u4 running at 16 MHz, this board has: 9 channels of 10-bit ADC, 5 PWM pins, 12 Digital I/O pins support UART and I2C communication.

NodeMcu: It is a IoT platform based on the microcontroller ESP8266, running at 40 MHz, this board has: 1 channel of 10-bit ADC, 16 Digital I/O pins, support UART, I2C and Wi-Fi communication.

3.2   Sensors

Gy-85: The module consists of three independent sensors: accelerometer ADXL345, gyroscope ITG3200 and magnetometer HMC5883L. The construction of the module requires the application of digital filters to achieve a correct reading of the turning angles, resulting in a small processing consumption, but this increases as the number of sensors increases.

Gy-521: The sensor module consists of the integrated MPU-6050, which internally has the accelerometer and gyroscope sensors, facilitating the process of obtaining data. In addition, it consists of a digital motion processor (DMP), which calculates internally the angles of rotation, thus allowing the connected microcontroller to read data in a simple way, omitting complex calculations requirement.

The sensor chosen for the project was the GY-521, due to the existence of greater support in terms of software, within which it is possible to mention the library developed for Arduino, giving simplicity to the handling of the sensors, also, due to the processor, saves processing time and formidably facilitates the reading of information.

3.3   Connection Between Arduino Pro-Micro and MPU6050

The circuit implemented to measure the angles of rotation in the three axes was composed of an Arduino Pro-Micro and a sensor module GY-512. The communication between board and sensor uses the I2C protocol, for that reason a logical address is required in the sensor device, which can be assigned by activating or deactivating the sensor pin AD0, if it is low digital level the address it will be 0x68, otherwise it will be 0x69.

About the processing of the data from the sensor, there are two options, the first one is to work with the unprocessed values of the sensor, which was explained in the least accurate method; the second one is to use the Digital Movement Processor (DMP) integrated in the sensor, which sends the processed data, allowing a direct and fast reading of the angles.

4   Communication

4.1   Communication Type Selection

Transmission of data by means of cable limits the mobility of the prototype, for this reason it is necessary to send the data wirelessly, the present alternatives were transmission via Wi-Fi or Bluetooth.

The transmission by Bluetooth requires the use of an external module, in addition the process of transmission and communication with Matlab sometimes presented errors and it was required to restart Matlab in order to reestablish communication.

In the Wi-Fi transmission, the ESP8266 could be used due to the large support existing and the existing of the board in the market, reasons why the NodeMcu module was considered to use it. This development board supports the processing of data and at the same time transmission over Wi-Fi. This facility and with the previous knowledge that in Matlab exist commands to handle the communication by Wi-Fi in a simple way, it is chosen to use the mentioned board.

4.2   Wi-Fi on the NodeMcu Board

The ESP8266 module has the capability to mount a Wi-Fi network, allowing the computer to connect easily and directly without the need for an extra device. The WiFi network to be established, must have the basic configuration parameters, such as: the network name, the password (optional) and the port to be used for communication.

4.3   Communication Between Matlab and NodeMcu

The Matlab software has commands to read data in a network, this command is: *webread* which sends a request to the server module, in this case the NodeMcu, which processes that request, to later respond and/ or perform some action, depending on the program code.

4.4   Connection Between NodeMcu and Sensors

The system to be implemented requires the reading of the angles described by the lower extremities, each one has three sensors that allow to monitor the inclination angles of the thigh, calf and foot, resulting in a total of six sensors, which must be controlled and read in an orderly manner.

The reception of the data presented difficulties, due to the addresses configured in the sensors to communicate by I2C, for that reason digital pins of the NodeMcu board were used, to control the activation and routing data, the connections between sensors and digital pins are shown in Fig. 1.

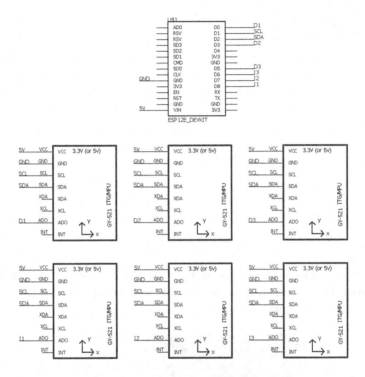

Fig. 1. Connection scheme NodeMCU and Gy-521 Sensors

5   System Construction

5.1   Physical Structure of the Suit

The inertial sensors and the main processing board are located individually in 3D structures printed, they have velcro straps to be attached easily and quickly to the body of the user. The location of the mentioned modules can be seen in Fig. 2.

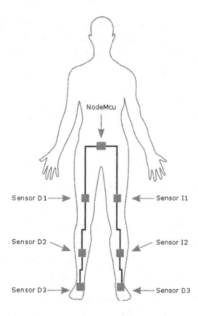

Fig. 2. Location of sensors

The structure of modules was designed in SolidWorks and then printed in 3D with PLA material. The sensors are soldered to a board which has pins for the connection of the data buses, as can be seen in Fig. 3.

Fig. 3. Sensor module construction

The sensor modules are interconnected via a seven-wire data bus. Two wires are dedicated to the 5 V supply, two ones for the I2C communication and three ones for the required digital activation, for the addressing of each sensor at the moment of read it. The cables distribution is in Fig. 4 for better appreciation.

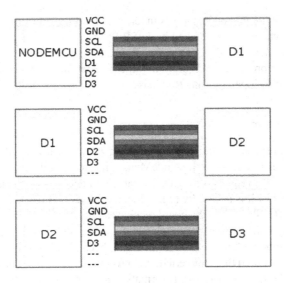

Fig. 4. Connection of sensors via bus

5.2 Suit Processing Program

In terms of communication, the NodeMcu with its internal program is responsible for reading the data from the sensors, processing the requests from the program in Matlab and transmit the data to the computer wirelessly.

The microcontroller board program starts with the calibration process of the sensors, allowing a reliable reading of the values, then proceeds to the main loop shown in Fig. 5. The board directs the sensor to be read by the digital pins, as mentioned in previous sections, and starts the reading process of the selected sensor, both steps are repeated until reading the six sensors, once stored the data, it continues the processing of requests in which verifies the existence of requested information of an external device, if it exists, it sends the data, with this step ends the cycle, giving way to the beginning of a new one.

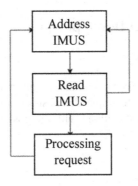

Fig. 5. Flow chart executed in the NodeMcu

The handling of the mpu6050 sensors in terms of reading is accomplished using the i2cdevlib library which was developed by Jeff Rowberg, and it is an open license. One consideration that must be taken before beginning to read the inertial sensors is their calibration, for this process, configuration values are required which can be obtained through the code developed by Luis Ródenas.

5.3 Matlab Program

The application developed in Matlab is shown in Fig. 6, and each step is described below. The program makes a request to the NodeMcu, using for this the command *webread*, which allows to send a request through the established network by the microcontroller board, to achieve this, it is necessary to indicate the IP address of the NodeMcu which by default is 192.168.4.1. When the board receives a request, it responds by sending the concatenated data of the six sensor modules into a single string of characters. The data received in the application are read in text format, because of this, they are organized and stored in an array, and then converted into a format of numbers. The ordered values are entered into the homogeneous transformation matrix corresponding to the human leg model, the resulting values of said matrix are used to generated a graph in the application and with this to emulate the position of the user's legs, then the process is repeated, running cyclically until the user stops it.

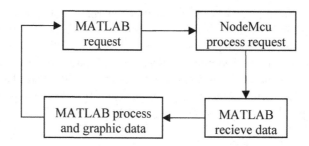

Fig. 6. Flow chart executed in MATLAB

6 Computational Model Development

6.1 Direct Kinematic Model

In the computer simulation process, direct transformation matrices based on the Denavit-Hartenberg algorithm are used to graph the position adopted by the user's legs. In Fig. 7, the right leg joints are listed along with the position where the inertial sensors are placed.

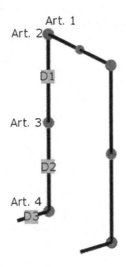

Fig. 7. Position of the inertial sensors in the user's body

The direct transformation matrix corresponding to the right leg can be seen in Table 1, where the values of theta angles $q1$ and $q2$ correspond to the values measured by the sensor $D1$, the angle $q3$ comes from the sensor $D2$ and the angle $q4$ is given by sensor $D3$. The distances $L2$ and $L3$ are the lengths of the thigh and leg respectively.

Table 1. Matrix direct transformation of the right leg

Art.	Θ	d	a	α
1	q1	0	0	−90
2	q2	0	L2	0
3	q3	0	L3	0
4	q4	0	0	0

6.2   GUI Developed in Matlab

A GUI was developed in Matlab, which performs the functions of processing values of the sensors and graphically reconstructing the movement of the lower limbs of the human body as seen in Fig. 8.

The main parts of the application are four, the table where the animation is plotted and three functions which are responsible for:

- Connect: establishes the connection between the program in Matlab and the NodeMcu.
- Graph: starts the process of simulation of movements with the digital model.
- Stop: interrupts the communication established with the NodeMcu, and stops the simulation process.

In addition, it has two textboxes, in which the values of the angles measured by the sensors *D1* and *D2* are printed, in order to verify the reception of the information and its status.

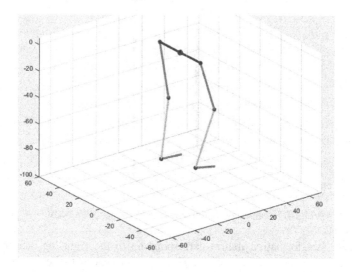

Fig. 8. Software reconstructing the position of the lower limbs

7   Results

The range of the wireless network established by the NodeMcu board is 10 m away from the computer, showing a good performance, for this test, the board was powered by a portable cell phone charger, connected by the micro-USB cable. In an open area, the user wore the suit while walking away from the computer, which continues receiving data without presenting problems.

A user wore the suit inside an office, where he walked through an area with three meters in length, the movements along the way consisted of: walking, marching, backing. During this test, the suit achieved the position of the lower limbs of the user without the difficulty, reconstructing the movement in the Matlab model, in which no other novelty appeared an exception of the existence of a slight latency.

The present delay in motion capture and simulation is due to the process of handling the sensors made by the microcontroller board, which consists of addressing one sensor at a time, proceed to read it and then continue with the following one. This process is carried out until it finished reading the six modules, then, the process of sending data is executed. Measurement of latency in the process was quantified using digital video, for which the user and the running program were recorded. These videos were taken to an editor program where they were synchronized, to enhance several observations allowing to appreciate the latency, which does not exceed 0.5 s.

The tests were performed by a user with 173 cm height, who walked on a flat surface, without obstacles, guided by a metronome configured at a speed of 40 ppm (pulses per minute), the duration of the tests was about 12 s. The graphs resulting from the data measured in the tests were compared with graphs obtained from a simulation of the analysis of a person's gait cycle [8]. The graphs are similar, although the speed of movements in tests were different, despite this, the shape of the peaks and the deviations are similar, this is shown in Fig. 9.

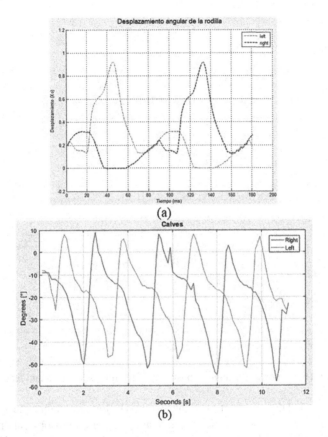

Fig. 9. Contrast between data simulated and measured; (a) Knee angular displacement [8] (b) Calves angular displacement

The data obtained are plotted in three figures, each one, to compare the angular positions of the thighs, calves and feet of the user, presented in Fig. 10. The angular positions existing between the user's thighs converge to −6.5° and −4.2° when aligning the legs, the offset time between peaks is around 1.5 s. The positions of the left and right calves present peaks at 8°, and converge at −14.25° and −18.5°, in addition, the offset time between the peaks of the positions is around 1.4 s. The peaks present in the graphs of the user's foot positions have an offset of approximately 1.6 s. The vertical offset observed between the two graphs is due to an adjustment error between the sensor and the user's foot, because this will require modification of the initial calibration step. The graphs mentioned allow us to understand the offset between the lower extremities and to measure the maximum and minimum angles produced by the user when walking.

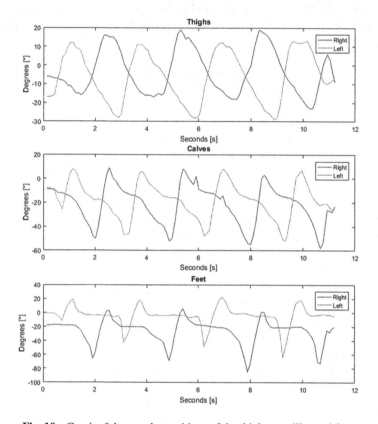

Fig. 10. Graph of the angular positions of the thighs, patrillas and feet.

A relevant part of the construction of the device is its low-cost, being the approximate value to the $160, which costs the NodeMcu board, six inertial sensors, battery, connection cables and suit manufacturing, despite of its limited characteristics, it is similar in functionality to commercial systems such as the case of the Biomechanics Laboratory [9], which price varies from $23,000 to $52,000, depending on the required version, so it is an excellent cost-benefit ratio.

8   Conclusions

The system developed has favorable results in terms of cost-benefit, since building a system of this type does not require very expensive elements and the implementation of the same is not complicated, in addition, it can improve the design and even extend it to other parts of the body without raising the cost considerably.

The electronic and physical characteristics of the model limit it to be used in activities which involve moderate movement of the lower extremities like walking and jogging, if the device is used in activities that require speed movements, the cables could break.

The switching of the sensors to be addressed does not have a good performance, for the reason they generate slight delays when simulating the model in the computer, therefore, the speed of the system response is limited, and this is also reflected in responding to requests from the computer. Due to the above it can be said, it is convenient to dedicate a device for reading sensors and one for wireless communication.

9 Future Work

The prototype presented in this work is in its first version, in the future is planned to make some improvements and updates such as accelerating the reading of the data, for which it will be restructured the system incorporating small microcontroller boards in each module, it means, each sensor will be connected individually to a single board, the same that will communicate wirelessly with the main NodeMcu of the suit, and this will be the only one to handle the requests made by the computer, something similar to establishing a network of sensors with a central node.

As for the range of wireless signals, if it is necessary to read data over long distance, the only way to improve it will be to use other microcontroller boards with greater range, that is to say improved versions of the board used in this work consisting of external antennas.

This prototype could be used in the rehabilitation of patients who have suffered a lesion in their lower limbs, the therapies they receive could use the sensorial suit to improve their efficiency, in addition this prototype would allow a history of patient evolution in detail.

The data are affected by the coupling of sensory modules with the different anatomical parts of the user, so it is proposed to develop a better initial calibration system.

References

1. Roetenberg, D., Luinge, H., Slycke, R.: Xsens MVN: full 6DOF human motion tracking using miniature inertial sensors. Xsens Technologies, April 2013
2. Dinua, D., Fayolasbc, M., Jacquetbc, M., Leguybc, E., Slavinskib, J., Houelc, N.: Accuracy of postural human-motion tracking using miniature inertial sensors. Procedia Eng. **147**, 655–658 (2016)
3. Zihajehzadeh, S., Park, E.: A novel biomechanical model-aided IMU/UWB fusion for magnetometer-free lower body motion capture. IEEE Trans. Syst. Man Cybern. Syst. **47**, 927–938 (2017)
4. Zheng, Y., Chan, K.C., Wang, C.C.: Pedalvatar: an IMU-based real-time body motion capture system using foot rooted kinematic model. In: IEEE/RSJ International Conference on Intelligent Robots and Systems (IROS 2014) (2014)
5. Mota, F.A.O., Biajo, V.H.M., Mota, H.O., Vasconcelos, F.H.: A wireless sensor network for the biomechanical analysis of the gait. In: 2017 IEEE International on Instrumentation and Measurement Technology Conference (I2MTC) (2017)

6. Chen, C., Jafari, R., Kehtarnavaz, N.: A survey of depth and inertial sensor fusion for human action recognition. Multimedia Tools Appl. **76**, 4405–4425 (2017)
7. Park, Y.L., Chen, B.R., Pérez-Arancibia, N.O., Young, D., Stirling, L., Wood, R.J., Goldfield, E.C., Nagpal, R.: Design and control of a bio-inspired soft wearable robotic device for ankle–foot rehabilitation. Bioinspir. Biom. **9**(1) (2014)
8. Gavilanes, J., Pazmiño, A., Pérez, M., Tinoco, J.: Análisis del ciclo de marcha bípedo como base de la rehabilitación física en miembros inferiores (2016)
9. Biomec. http://www.biomec.com.co/Laboratorio-deportivo-3d.html

Mammogram Classification Schemes by Using Convolutional Neural Networks

Danny Soriano[1], Carlos Aguilar[1], Ivan Ramirez-Morales[2],
Eduardo Tusa[1]($\boxtimes$), Wilmer Rivas[1], and Maritza Pinta[1]

[1] Unidad Académica de Ingeniería Civil, Universidad Técnica
de Machala, Machala, El Oro 070210, Ecuador
{dosoriano_est,caaguilarn_est,etusa,wrivas,mpinta}@utmachala.edu.ec
[2] Unidad Académica de Ciencias Agropecuarias, Universidad Técnica
de Machala, Machala, El Oro 070210, Ecuador
iramirez@utmachala.edu.ec

Abstract. This work presents the comparison of two schemes of mammogram classification based on convolutional neural networks (CNN). The main difference between these two classification schemes relies on the number of bits per image pixel, the feature extraction techniques and the number of neurons in the fully connected layer. We use 1070 mammograms from the Digital Database for Screening Mammography (DDSM), which are divided into two categories: benign and malignant mammograms. We use CNN for classification by applying the open source library TensorFlow which is configured on the high level library Keras. In order to tune our classification model parameters, we apply random and grid search algorithms, by combining the batch size, the number of layers, the learning rate and three optimizers: Adadelta, RMSProp and SGD. We evaluate the classification algorithm performances through the accuracy and two loss functions: Categorical Cross-Entropy and Mean Squared Error. The model with the best accuracy has 85.00%, and a mean squared error of 15.00%.

Keywords: Breast cancer · Convolutional neural network
Machine learning · Mammography · TensorFlow

1 Introduction

The effects of cancer have significant implications around the world. According to statistics from the American Cancer Society, there were 14.1 million new cancer cases and 8.2 million cancer deaths worldwide in 2012. In the US, there will be an estimated 1.688.780 new cancer cases diagnosed and 600.920 cancer deaths in 2017. In Ecuador, the increase of advanced cases reflects a poor coverage of impoverished populations, mainly, in rural areas. According to Godoy et al. [1], 30 of 100.000 people are diagnosed each year with breast cancer in Ecuador. Approximately, half of these cases are in advance stage, which decreases the likelihood of successful treatment and survival.

© Springer International Publishing AG 2018
M. Botto-Tobar et al. (Eds.): CITT 2017, CCIS 798, pp. 71–85, 2018.
https://doi.org/10.1007/978-3-319-72727-1_6

The incidence rate of breast cancer in Ecuador has been growing over the last years, reaching up to 32.7 in 2012 [2]. The role of the early diagnostic techniques becomes imperative for saving lives. Screening mammograms are used to detect abnormalities in women who have no apparent symptoms. Diagnostic mammography is applied for women who present with clinical signs and symptoms. The recommendation of the American College of Radiology is a more comprehensive auditing of outcomes associated with all mammograms, with statistics prepared separately for screening and diagnostic mammography [3].

The research area of computer vision and machine learning has reported numerous algorithms covering medical image registration, segmentation and edge detection for medical image content analysis, computer-aided diagnosis (CAD) with specific coverage on mammogram analysis towards breast cancer screening, and other applications [4]. This work presents the comparison of two schemes of mammogram classification based on CNN. We test our algorithms by using the Digital Database for Screening Mammography (DDSM), in order to discriminate two categories: benign and malignant mammograms.

The paper is organised as follows: Sect. 2 describes the theoretical background and related works, Sect. 3 explains the materials and methods, Sect. 4 explains the experimental results. Finally, Sect. 5 discusses and concludes the paper, and provides possible directions for future work.

2   Theoretical Background and Related Works

The task of mammogram classification has been approached by comparing different learning algorithms widely available in computational libraries. Kamalakannan et al. [5], evaluate the sensitivity, specificity and accuracy on seven classifier techniques: Decision Tree (DT), K-Nearest Neighbour (KNN), Fuzzy K-Nearest Neighbor (FKNN), Naive Bayes (NB), Artificial Neural Network (ANN), Ensemble and Support Vector Machines (SVM) by selecting proper region of interest (ROI) from mammograms, whose database is not mentioned explicitly.

Don et al. [6] extract the salient features such as Fractal Dimension (FD) and Fractal Signature (FS) as texture descriptors. For classification purposes, a trainable multilayer feed forward Neural Network (NN) has been designed and compared with K-Means. The algorithm reveals a good performance rate of 98% by using the DDSM and the Mammographic Image Analysis Society (MIAS) dataset for discriminating in four tissue density categories.

Jankulovski et al. [7] use 326 annotated images from MIAS database to classify normal and abnormal tissue. While they compare three supervised classifiers: SVM, KNN and Random Forest (RF), six different feature descriptors are evaluated: Local Binary Pattern (LBP), Gray Level Difference Method (GLDM), Gray Level Run Length Matrix (GLRLM), Haralick, Gabor filters and a combined descriptor. The best results were obtained when the images were described using GLDM together with the SVM as a classification technique.

Xie et al. [8] present a novel CAD system for the diagnosis of breast cancer based on Extreme Learning Machine (ELM). They implement a model of multidimensional feature vectors, where feature selection is done by SVM and ELM. The algorithm classify malignant masses from benign ones from DDSM and MIAS database. Authors compare the classification performance with SVM and Particle Swarm Optimization-Support Vector Machine (PSO-SVM). The system achieve an average accuracy of 96.02%.

Important contributions for mammography classification have been implemented by different authors. Taghanaki et al. [9] introduce a novel multi-objective optimization of deep auto-encoder networks, in which the auto-encoder optimizes two objectives: Mean Squared Reconstruction Error (MRE) and Mean Classification Error (MCE) for Pareto-optimal solutions. These two objectives are optimized simultaneously by a non-dominated sorting genetic algorithm. They use 949 X-ray mammograms categorized into 12 classes, obtaining a classification accuracy of up to 98.45%.

Khan et al. [10] propose the concept of Cartesian Genetic Programming (CGP) for training both differentiable and non-differentiable parameters of Wavelet Neural Networks (WNNs). They use a representative subset of 200 areas of benign and malignant tumors from the DDSM dataset. The proposed WNNs perform competitively in comparison to several other methods.

Magna et al. [11] investigate the properties of a classifier based on an ensemble of Adaptive Artificial Immune Networks (A^2INET) applied to original mammography image from DDSM and MIAS datasets in order to detect bilateral asymmetry, which is known to be correlated with increased breast cancer risk. Classification models were trained using a set of descriptors measuring the degree of similarity of paired regions of the left and right breasts. The accuracy level is 0.90, sensitivity is 0.93 and specificity is 0.87.

Pratiwi et al. [12] classify various type of breast cancers into benign and malignant abnormalities by using Radial Basis Function Neural Network (RBFNN) and GLCM texture based features. Instead of using 14 Haralick descriptors, the most dominant four are used: ASM, Correlation, Sum Entropy, and Sum Variance. They use the MIAS dataset to obtain an accuracy of 93.98%.

Buciu and Gacsadi [13] use Gabor wavelets based features extracted from mammograms representing normal tissues, or benign and malign tumors. Once features are detected, Principal Component Analysis (PCA) is further employed to reduce data dimensionality. To an end, directional properties and frequency spectrum of those features are analyzed with respect to the classification performance by employing multiclass support vector machines as classifier. For comparison, as baseline, PCA was also applied directly to the data set with no feature filtering. The directional properties of Gabor wavelets provided by their orientation are important issues to discriminate mammogram tumor types.

Khan et al. [14] contribute to the previous work by finding the optimal parameters of Gabor filter banks based on an incremental clustering algorithm and Particle Swarm Optimization (PSO). They employ SVM with Gaussian kernel as a fitness function for PSO. The effect of optimized Gabor filter bank was evaluated on 1024 ROIs extracted from DDSM dataset. The proposed method enhances the performance and reduces the computational cost.

Srinivasan and Venkata [15], use 322 images from MIAS database to classify mammograms in three categories: normal, benign and malignant. They select 180 images (60 images for each class) to train the algorithm of Discrete Gabor Wavelet Transforms based on Hidden Markov Model for classification. The performance of their technique yields 90% of accuracy.

2.1 Neural Networks (NN)

These prediction models are a set of interconnected artificial neurons that perform the functions of learning, memorization, generalization or abstraction of features; by posing a computational model similar to the functioning of the human brain. NN allow excellent results in applications where the inputs to the model contain noise, randomness or are incomplete, being used for text-to-speech processing, or for character and image recognition, and are also used in the robotics area.

The basic structure of a neuron can be theoretically set by $X = \{x_i, i = 1, 2, ..., n\}$ as the inputs to the neuron and Y represents the output. Each input is multiplied by its weight w_i, a bias b is associated with each neuron and their sum goes through a transfer function f [4]. The relationship between input and output can be described as follows in Eq. (1)

$$Y = f\left(\sum_{i=1}^{n} w_i x_i + b\right) \tag{1}$$

Several approaches have used NN for breast cancer detection in mammography images. Lucht et al. [16] test the performance of NN for the classification of signal-time curves obtained from breast masses by dynamic MRI. Signal-time courses from 105 parenchyma, 162 malignant, and 102 benign tissue regions were examined. Four neural networks corresponding to different temporal resolutions of the signal-time curves were tested. Discrimination between malignant and benign lesions is best if 28 measurement points are used (sensitivity: 84%, specificity: 81%). All examined networks yielded poor results for the subclassification of the benign lesions into fibroadenomas and benign proliferative changes.

Setiawan et al. [17], propose a mammogram classification using Law's Texture Energy Measure (LAWS) as texture feature extraction method. NN is used as classifier for normal-abnormal and benign-malignant images. Training data for the mammogram classification model is retrieved from subset of 327 images of MIAS database. Result shows that LAWS provides better accuracy than other similar method such as GLCM. LAWS provide 93.90% accuracy for normal-abnormal and 83.30% for benign-malignant classification.

The application of NN in problem solving is necessary to establish a structure of convolutional layers (feature extraction) and fully connected (classifier) that apply learning algorithms and validation [18]. This is why, our approach is based on Convolutional Neural Networks.

2.2   Convolutional Neural Networks (CNN)

These are special type of NN where instead of having weights for each and every input, the weights are shared and are convolved across the input as a moving window [19]. This convolutional property along with a pooling layer achieves translation invariance, which especially suits images. Our mammogram classification schemes are based on a CNN with the following model parameters [20]:

- **Convolutional layer** uses a filter, which is an array of weights, to slide across the input from the previous layer in order to compute the dot product of the weights and the entries in the input. These weights are learnt using backpropagation of errors. An activation function, which applies element-wise non-linearity, is applied to produce a feature map, where each entry can be considered as an output of a single neuron from a local small region of the input. Equation (2) provides the mathematical expression for convolution process in case both the filter and input are two-dimensional [21].

$$O^l_{xy} = \sum_{i=0}^{r-1}\sum_{j=0}^{c-1} F_{ij}I^{l-1}_{(x+i)(y+j)} \tag{2}$$

where F is a filter of size $r \times c$, I is the input from the previous layer $l-1$, O is the output at the current layer l (after convolution and before applying the activation function) and x and y represents the starting indices of row and column for the receptive field of F with respect to I.

- **Activation function** is a non-linear function such as sigmoid or ReLU, which is applied to elements of the convolution.
- **Pooling layer** reduces the computational complexity of a CNN when one or more pooling layers are applied to the feature maps produced by the convolutional layers, by decreasing the size of the maps. Two commonly used methods are max pooling and average pooling.
- **Output layer** consists of as many nodes as the number of classes in the dataset. We use Softmax function for classification at the output.
- **Number of epochs** defines the number of times for training and validating the neural network to be executed. An algorithm may take thousands of epochs to converge to a combination of weights with an acceptable level of accuracy.
- **Batch size** defines the number of samples in our dataset, which will be loaded and propagated during training and validation of the neural network.
- **Learning rate** controls the size of weight and bias changes in learning of the training algorithm. It is a value that must be defined low enough for the neural network to converge, but high enough in order to avoid spending too much time in training it.
- **Number of hidden layers** are fully connected layers which have a specific weight for each defined neuron, which is adjusted as the training times are executed. Each neuron has its activation value which is calculated based on its input values and its weights. This calculation returns a value that serves as input to the final layer using the Softmax function, which classifies mammograms into benign and malignant.

The feature extraction performance in mammography images of our CNN model presents two re-training techniques known as Transfer-learning and Fine-tuning on the Inception-v3 model [22] launched by Google. Inception-v3 uses the weights of its network to perform the task of classification in a mammography dataset distributed in two classes: benign and malignant cancer. It is necessary to use the following techniques considering the size and the similarity of training data:

- **Transfer-learning** is a technique used to deal with small or large amounts of labeled information from a source domain to a destination domain, in order to build an efficient prediction model. The Inception-v3 CNN model has been pre-trained by using the imageNet dataset, to freeze its layers making them non-trainable. Then, the last layer is removed fully connected or Softmax. A new layer is added fully connected, taking the rest of the network for feature extraction and for training the model.
- **Fine-tuning** is a process to take a network model that has already been trained for a given task, and make it perform a second similar task.

The optimization algorithms are necessary arguments to elaborate a NN model in Keras, in such a way that the gradient descent is tunned properly. Our models are tested by the following optimizers:

- **Adadelta** is an optimization algorithm used to control the gradient descent. It is very adaptive dynamically over time because it only needs first order information and occupies low computational cost, which makes it a very useful optimizer for NN models [23].
- **RMSprop** has a different operation to the other optimizers, because it divides the learning rate for a weight by a running average of the magnitudes of recent gradients for that weight [24].
- **SGD**, the Stochastic Gradient Descent optimizer does not recalculate the weights using all the samples. On the contrary, it only uses the input sample to perform this process, allowing the weights to be updated more frequently, providing a faster convergence [25].

The evaluation of the different experiments of our algorithms is based on three metrics: Accuracy (ACC) [26], Categorical cross-entropy (CCE) [27], and Mean squared error (MSE) [28].

3   Materials and Methods

3.1   Database

The dataset for training and evaluating our approach was obtained from DDSM dataset [29, 30], which belongs to the University of South Florida. We identify two types of cases: malignant and benign mammograms. In each downloaded directories, there are 5 files corresponding to digitized mammograms in two different projections: Cranial-Caudal (CC) and Mediolateral-Oblique (MLO) in "LJPG" format. In addition to the images, there is an ".ics" file containing detailed information for each case, regarding patient data and image resolution. The digitized mammography in the "LJPG" format is converted to any standard image format by using a repository hosted in GitHub [31]. Previously, it is necessary to install a Linux environment called Cygwin that requires two libraries: Ruby and Imagemagick. The steps for image file format conversion are:

1. Select the file associated to the cases to convert.
2. Run the *jpeg.exe* file for each of the mammograms scanned in LJPEG with the following command: *./jpeg.exe -d -s [filename]*. A file with the same name as the original will be created but with a ".1" extension.
3. Run *ddsmraw2pnm.exe* with the previously created file by using the command: *./ddsmraw2pnm.exe [created file] [height] [width] [lumisys/dba/howtek]*. The last 3 fields of this command are extracted from the ".ics" file corresponding to the image of the selected case. The output is a file with ".pnm" extension.
4. Apply the command: *convert [file created] -resize [width] x [height]^ -gravity center -extent [width] x [height] [new file name] .jpg*. The height and width resolution are according to the ".ics" file. The last parameter corresponds to the new filename with its respective format.

After this process, we obtain the digitized mammograms in the selected image format, in this case, JPG. We then select the mammograms to trim the ROI that represents the affected tissue, as we observe in Fig. 1. Each ROI is obtained manually, with reference to database, which provides all relevant information. The ROI is resized to 299 × 299, so the abnormal regions are contained in the image and are labeled as benign or malignant mammograms.

Fig. 1. Dataset of ROIs for benign and malignant mammograms

3.2 Methodology

In the previous stage, we obtain 1070 images, which are divided into 535 mammograms for each class: benign and malignant. Two schemes or models are defined during preprocessing. Model 1 uses a dataset of 16-bit grayscale images, while the image data for Model 2 are obtained by converting the grayscale image from 16-bit to 8-bit through the OpenCV Library. These processes are differentiated in Fig. 2.

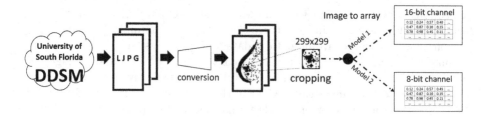

Fig. 2. Stages for preprocessing ROIs obtained from the DDSM dataset

This configuration creates vectors with the pixel values for each image, as we describe below:

1. Upload image from your directory.
2. Define the number of bits per channel for Model 1 and 2.
3. Reshape all uploaded images in a list of 89401-dimensional vectors (299×299 image), which is an array format obtained through library Numpy.
4. Define the pixel values in "float32" format and save them in other vector.
5. Normalize the pixel values of the entire vector between 0 and 1.
6. Create a vector of labels with a size proportional to the total number of images in the training subset. A label value of 0 is assigned for benign cases and 1 for malignant cases.
7. Divide the data into two parts, 90% for training and 10% for validation.

Inception-v3 contains a pre-trained CNN to extract features of the images with a low computational cost and to work in scenarios of handling large amounts of data [32]. Figure 3 shows the stage of feature extraction in Model 1 and 2. These methods help to build a NN model with greater stability and consistency, due to the fact, it modifies the values of the weights and biases until the last layer is stabilized in order to reconvert the rest of them [33]. The scheme of classification is presented Fig. 4.

4   Experimental Results

For the development of our classification schemes, we use the machine learning library of Google, Tensorflow [34], that is configured to work on the high level library Keras. The models are run on a Dell inspiron 2350 computer running Windows 10 SL with an i7-6700 processor with a clock speed of 2.60 GHz with 12 GB of RAM and an Nvidia GeForce 940M GPU with 4 GB of RAM. The proposed models were evaluated in terms of accuracy and two loss functions. In Table 1, we show a summary of the main characteristics between model 1 and model 2.

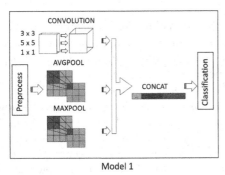
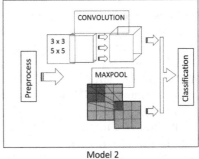

Fig. 3. Stage of feature extraction in the model Inception-v3. Model 1 uses three size of filters: 5×5, 3×3 and 1×1. The pooling layer applies the techniques: max pooling and average pooling. Model 2 uses two size of filters: 5×5 and 3×3. The pooling layer applies max pooling.

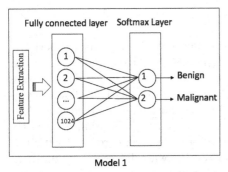
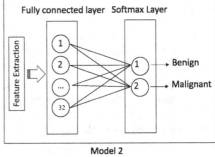

Fig. 4. Scheme of our proposed CNN with fully connected layer and Softmax as the output layer. Model 1 has a fully connected layer of 1024 neurons, while Model 2 presents 32 neurons.

Table 1. Summary of main differences between model 1 and model 2

Model	Input dimension	Feature extraction	Classification
Model 1	$299 \times 299 \times 3$ array in 16-bit channel	3×3 Convolution 5×5 Convolution Max pooling	1024 to 2 neurons in fully connected layer
Model 2	$299 \times 299 \times 1$ array in 8-bit channel	1×1 Convolution 3×3 Convolution 5×5 Convolution Max pooling Average pooling	32 to 2 neurons in fully conected layer

4.1 Random Search

We implement the search for optimal combination of model parameters by applying random search, which consists of performing a random combinations of parameters for both models, taking into account a loss function and accuracy. Once the model is selected based on its performance, a grid search is focused on tuning the model parameters. The accuracy results for model 1 are higher by using the optimizers SGD and Adadelta. On the other hand, the loss function provides better results with MSE. The accuracy values of model 2 are around 70%, but the loss function values obtained by model 2 are not better for those generated in model 1. At this point, we consider the values of accuracy for the validation of both models around 70%. However, the loss function allows us to identify better results in the parameter combinations in model 1. Since we have to select the best combination for both models, we identify the best values of loss function and accuracy for model 1 at 0.27 and 0.78, respectively. While the best results of loss function and accuracy for model 2 are 0.48 and 0.75, respectively. Model 1 offers potential results for experimenting new model parameter combinations by applying grid search technique.

4.2 Grid Search

For this process, we use the grid search technique [35] which consists of performing a search through a sweep defined parameters: Number of layers to freeze: 50, 120, 249; Batch Size (BS): 8, 16; Optimizer: RMSprop, SGD, Adadelta; Loss Function: CCE and MSE; and Learning Rate (LR): 0.01, 0.001. It allows to estimate the model performance in sequence for each parameter combination. These results are mainly obtained from variations in learning rate, optimizers and the number of Inception-v3 layers to freeze. From this, we compare sets focused on the SGD optimizer, which provided better results, with different configurations in learning rate, loss function and the number of frozen layers of Inception-v3. As shown in Table 2, the best results in the loss value is obtained with a learning rate configuration of 0.001 and with a smaller number of frozen layers of Inception-v3, all with the CCE loss function.

The results reflected in Table 3 exceed those obtained in Table 2. This improvement is given by the MSE loss function by selecting a higher learning rate of 0.01, and a smaller number of frozen layers of Inception-v3.

Then, we apply a second grid search, maintaining the Batch Size, the Optimizer, and fully connected layer model parameters for all combinations, but we vary learning rates only: 1, 1.0, 0.5, 0.05; the loss functions are MSE and CCE; and the number of layers to freeze from Inception-v3 model: 0, 10, 20, 30, 40, 50, 60, 70, 80, 90; obtaining a total of 80 models to test. As we see in Table 4, we obtain better results by training more layers of the Inception-v3 model, as we apply the SGD optimizer. The CCE loss function does not offer promising results.

In the same way, Table 5 presents that both loss function and learning rate have a great influence on the values obtained during the training. We identify the optimal combination as the model parameters number 7 of Table 5.

Table 2. First grid search results with categorical cross-entropy function.

N.	BS	LR	Optimizer	Freeze	Hidden layer	Min loss	Max acc	Epoch
1	16	0,01	SGD	50	1024	0,46	0,78	6
2	8	0,01	SGD	50	1024	0,48	0,79	3
3	16	0,01	SGD	172	1024	0,50	0,76	1
4	8	0,01	SGD	172	1024	0,51	0,79	4
5	16	0,01	SGD	249	1024	0,52	0,74	3
6	16	0,001	SGD	50	1024	0,46	0,77	11
7	16	0,001	SGD	249	1024	0,48	0,76	16
8	**8**	**0,001**	**SGD**	**172**	**1024**	**0,47**	**0,79**	**19**
9	8	0,001	SGD	249	1024	0,49	0,75	15
10	8	0,001	SGD	50	1024	0,51	0,77	12

Table 3. First grid search results with mean squared error function.

N.	BS	LR	Optimizer	Freeze	Hidden layer	Min loss	Max acc	Epoch
1	**16**	**0.01**	**SGD**	**50**	**1024**	**0,14**	**0,81**	**5**
2	8	0,01	SGD	50	1024	0,14	0,79	7
3	16	0,01	SGD	172	1024	0,15	0,76	2
4	8	0,01	SGD	249	1024	0,16	0,76	6
5	16	0,01	SGD	249	1024	0,16	0,77	12
6	8	0,01	SGD	172	1024	0,17	0,77	11
7	16	0,001	SGD	172	1024	0,15	0,79	15
8	16	0,001	SGD	50	1024	0,16	0,74	11
9	16	0,001	SGD	249	1024	0,18	0,76	7
10	8	0,001	SGD	172	1024	0,18	0,72	6

Table 4. Second grid search results with categorical cross-entropy function.

N.	BS	LR	Optimizer	Freeze	Hidden layer	Min loss	Max acc	Epoch
1	8	0,05	SGD	0	1024	0,62	0,68	1
2	8	0,05	SGD	10	1024	0,49	0,78	4
3	8	0,05	SGD	20	1024	0,51	0,83	9
4	8	0,05	SGD	30	1024	0,50	0,81	8
5	8	0,05	SGD	40	1024	0,54	0,75	2
6	**8**	**0,05**	**SGD**	**50**	**1024**	**0,37**	**0,83**	**6**
7	8	0,05	SGD	60	1024	0,43	0,78	1
8	8	0,05	SGD	70	1024	0,54	0,71	1
9	8	0,05	SGD	80	1024	0,59	0,74	4
10	8	0,05	SGD	90	1024	0,50	0,78	11

Table 5. Second grid search results with mean squared error function.

N.	BS	LR	Optimizer	Freeze	Hidden layer	Min loss	Max acc	Epoch
1	8	0,05	SGD	0	1024	0,15	0,82	7
2	8	0,05	SGD	10	1024	0,14	0,83	6
3	8	0,05	SGD	20	1024	0,16	0,80	7
4	8	0,05	SGD	30	1024	0,15	0,79	9
5	8	0,05	SGD	40	1024	0,13	0,83	9
6	8	0,05	SGD	50	1024	0,14	0,81	5
7	**8**	**0,05**	**SGD**	**60**	**1024**	**0,13**	**0,85**	**7**
8	8	0,05	SGD	70	1024	0,15	0,78	1
9	8	0,05	SGD	80	1024	0,15	0,81	2
10	8	0,05	SGD	90	1024	0,13	0,84	9

5 Discussion and Conclusions

As we observe in Table 6, we summarize a comparison of binary classification performance schemes based on accuracy among different approaches revised previously in Sect. 2. Among those tested proposals with the DDSM database, our implementation offers promising results for benign and malignant classification.

Table 6. Comparison of our best result with respect to other revised binary mammogram classification approaches

Approach	Database	Classification algorithm	Accuracy
Jankulovski et al. [7]	MIAS	RF + GLDM	99.08%
Xie et al. [8]	DDSM + MIAS	PSO-SVM	96.02%
Pratiwi et al. [12]	MIAS	RBFNN + GLCM	93.98%
Setiawan et al. [17]	MIAS	NN + LAWS	93.90%
Our approach	DDSM	CNN	85.00%
Khan et al. [10]	DDSM	CGP	73.05%

We compare two schemes of mammogram classification that discriminate two categories: benign and malignant cancer, by using CNN as classifier. We evaluate the algorithm performances by the accuracy and two loss functions: MSE and CCE, from which; MSE registers the lowest loss value. We implement the optimizers given by the algorithms: Adadelta, Rmsprop and SGD, being the latter the most promising of them, because it obtains the greatest accuracy among the different parameter combinations. The learning rate, whose values were among 0.001, 0.01, 0.1, 1 and 0.05; generates better results when it is 0.05. The best accuracy results required a less amount of epochs. From the literature review, CNN reveals important advantages for low computational cost, due to the fact that we define a small batch size, which requires less memory. However, a small batch size allows less accurate estimation of the gradient. Based on the results presented in Table 6, our future work focuses on the study of feature descriptors by adding texture information. Several researches have shown the use Gabor bank filters, GLCM, Haralick texture descriptors provide effective results. These improvements in our system can advance in a next level by increasing the number of categories to classify mammograms. The use of Breast Imaging Reporting and Data System (BIRADS) from the DDSM dataset is an important resource of breast cancer diagnosis in order to identify other subcategories of malignant cancer.

References

1. Godoy, Y., Godoy, C., Reyes, J.: Social representations of gynecologic cancer screening assessment a qualitative research on ecuadorian women. Revista da Escola de Enfermagem da USP **50**(SPE), 68–73 (2016)
2. López-Cortés, A., Echeverría, C., Oña-Cisneros, F., Sánchez, M.E., Herrera, C., Cabrera-Andrade, A., Rosales, F., Ortiz, M., Paz-y Miño, C.: Breast cancer risk associated with gene expression and genotype polymorphisms of the folate-metabolizing mthfr gene: a case-control study in a high altitude ecuadorian mestizo population. Tumor Biol. **36**(8), 6451–6461 (2015)
3. Sprague, B.L., Arao, R.F., Miglioretti, D.L., Henderson, L.M., Buist, D.S., Onega, T., Rauscher, G.H., Lee, J.M., Tosteson, A.N., Kerlikowske, K., et al.: National performance benchmarks for modern diagnostic digital mammography: update from the breast cancer surveillance consortium. Radiology **283**(1), 59–69 (2017)
4. Jiang, J., Trundle, P., Ren, J.: Medical image analysis with artificial neural networks. Comput. Med. Imaging Graph. **34**(8), 617–631 (2010)
5. Kamalakannan, J., Thirumal, T., Vaidhyanathan, A., MukeshBhai, K.D.: Study on different classification technique for mammogram image. In: 2015 International Conference on Circuit, Power and Computing Technologies (ICCPCT), pp. 1–5. IEEE (2015)
6. Don, S., Chung, D., Revathy, K., Choi, E., Min, D.: A new approach for mammogram image classification using fractal properties. Cybern. Inf. Technol. **12**(2), 69–83 (2012)
7. Jankulovski, B., Kitanovski, I., Trojacanec, K., Dimitrovski, I.: Mammography image classification using texture features (2012)
8. Xie, W., Li, Y., Ma, Y.: Breast mass classification in digital mammography based on extreme learning machine. Neurocomputing **173**, 930–941 (2016)
9. Taghanaki, S.A., Kawahara, J., Miles, B., Hamarneh, G.: Pareto-optimal multi-objective dimensionality reduction deep auto-encoder for mammography classification. Comput. Methods Programs Biomed. **145**, 85–93 (2017)
10. Khan, M.M., Mendes, A., Zhang, P., Chalup, S.K.: Evolving multi-dimensional wavelet neural networks for classification using cartesian genetic programming. Neurocomputing **247**, 39–58 (2017)
11. Magna, G., Casti, P., Jayaraman, S.V., Salmeri, M., Mencattini, A., Martinelli, E., Di Natale, C.: Identification of mammography anomalies for breast cancer detection by an ensemble of classification models based on artificial immune system. Knowl.-Based Syst. **101**, 60–70 (2016)

12. Pratiwi, M., Harefa, J., Nanda, S., et al.: Mammograms classification using gray-level co-occurrence matrix and radial basis function neural network. Procedia Comput. Sci. **59**, 83–91 (2015)
13. Buciu, I., Gacsadi, A.: Gabor wavelet based features for medical image analysis and classification. In: 2nd International Symposium on Applied Sciences in Biomedical and Communication Technologies, 2009. ISABEL 2009, pp. 1–4. IEEE (2009)
14. Khan, S., Hussain, M., Aboalsamh, H., Mathkour, H., Bebis, G., Zakariah, M.: Optimized gabor features for mass classification in mammography. Appl. Soft Comput. **44**, 267–280 (2016)
15. Srinivasan, M., Venkata, H.P.: Towards better veracity for breast cancer detection using gabor analysis and statistical learning. In: 2014 13th International Conference on Control Automation Robotics & Vision (ICARCV), pp. 1864–1869. IEEE (2014)
16. Lucht, R.E., Knopp, M.V., Brix, G.: Classification of signal-time curves from dynamic MR mammography by neural networks. Magn. Reson. Imaging **19**(1), 51–57 (2001)
17. Setiawan, A.S., Wesley, J., Purnama, Y., et al.: Mammogram classification using law's texture energy measure and neural networks. Procedia Comput. Sci. **59**, 92–97 (2015)
18. Blas, M.J., Sarli, J.L., Díaz Ferreyra, N.E.: Redes Neuronales Artificiales Aplicadas al Reconocimiento de Caracteres Morse (2013). https://doi.org/10.13140/2.1.2233.4247
19. Wahab, N., Khan, A., Lee, Y.S.: Two-phase deep convolutional neural network for reducing class skewness in histopathological images based breast cancer detection. Comput. Biol. Med. **85**, 86–97 (2017)
20. Qayyum, A., Anwar, S.M., Awais, M., Majid, M.: Medical image retrieval using deep convolutional neural network. Neurocomputing **266**, 8–20 (2017). https://doi.org/10.1016/j.neucom.2017.05.025. ISSN 0925-2312
21. Arevalo, J., González, F.A., Ramos-Pollán, R., Oliveira, J.L., Lopez, M.A.G.: Representation learning for mammography mass lesion classification with convolutional neural networks. Comput. Methods Programs Biomed. **127**, 248–257 (2016)
22. Szegedy, C., Vanhoucke, V., Ioffe, S., Shlens, J., Wojna, Z.: Rethinking the inception architecture for computer vision. In: The IEEE Conference on Computer Vision and Pattern Recognition (CVPR), June 2016
23. Zeiler, M.D.: Adadelta: an adaptive learning rate method. arXiv preprint arXiv:1212.5701 (2012)
24. Hinton, G., Nitish S., Kevin S.: Neural networks for machine learning lecture 6a overview of mini-batch gradient descent (2012)
25. Raschka, S.: Stochastic downward gradient (2017)
26. Leal, Y., Gonzalez-Abril, L., Ruiz, M., Lorencio, C., Bondia, J., Vehi, J.: Un nuevo enfoque para detectar mediciones de glucosa erróneas en los sistemas de monitor-ización continuos de glucosa. In: JARCA 2012, vol. 15, p. 17 (2012)
27. Liu, H., Meng, J., Wang, H., Qiu, S.: Application of cross entropy algorithm in combination forecasting model. In: 2016 2nd IEEE International Conference on Computer and Communications (ICCC), pp. 1289–1293. IEEE (2016)
28. Jensen, J.R., Christensen, M.G., Jakobsson, A.: Harmonic minimum mean squared error filters for multichannel speech enhancement. In: 2017 IEEE International Conference on Acoustics, Speech and Signal Processing (ICASSP), pp. 501–505. IEEE (2017)

29. Heath, M., Bowyer, K., Kopans, D., Kegelmeyer Jr., P., Moore, R., Chang, K., Munishkumaran, S.: Current status of the digital database for screening mammography. In: Karssemeijer, N., Thijssen, M., Hendriks, J., van Erning, L. (eds.) Digital Mammography, vol. 13, pp. 457–460. Springer, Dordrecht (1998). https://doi.org/10.1007/978-94-011-5318-8_75

30. Heath, M., Bowyer, K., Kopans, D., Moore, R., Kegelmeyer, W.P.: The digital database for screening mammography. In: Proceedings of the 5th International Workshop on Digital Mammography, pp. 212–218. Medical Physics Publishing (2000)

31. Rose, C.: Digital database for digital mammography software (2016)

32. Lee, H., Lee, B.T.: Selective inference for accelerating deep learning-based image classification. In: 2016 International Conference on Information and Communication Technology Convergence (ICTC), pp. 135–137. IEEE (2016)

33. Lu, Y., Chen, L., Saidi, A., Dellandrea, E., Wang, Y.: Discriminative transfer learning using similarities and dissimilarities. IEEE Trans. Neural Netw. Learn. Syst. **PP**(99), 1–14 (2017). https://doi.org/10.1109/TNNLS.2017.2705760

34. Abadi, M., Barham, P., Chen, J., Chen, Z., Davis, A., Dean, J., Devin, M., Ghemawat, S., Irving, G., Isard, M., et al.: Tensorflow: a system for large-scale machine learning. In: OSDI, vol. 16, pp. 265–283 (2016)

35. Pontes, F.J., Amorim, G., Balestrassi, P.P., Paiva, A., Ferreira, J.R.: Design of experiments and focused grid search for neural network parameter optimization. Neurocomputing **186**, 22–34 (2016)

Risk Analysis of Implanted Electronic Devices in Human Beings

Enrique Ferruzola-Gómez(✉) [iD], Johana Duchimaza-Supliguicha [iD],
Oscar Bermeo-Almeida [iD], Charlles Pérez-Espinoza [iD], Teresa Samaniego-Cobo [iD],
and William Bazán-Vera [iD]

Computer Science Department, Faculty of Agricultural Sciences, Universidad Agraria del
Ecuador, Av. 25 de Julio y Pio Jaramillo, P.O. BOX 09-04-100, Guayaquil, Ecuador
{eferruzola,jduchimaza,obermeo,cperez,tsamaniego,
wbazan}@uagraria.edu.ec

Abstract. This paper is a guide to risk analysis of implanted electronic devices in humans. The development of science and technology made global changes about dangers that threaten the security of humanity, however, in recent years there had arisen a new field of analysis for these implanted devices, contributing important elements. In this research, the authors tried to collect all the technological aspects concerning for some electronic devices that can be implanted in the body that can be hacked, to identify the possible computer attacks that they could suffer. The author's research different threats to which these electronic devices are exposed and how to find the way to reduce such threats and vulnerabilities. As well as to differentiate the types of attacks, the way that they operate and how they affect its operational function processes denoting an operational impact of these, such as an analysis of the prevention, detection, and mitigation of the main vulnerabilities.

Keywords: Mitigation risk · Security · Electronic devices · Security attacks
Vulnerabilities

1 Introduction

Today, the issue of electronic devices implanted in humans has become a current reality. All of these have a important use in our body; an example of these devices is the use of pacemakers in medical science. There are complex systems that can be injected into the brain and they mitigate or limit the effects of Parkinson's.

The creation of these types of electronic devices capable of being implanted in the human body is not a simple task. These types of development and implantations have to measure the state of human being tissues.

These implantations in the human body have many benefits, for instance obtaining better control of particular system functions that are using these implanted electronic devices, but like all technology, these bring some risks. Benefits can be obtained in several aspects, but also, the human being is exposed to possible risks of either security or intrusion of computer viruses. There are many examples like in the United States

© Springer International Publishing AG 2018
M. Botto-Tobar et al. (Eds.): CITT 2017, CCIS 798, pp. 86–99, 2018.
https://doi.org/10.1007/978-3-319-72727-1_7

Sanitary's Law which requires all citizens that are going to have these implantations must have a radio frequency chip, which allows the storage and data retrieval with the location and situation of the individual, so it is considered beneficial for find missing persons.

These devices are beneficial in certain aspects, but in the society the fact of being observed or monitored produces too much insecurity, because the implants whether these are electronic devices can be infected by some computer virus, and this could affect computer devices that are close to the human being who carries the implant.

1.1 Background

Today the implantation of a microchip as an identifier placed under the skin is a step closer to the future, and if this chip has a network access, it can be used for many different functions, making humans connect to the universal network: called the Internet [5].

The possibility that a company puts chips or microchips inside employees bodies to open or close doors or maybe to access their computers, would generate a sense of loss of freedom and privacy in terms of concepts of culture in society; where technology and government play an important role because they could control in a certain way the carriers of such devices.

There are companies in other countries such as Russia and Germany, which have a higher technological level. They refuse to be tracked through electronic devices implanted inside their body. But in other countries like Belgium, software companies that are specializing in digital marketing broke that cultural enigma and the use of implanted access chip is an obligation for its employees. Also, they use similar devices to identify their pets; this technology is based on radio frequency identification and memory of 868 bytes [7].

For the case of humans, a chip can be inserted in hand, between the index finger and the thumb finger. These chips are used to verify the registration like their identification that is controlled by a PC or mobile application. Also, they can be used for location purposes, and they can simply replace identity cards.

There are minimal implants that have a certain similarity to a tattoo machine needle, and you only felt a small prick leaving just a small mark on the skin. In certain cases they can be distinguished as a small protuberance. The companies that make these types of implants are supported by a wireless technology in turn to benefit the product impact.

The application of implants of electronic devices in humans has been considered useful to a large extent of people that want to replace passports, bank cards or perhaps transportation subscriptions, and also, the making of medical information records [23].

A clear example is from Dr. Mark Gasson at the University of Reading, he implemented a chip in his hand that allowed him to pass through the security doors of his laboratory, and this chip does not interfere with the use of the cell phone [29].

But what made this chip special? Was the fact that Gasson transmitted a virus from his computer, and later he proved that such virus could be transmitted from the chip to other electronic devices. Dr. Gasson admitted that the test was a proof of principle but he thought it had important implications for a future where medical devices, such as pacemakers and implants become more sophisticated and risk being contaminated by other human implants [30].

1.2 Official Computer Security Organizations

Several official agencies are responsible for risk prevention and assistance to all incident treatments, such as the Computer Emergency Response Team, the Software Coordination Center and the Institute of Engineering at Carnegie Mellon University. The Institute of Engineering at Carnegie Mellon University is an alert and reaction center against computer attacks that can attack companies or their administrators where they usually handle a large amount of information. And in the United States, there are other organizations that permit the use of these electronic devices, such as:

- Center for Medicare and Medicaid Services (CMS)
- Food and Drug Administration (FDA)
- Department of Health and Human Services (HHS)
- Department of Defense (DoD)
- Department of Veterans Affairs (VA)
- Department of Homeland Security (DHS)

1.3 Analysis of Vulnerabilities for Risk Mitigation

To protect the evolving threats, is necessary to create a protection strategy that covers the safety of these implanted electronic devices because they are not like cell phones that you can change, they are inside of a person [11]. Device manufacturers must strive to improve upon recent advances, ensuring that security concerns are considered throughout the design process and not relegated to an afterthought, and should cooperate with security researchers who seek to responsibly disclose design flaws. Regulatory bodies must balance the use of their powers to encourage good neurosecurity practices with the risk of impairing real-world security through overly burdensome regulations [31].

From the research point of view, the analysis and mitigation of risks in electronic devices become a verification method working like real networks, with savings in equipment and device costs. The analysis and evaluation of the vulnerabilities on electronic devices implanted in the human body that allowed identifying of some types of attacks and identified preventive security measures to avoid them.

The alteration of technological devices is very frequent because we have technological advances that make easier the access to the information of how these systems are constructed. This information has allowed the ways of violating the security of these devices. Organizations that have their structure for their computer systems must implement security policies to allow them to use different methodologies and mitigation tools to reduce the loss or manipulation of data [8].

1.4 Recognition of Vulnerabilities in Targeted Attacks Directed to Humans Through Technological Devices

Like most attacks on technological devices, attempts are made to manipulate the information or alter its normal process of operation; other attacks are much more selective. Malware creators may attempt to attack only a few companies to obtain certain credentials or data, and prepare attacks with care through previous investigations and acknowledgments. These attacks may consist of many emails that contain infected attachments designed to certain recipients. Selective attacks are usually aimed for malicious programs that are distributed to some technological devices for certain people or companies that may not know about them and they are hidden even without using advanced polymorphism techniques [4].

Risk assessment is probably the most important step in a device deployment process and also, the most difficult and most likely to make mistakes. Once risks have been identified and evaluated, the next step is to prevent the wrong use of these devices. The manufacturers have the obligation of creating the best plan for not harm human health: the mitigation policies and the mitigation procedures. Part of the difficulty in risk management is that the measurement of these two parameters; because if they failed, the implanted electronic device could affect the life of the person who carries it [10].

It is important to know how a human can recover from a possible disaster that may lead to a violation of this type of implant. It is indispensable to contemplate the preventive actions that are necessary for this purpose and risk calculation must be carried out regularly. But not only for identification of significant threats that affect the operations of vulnerabilities and the degree of exposure to risk, but it is also, necessary to identify the controls to be introduced to minimize impact damage [1].

2 Types of Electronic Devices Implanted in Humans

2.1 Brain Implant

Recognized also, as a neural implant, it is a technological device that connects directly to the brain, it usually placed on the surface of the brain, or maybe it is connected to the cerebral cortex. A common goal of modern brain implants and current research of them is to develop a biomedical prosthesis to replace areas of the brain that are dysfunctional because of head injuries or strokes. This includes sensory substitution, for example, in vision. Other brain implants are used in animal experiments only to record brain activity. Some brain implants require the creation of interfaces between neural systems and computer chips. This topic is part of a wider field of research called brain-computer interfaces [14].

Neuroimplants are used to treat a wide range of neurological and psychiatric conditions, such as Parkinson's disease, chronic pain, depression, etc. and will likely be used for an even wider range of ailments, as well as a way to correct "abnormal moral behavior," in the future [31]. These implants, therefore, have the potential of being switched off or made to function in undesired ways by unauthorized persons, leading to tissue damage, increased pain, altered impulse control, unwanted mental conditioning, and more, all to the detriment of the people who need these implants [24].

2.2 Insulin Pump

An insulin pump is a small electronic device that holds a reservoir of insulin [32]. It is about the size of a cell phone and is worn 24 h a day. An insulin pump can help to manage diabetes. By using an insulin pump, a person can match his insulin to his lifestyle, rather than getting an insulin injection and matching his life to how the insulin is working [33]. It is important that the person has realistic expectations about pump therapy. It is not a cure for people who require insulin to manage their diabetes but is a way of delivering insulin that may offer increased flexibility, improved glucose levels and improved quality of life. There are two types of these pump devices:

1. Traditional Insulin pumps have an insulin reservoir (or container) and pumping mechanism and attach to the body with tubing and an infusion set. The pump body contains buttons that allow you to program insulin delivery for meals, specific types of basal rates, or suspend the insulin infusion, if necessary [34].
2. Insulin patch pumps are worn directly on the body and have a reservoir, pumping mechanism, and an infusion set inside a small case. Patch pumps are controlled wirelessly by a separate device that allows programming of insulin delivery for meals from the patch [34].

In this type of electronic device, there is one function called CGM system for the pump the insulin and this function works like SCADA/ICS system [26]. In 2011 one researcher found that there was a malware named Stuxnet that damage this SCADA/ICS system. With this information, the same researcher tried to hack this electronic device, and he noticed that this malware affected the insulin pump making the centrifuge spin too fast and this could cause a patient's death [25].

2.3 Verichip

This electronic chip was the first implant created for humans that was approved by the US Food & Drug Administration. In 2004 it was a nano-chip with information about its human carrier, which has been recorded and could be recovered by radio frequency identification (RFID) system. It was marketed by VeriChip Corporation, a subsidiary of Applied Digital Solutions [9].

With an approximately double size of the length of rice, the device is normally implanted above the triceps area. Once scanned and used the correct frequency, the VeriChip responds with a unique 16-digit number, which can be linked with information about the user, and stored in a database for identity verification, access to medical records and other uses. The insertion procedure is performed under local anesthesia in a doctor's office and once inserted it is invisible to the eye. Implemented as a device used for identification by a third party, it has generated controversy and debate [5].

Many researchers think that the Verichip should only be used exclusively for identification, and not authentication or access control. Because if an attacker or a hacker capable of scanning a implanted VeriChip, eavesdropping on its signal, or simply learning its serial number can create a spoof device whose radio appearance is indistinguishable from the original [21]. Hackers use the analysis of a cryptographically for RFID signal, that help them to interfere the signal and steal the information and also, for sending a wrong information [22].

2.4 Cardiac Pacemaker

It is a small device operated with batteries. It perceives when the heart is beating irregularly or very slowly. It sends a signal to the heart, which makes it, beat correctly.

Description [2]

The weight of the newer pacemakers is one ounce (28 g). Most pacemakers have two parts:

- The generator that contains the battery and the information to control the heartbeat.
- The leads that are wires that connect the heart to the generator and carry the electrical messages to that organ.

A pacemaker should be implanted under the skin. In most cases, this procedure takes about 1 h. You will be given a sedative to help you to relax because you will be awake during the procedure.

The doctor makes a small incision. This incision is on the left side of the chest below the collarbone. Then the pacemaker generator is placed under the skin at this location. The generator can also be placed in the abdomen, but this not so common [13].

Using live x-ray images to see the area, the doctor places the leads through the incision, into a vein and then to the heart. The leads are connected to the generator. The skin is closed with sutures. Most people go home after one day.

The pacemakers that are used only in medical emergencies are

Transcutaneous Pacemakers: Used in medical science to extend the human life prognosis in case of heart problems. The materials used in its application are: Lifepak-10 monitor/monitoring electrodes, pacemaker cable, self-adhesive pacemaker electrodes, Scissors, gauze.

Transvenous pacemakers: These pacemakers generate an electric impulse that triggers the myocardial depolarization to subsequently triggering the mechanical activity.

2.4.1 Techniques Used in the Application of a Pacemaker

Firstly the patient is placed in a comfortable position. It is also mentioned that both the patient and the monitor should be far away from power cables, stretcher rails, etc. That is for preventing the interference that can generate the different electrical sources [12].

If the patient has pain or a discomfort reaction, the doctor should use analgesics or sedation. The doctor puts some adhesive electrodes that are from the pacemaker to the patient's body; in the case that the patient has an excess of hair in the thorax will proceed to cut (not to shave avoiding the possibility of obtaining cuts in the skin).

2.4.2   The Positions in Which the Electrodes Will Be Placed

From the techniques used in the application of a pacemaker we can identify the different positions in which they can be implanted in humans, we have the anterior-posterior position where the negative electrode is placed in the left anterior part of the thorax (just in the middle) where the xiphoid aphorisms and the left nipple are located. This position corresponds to the position V2–V3 of the ECG. And the positive electrode is placed on the left posterior part of the thorax, just below the paravertebral scapula.

Another of the most common positions is the anterior-anterior position where the negative electrode is placed in the left side of the thorax, which is in the middle winged region of the axilla. And the positive electrode is located in the right anterior part of the thorax just in the subclavicular area. It is taken into this position like second choice at the moment of being applied since this type of position interferes with the placement of the so-called defibrillation pads, and for this reason, there are problems of stimulation in the pectoral muscle. After the placement of the pacemaker, the electrodes of the electronic device that is implanted in the human. The pacemaker cable must be connected to the pacemaker connector on the side of the defibrillator and monitor [2].

It is important to indicate that to activate this device MARC must be pressed until the corresponding indicator lights up, and then it starts its operation. After initiation, the desired pacemaker frequency is selected. Usually, the power-on frequency starts with 40 bpm. It is necessary to proceed to observe the screen, where the device will be controlled; on this screen it will show stimulation indicators. If one case that the pacemaker needs changes in stimulation levels, the wavelength must be observed and modified with the AMPEG button [8].

Once selected and determined the wave amplitude in the stimulation is activated by pressing START/STOP. As a final indication, this will flash, and a positive signal will appear with each stimulation on the screen. From there you can slowly increase the current as the current level starts at 0 mA; the kaleidoscope should be observed to demonstrate the electrical stimulation capture. Finally, the patient's pulse must be checked to verify the mechanical capture. After this to end the stimulation, press START/STOP again or press MARC to turn the indicator light off.

Temporary pacemakers are usually implanted by bradyarrhythmias or tachyarrhythmias refractory to conservative treatments, or when hemodynamic or clinical instability occurs. If we add that the indications are much less clear than those of definitive cardiac pacing, we find that the decision to implant a intravenous pacemaker is always complicated and risky, so we must avoid overuse of this type of stimulation. To cope with this situation, we must use a better knowledge of the arrhythmias that make us consider the implant, evaluate less aggressive alternatives, such as transcutaneous pacemakers, and use new technologies such as ultrasound, which will facilitate the development of this technique.

The risk in these pacemakers is that can be updated by remote connection, and by this way, the hackers could damaged it. In 2017, two researchers of WhiteScope performed a security evaluation of the implantable cardiac device. They said that the inherent architecture and implementation interdependencies are susceptible to security risks that have the potential to impact the overall confidentiality, integrity and availability of the pacemaker [27].

3   Risk of Using These Electronic Devices

The evolution of science and technology in electronic devices had given us many advances and unprecedented developments in the history of mankind. However, the adoption of these new forms and technologies bring risks in certain mechanisms. Many times we only see the benefits of technologies and not the security of them.

Knowing this we can talk about technological risks. The probability that an object, equipment, material, process, substance or a phenomenon due to the interaction of these, cause a certain number of consequences to health, economy, and environment. When these interactions make real, occurred accidents produced by these technologies showing the weaknesses. The vulnerabilities of the technological elements play an important role in the dynamics of risk construction. Because different electronic devices are capable of generating technological threats in the body of the human being, but they are associated with external events can aggravate the situation [13].

In 2012, the Forbes Magazine, which is the most important Financial Magazine in the United States, published one article about hacking technological devices. In this paper, a researcher called Jerome Radcliffe demonstrated how to hack an insulin pump using an Arduino module that cost less than $20. An insulin pump cost approximately $250 per month. In April of the same year another researcher, Barnaby Jack, a security researcher at McAfee, demonstrated a system that could scan for and compromise insulin pumps. The difference with the other device is that this one can communicate wirelessly. He demonstrated that with a single push of a button on his laptop, he could have any pump within 300 ft dump its entire contents, without even needing to know the device identification numbers [37].

In October at a different conference, the same researcher Barnaby Jack, showed how using his laptop could reverse-engineer a pacemaker and could deliver an 830-V shock to a person's device from 50 ft away. In this conference, a professor of the University of Michigan called Kevin Fu explained that this happened because old pacemakers were running on an old OS, perhaps as old as Windows 95 to protect critical medical apps. These systems can be infected by worms that are 5 to 10 years old and said that manufacturers are also, a big part of the problem. Because some manufacturers refuse to allow OS updates or security patches. The manufactures can do more to protect these electronic devices and their data for potential exploit.

3.1   Different Threats in Technological Devices that Affect Its Control Mechanism

The functioning of an electronic transmission device must be considered important because many times this functioning is unpredictable and alters its control.

- Users: this is the biggest problem if we talk about a computer system security. In some cases their actions cause security problems, although in most cases, it is because they have oversized permissions, they have not been restricted from unnecessary actions, etc.
- Malicious programs: programs aimed to harm or to make illicit use of system resources. They are installed on the computer, opening a door to intruders or worse

for modifying the data. These programs can be a computer virus, a computer worm, a Trojan, a logic bomb, a spyware program or spyware, generally known as malware.

- Programming Errors: Most programming errors that can be considered as a computer threat are due to their condition of being used as exploits by hackers, although there are cases where the bad development is in itself a threat. Updating patches of operating systems and applications helps prevent such threats.
- Intruders: people who get access to our data or programs, that are not authorized such as crackers, defacers, hackers, script kiddie or script boy, viruxers, etc.
- A sinister: a bad manipulation or bad intention can damage the devices and also, programs.
- Internal technical staff: system technicians, database administrators, development technicians, etc. The reasons that are among in this list are because they had: internal disputes, labor problems, dismissals, for profit, espionage, etc.
- Electronic or logical failures of computer systems in general.
- Intercepting Telemetry: This is an important issue that can produce many errors on electronic devices like the pacemakers. It could make a magnetic field of sufficient strength to loss of data. The old pacemakers send data over 175 kHz at FM band, and if some device with the same frequency it could predict signal (in place of a heartbeat), making data that appeared as a periodic binary noise.

4   Methodology

4.1   Process

In this research, the authors used some articles based on the scientific study of the use and analysis of electronic devices implanted in humans. They used a method to explain this methodology [20]. This paper used a complexity scientific inquiry that helps for writing this part of the paper for being clear and orderly to avoid confusion and ambiguity. It has five steps: (i) Describing the materials used in the study, (ii) explaining how the materials were prepared, (iii) describing the research protocol, (iv) explaining how measurements were made and what calculations were performed, (v) and for the last stating which statistical tests were done to analyze the data. And in this paper, the authors did not use calculations neither the stating.

First, the authors read some papers that had a list of implanted electronic devices in human beings [15–19, 24] and took the most important implanted electronic device. There were many of these implanted devices, but only a few had a processor or the main board. The second issue that the authors did was choosing the electronic devices that had motherboards that can be hacked by other computers.

In Table 1 the authors put the list of the implanted electronic devices that they found in papers, and for this research, they only chose the ones which can be hacked.

Table 1. Implanted electronic devices in human beings

Device class	Devices	Can be hacked?
Pumps	Pharmacological agents	No
Pumps	Chemotherapy agents	No
Pumps	Insulin Pumps	Yes
Neurostimulators	GES	No
Neurostimulators	Brain Implant	Yes
Neurostimulators	DBS	No
Neurostimulators	Spinal Cord Neurostimulator	No
Cardiac	Transcutaneous Pacemaker	Yes
Cardiac	Transvenous Pacemaker	Yes
Cardiac	ICD	Yes
Cardiac	Verichip (For identified people)	Yes

In Sect. 2, in each paragraph of these electronic devices, the authors put how can hackers could malfunction those. Some of these can be hacked by Wifi, Bluetooth inclusive RFID.

Other scientific articles such as the article titled "Microchip in Humans - A Reality" by Babette Josephs authors, Tommy Thompson published on The Financial World of Guatemala magazine helped the authors for support the investigation.

5   Conclusions

With the results of this research, the authors intended to contribute to the knowledge of the many kinds of attacks that are made through electronic devices, attacks through their vulnerabilities found these days. It has been created at the same time that technology evolves and innovates with new tools that allow adaptation to an environment and meeting needs. There are a lot of frauds in computer devices that usually were developed to deceive or harm a person to acquire their benefit, that become a criminal act. There are solutions such as the mitigation that allow the detection of deficiencies of a computer system, the mitigation checks out the different aspects like policies, personnel, security to achieve an efficient plan and response to any necessary situation for the human being.

The confidentiality of the data and processes that are stored in the system of the electronic device implanted in the human body can be violated and can be manipulated by another person in the world. But they cannot connect to Wi-Fi or Bluetooth, the implanted electronic devices work with connections that you have to be within a short distance to access them, and also, the data is encrypted and can be protected by a simple or complex password.

The implantation of electronic devices constitutes a difficult decision situation, because its indications are not so clear, that the clinical experience is more important than the scientific evidence. As a general rule, they should be implemented in case of clinical and hemodynamic instability when someone has bradyarrhythmias and tachyarrhythmias and when other more conservative treatments fail because it is a technique with some complications, some of which may be fatal. To avoid them, a person has to have good training in these implantations, and also, the person has to have an ultrasound exam if it will be necessary.

One significant problem is the proliferation of software that controls medical devices. Day after day is increasingly available through and exposed to cyber security risks on the Internet. These risks include that many hackers could decode this software and use to control these electronic devices. We can find on internet from radiological imaging software to custom embedded software that is found in pacemakers that have remote connectivity that in many cases are Wifi connections.

There are concurrently increased risks of both unintentional interference and malicious tampering conducted with these same communication channels. So the manufacturers have to create or secure this software that controls these electronic devices implanted in our body or control some part of our organism.

Fortunately since 2013, in the United States, the Food and Drug Administration (FDA) began more seriously evaluating device cybersecurity as criteria for product approval, and has updated it since. The FDA largely based its guidance on the National Institute of Standards and Technology's (NIST) 2014 Framework for Improving Critical Infrastructure Cybersecurity. NIST is currently working on revisions, and also, released a separate landmark document that details a fundamental approach to developing secure and trustworthy digital systems. It is not enforceable, but it is a start.

6   Recommendations

In this paper, the authors show many different types of electronic devices implanted in the human being, through this how to identify the behavior of each of them, according to its functionality and application at the moment of the implantation process.

The respective authorities have shown their concerns about the possible loss of control over the data generated because this data could be automatically transmitted and then is a huge possibility that this information could be combined and analyzed, and used for secondary or anti-treatment purposes.

It is recommended that when someone has to buy an implantable electronic device, the person has to ask about if this device has security properties like:

- Authentication. If one intruder wants to enter to the device SO the identity of parties must be correctly established before performing any other operation.
- Encrypted Data. Either stored in the device or being communicated through the wireless link, can only be modified by authorized functions that decrypt this data.
- Authorization. This operation must be executed only if the requester has sufficient privileges to order it.

For implementing a program to manage cybersecurity risks, manufacturers should, among other things, have a way to monitor and detect cybersecurity vulnerabilities in their devices. Establish a process for working with researchers and other stakeholders to get information about potential vulnerabilities, such as the use of techniques such as firmware packing, obfuscation and encryption make those electronic devices much more difficult to reverse engineer firmware.

In 2013, researchers at Purdue and Princeton universities had created a prototype firewall to block hackers from interfering with wireless medical devices. This prototype system called MedMon, for a medical monitor, which acts as a firewall to prevent hackers from hijacking the devices. They demonstrated how MedMon could protect a diabetes system consisting of a glucose monitor and an insulin pump, which communicate with each other wirelessly [28].

This paper also refers, that some technologies are designed specifically to track humans especially for those that have electronic device in their bodies. Today software is capable of performing real-time observation, with the possibility of up to Make predictions about future events or perhaps sends signals to their control stations depending on its available technology. And the manufacturers have to encrypt these signals so that only they can access.

References

1. Castillo, A.: Riesgos tecnológicos y seguridad aparente: revisión y análisis para definición y reconocimiento (2013). http://www.laccei.org/LACCEI2013-Cancun/RefereedPapers/RP284.pdf
2. López, A., Macaya, C.: Libro de la salud cardiovascular del hospital clínico San Carlos y la Fundación BBVA. BBVA (2015)
3. Estacio, J.: Los riesgos tecnológicos en el DMQ: la paradoja del desarrollo urbano y el síndrome de nuevos escenarios de riesgos y desastres (2015). http://www.flacsoandes.edu.ec/biblio/shared/biblio_view.php?bibid=111097&tab=opac
4. García, C.: Seguridad en Smartphone Análisis de riesgos de vulnerabilidad y auditorias dispositivos (2017). http://openaccess.uoc.edu/webapps/o2/handle/10609/60705
5. Gasson, M.: Dispositivos electrónicos en el cuerpo humano. Cuerpo Humano Electrónico, pp. 13–17 (2015)
6. Gil, E.: Ciencias para llevar. Obtenido de Nano-básculas para pesar virus y bacterias en la detección de enfermedades, 10 June 2017. https://blogs.20minutos.es/ciencia-para-llevar-csic/
7. Mejía, C., Ramírez, M.: Vulnerabilidad, tipos de ataques y formas de mitigarlos en las capas del modelo OSI en las redes de datos de las organizaciones. PEREIRA: Universidad Tecnológica de Pereira - facultad de ingenierías eléctrica, electrónica, física y ciencias de la computación (2015)
8. Páu, M.: Medio humano, medio máquina. La vanguardia, pp. 20–28 (2015)
9. Perazo, C.: Chips bajo la piel. La Nación, pp. 20–25 (2014)
10. Ruiz, A.: Foros de la virgen. Obtenido de Militares están desarrollando microchips para implantaren el cerebro, 6 September 2014. http://forosdelavirgen.org/81431/en-que-estamos-respecto-a-la-implantacion-de-microchips-2014-09-06/
11. Sánchez, A.: Piel electrónica y super sensible (2015). http://cuerpohumanoelectronico.blogspot.com/2015/12/piel-electronica-y-super-sensible_29.html
12. Vásquez, T.: Medicina y actividad creadora. Obtenido de Estamos abocados a convertirnos en cíborgs? 26 June 2017. http://www.expansion.com/economia-digital/innovacion/2017/07/26/5977b44622601db35c8b4645.html

13. Vélez, A.: Tecnología avanzada ciencias médicas (2014). http://www.eltiempo.com/archivo/documento/CMS-14674255
14. Zapata, L.: Evaluación y mitigación de ataques reales a redes IP utilizando tecnologías de virtualización de libre distribución. In: INGENIUS, pp. 16–19 (2012)
15. Bazaka, K., Jacob, M.V.: Implantable devices: issues and challenges. Electronics 2(1), 1–34 (2013)
16. Petersen, B.T.: Implanted electronic devices at endoscopy: advice in a gray area. Gastrointest. Endosc. 65, 569–570 (2007)
17. Petersen, B.T., Hussain, N., Marine, J.E., et al.: Endoscopy in patients with implanted electronic devices. Gastrointest. Endosc. 65, 561–568 (2007)
18. Logan, J., Boushahri, A.: Cardiovascular implantable electronic devices. Hosp. Med. Clin. 6(1), 1–15 (2017)
19. Hiestand, B.: Cardiac implantable electronic devices. In: Peacock, W. (ed.) Short Stay Management of Acute Heart Failure. Contemporary Cardiology, pp. 285–294. Humana Press, Cham (2017). https://doi.org/10.1007/978-3-319-44006-4_22
20. Kallet, R.H.: How to write the methods section of a research paper. Respir. Care 49, 1229–1232 (2004)
21. Halamka, J., et al.: The security implications of verichip cloning. J. Am. Med. Inform. Assoc. 13(6), 601–607 (2006)
22. Bono, S., Green, M., Stubblefield, A., Juels, A., Rubin, A., Szydlo, M.: Security analysis of a cryptographically-enabled RFID device. In: 14th USENIX Security Symposium, pp. 1–16, Baltimore, Maryland, USA, July–August 2005
23. Hopkins, T.J.: FDA approves implantable chip to access medical records. BMJ Br. Med. J. 329(7474), 1064 (2004)
24. Pycroft, L., Boccard, S., Owen, S.L.F., Stein, J., FitzGerald, J., Green, A.L., Pereira, E.: Brainjacking: implant security issues in invasive neuromodulation. World Neurosurg. 92, 454–462 (2016). https://doi.org/10.1016/j.wneu.2016.05.010
25. Radcliffe, J.: Hacking medical devices for fun and insulin: breaking the human SCADA system. n.d. Black Hat, 20 April 2014. http://media.blackhat.com/bh-us-11/Radcliffe/BH_US_11_Radcliffe_Hacking_Medical_Devices_WP.pdf
26. Cruz, T., Queiroz, R., Simoes, P., Monteiro, E.: Security implications of SCADA ICS virtualization: survey and future trends (2016). https://doi.org/10.13140/RG.2.1.1064.2167
27. Rios, B., Butts, J.: Security evaluation of the implantable cardiac device ecosystem architecture and implementation interdependencies (2017)
28. Zhang, M., Raghunathan, A., Jha, N.K.: MedMon: securing medical devices through wireless monitoring and anomaly detection. IEEE Trans. Biomed. Circ. Syst. 7(6), 871–881 (2013). https://doi.org/10.1109/TBCAS.2013.2245664
29. Shirkhani, S.: What is the future of startups? (2012). http://shahramshirkhani.com/
30. Cellan-Jones, R.: BBC News - First human 'infected with computer virus' (2010). http://davidhuerta.typepad.com/blog/2010/05/bbc-news---first-human-infected-with-computer-virus.html
31. Zorz, Z.: Brainjacking: Hacking brain implants (2016). https://www.helpnetsecurity.com/2016/08/26/hacking-brain-implants/
32. NDSS Pump Consumables, Insulin pumps (2017). https://www.diabetesaustralia.com.au/insulin-pumps
33. Diabetes: How Do Insulin Pumps Work? (2015). http://www.diabetes.org/living-with-diabetes/treatment-and-care/medication/insulin/how-do-insulin-pumps-work.html
34. Aleppo, G.: Insulin Pump Overview (2016). https://www.endocrineweb.com/guides/insulin/insulin-pump-overview

35. Orangel y Sulma (2012). www.slideshare.net/Orangelescritura
36. PCRisk, Heart Stopping Vulnerabilities (2017). https://www.pcrisk.com/internet-threat-news/11295-heart-stopping-vulnerabilities
37. Wadhwa, T.: Yes, You Can Hack a Pacemaker (And Other Medical Devices Too) (2012). https://www.forbes.com/forbes/welcome/, https://www.forbes.com/sites/singularity/2012/12/06/yes-you-can-hack-a-pacemaker-and-other-medical-devices-too

Design and Construction of Self-driving Vehicle with Renewable and Non-polluting Energy

José Manuel Rosado Anzules$^{(\boxtimes)}$ ⓘ, Pedro Josue Mora Almeidaⓘ,
Joel Ricardo Muñoz Moranⓘ, and Nelly Karina Esparza Cruzⓘ

Universidad Técnica de Babahoyo, Ave Universitaria Km 2 ½ vía Montalvo,
Babahoyo, Ecuador
{jrosadoa002, pedromora522, jmunozm669,
nesparza}@utb.edu.ec

Abstract. Renewable energy is a contribution to society, it cares for the environment and helps the operation of machines at low cost. The prototype was designed with low-cost materials and to operate within the Technical University of Babahoyo campus. Our primary objective is to create a solar vehicle that uses clean energy and be capable of moving people with motor disability with the utilization of a voice recognition system. Tests were carried out with a real-size prototype obtaining satisfactory results, reaching speeds up to 8 km/h on flat surfaces with operating times of approximately 60 min when there are sunlight and 20 min at night.

Keywords: Arduino · Solar energy · Sustainable energy · Voice recognition
Experimental vehicle

1 Introduction

The primary purpose of this project is to promote the use of renewable and non-polluting energy; a subject that is of vital importance when it comes to the environmental situation of our planet. At present university institutions, both public and private, have a common problem: moving from one department to another or from one faculty to another one. It involves a considerable amount of time and effort. The problem becomes more difficult when there are people with some motor disability, or perhaps they are physically indisposed. Also, an even more worrying factor and of universal connotations refers to the environmental contamination provoked by vehicles most commonly used [1].

According to the 2010 census carried out by the INEC (Spanish acronym for Institute of Statistics and Censuses), in the city of Babahoyo, there were approximately 3182 people with motor disabilities. Therefore, a prototype vehicle like the one proposed in this project would be an affordable and efficient solution. The proposed energy is solar, taking into account that the transformation of sunlight using photovoltaic cells, which can be stored in accumulators for later use [2].

© Springer International Publishing AG 2018
M. Botto-Tobar et al. (Eds.): CITT 2017, CCIS 798, pp. 100–114, 2018.
https://doi.org/10.1007/978-3-319-72727-1_8

In 1977 Ed Passerini designed the first solar vehicle at the University of Alabama, however, in 1982 [10] the Australian Hans Tholstrup and racing driver Larry Perkins built the so-called solar car "BP Quiet Achiever" to cross from Perth to Sydney and started a competition between countries to improve prototypes. In 1985 the Swiss Urs Muntwyler created the first solar car competition called "Tour de Sol," which is still held in Europe. There are also other competitions such as the World Solar Challenge and the North American Challenge of Solar. Moreover, in Latin America, the most popular is the Solar Route in which yearly competes teams of universities and professionals.

Since 1990, University's the world has been designing and building solar vehicles. Major US universities such as Standford, Yale, Harvard lead the design and construction of solar vehicles. They have been built mainly for the purpose of competing in races, however, it is also possible to find models oriented to mobility and commercial viability, people with motor disabilities.

In Latin America, it is also possible to find solar vehicle construction projects. In 2014 the University Ecuadorian ESPOL participated in the Solar Race the Atacama with the hybrid vehicle 'Iron Trike'. In this edition, there were representations of Chile, Colombia, Ecuador, Bolivia, Japan. This competition aims to stimulate innovation in universities and companies, raise awareness of the importance of the use of renewable energy in our mobility. In 2016 the ESPE team of the University of the Armed Forces of Ecuador participated in the hybrid category.

The design of solar vehicles in Ecuador promises to be a market with great potential. The prototype proposed by U.T.B. was designed by a group of students and professors of the system's career. This team successfully participated in "Galardones 2017" and to improve it a multidisciplinary team including electronic, mechanical and other engineers will be formed.

In the development of this project, we used Arduino [11], which was born in Italy in 2005 under the concept of hardware and free software using the C++ programming language to control the inputs and outputs of data, easy to use and robust in its performance. There are some models available in the market: Arduino Uno, Arduino Mega, Arduino Nano, Arduino LilyPad, each have a different functionality for various projects. Regarding this project, it employs the Mega Arduino.

The need for a vehicle that transports people, which is environmentally friendly has become increasingly evident; therefore, its implementation will contribute efficiently and positively, to move from one place to another within a particular area.

A self-driving vehicle with renewable energy is designed and built to achieve a comfortable, safe, autonomous and non-polluting mode of transportation. It also contributes making transportation of people with motor disabilities or physical difficulties more comfortable and safe.

2   Related Work

Research and development of scenarios in the design and construction of solar vehicles have increased both a commercial and academic level. The following are the most relevant studies in the area of use of renewable energy in experimental vehicles:

Vilnitzky [8] designed a solar vehicle that can circulate in the city at a speed of up to 50 km/h, the electric battery solar is activated with a soft pedaling, and software controls the power of the vehicle, to fit the speed limits of each country. This car was built with aeronautical wood and recyclable plastic. Also, it uses solar panels and a battery.

González [10] created an autonomous vehicle that used solar energy with an embedded computer and sensors. It is able to follow a route without human help and is capable of reacting on its own to eventualities such as the appearance of obstacles along the way. It is also used in field investigations, due to it automatically sends data to a control center.

The Pampa Solar project [4], developed a prototype, made by teachers, students, and non-teaching staff, and it also participated in the Latin American competition for solar cars. This project won the first place to the most efficient use of solar energy because its systems utilize clean energies and zero emissions of pollutants to the environment.

In this work, we propose an autonomous solar vehicle that through sensors can react by itself to events such as automatic detection of obstacles, using renewable energy and operating by voice commands.

3   Methods

This section describes the hardware used in the implementation of the prototypes, the stages of the prototype, the android application and the functionality test.

3.1   Description of Materials

In this section the description of the elements to elaborate the prototype of a self-driving vehicle of real size is realized.

The total cost of the prototype is $1114.00 USD becoming an attractive price to the commercial market compared to its competitors like the Mö an electric vehicle [13] developed by Cooperativa Evovelo of Málaga(Spain) in February 2016 which approximately costs 4500 euros (Table 1).

3.2   Stages of the Prototype

The present study tries to create a vehicle with the appropriate characteristics to mobilize people automatically inside university campus, the search for similar investigations was done, and it is possible to summarize the stages of development in the following:

- Stage 1: Information gathering consisted of searching for the theoretical framework of this project in books, published articles, websites and interviews with experts in the areas of electronics and robotics, as well as reviewing statistical results at regional levels of disability and pregnant women.

Table 1. List of materials for the elaboration of the prototype in real size

Article	Quantity	Unit price	Total price
Square steel tube 3/4	3	$ 12.00	$ 36.00
One-quarter inch bearings	2	$ 22.00	$ 44.00
Tires 30 cm without tube	4	$ 15.00	$ 60.00
Round tube 1/4	1	$ 17.00	$ 17.00
Transmission kit (pinion, chain and catalina) of 43 teeth	2	$ 16.00	$ 32.00
Black spray paint	5	$ 2.00	$ 10.00
Wireless head set #800 (wireless microphone)	1	$ 125.00	$ 125.00
X100 mobile wireless speaker	1	$ 35.00	$ 35.00
Mega Arduino kit (Mega 2560 complete ultimate starter kit for Arduino)	1	$ 50.00	$ 50.00
Solar panel 100 W 24 V	1	$ 250.00	$ 250.00
Motorcycle battery 12 V	2	$ 60.00	$ 120.00
12 V Electric motor 1HP 1500 RPM	1	$ 50.00	$ 50.00
Stepper motors: mg995	3	$ 15.00	$ 45.00
Wifi module for Arduino Esp8266	2	$ 7.00	$ 14.00
GPS module for Arduino ublox NEO-6M-0-001	2	$ 55.00	$ 110.00
HC-05 bluetooth module for Arduino	2	$ 8.00	$ 16.00
Touch device with android operating system (phone or tablet)	1	$ 100.00	$ 100.00
Total			**$ 1114.00**

- Stage 2: Power calculations and electrical loads [9], it was necessary to elaborate some prototypes that allow establishing the ideal weight balance of structures and power of motors [3], together with the solar panel load and proper operation of batteries, losses voltage and design faults in the direction of the vehicle. A 2D model was developed for the primary structure of the vehicle (Fig. 1):

The power calculations were made based on the weight of the metal body that was 90 lb plus the average weight of a person of 120 lb, giving a total of 210 lb (Fig. 2).

To calculate the drag capacity of the motor [7], the horsepower (HP) is used and calculated using the following formula:

$$Pm = \frac{NxT}{5252} \tag{1}$$

$$1HP = 746 \ W \tag{2}$$

$$1 \ W = 0.00134 \ HP \tag{3}$$

Pm   = mechanical power in HP
N   = speed of revolutions per minute
T   = pair in foot pounds
5252 = constant in the English system

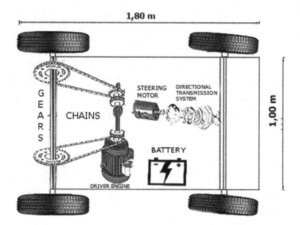

Fig. 1. 2D view of the actual size prototype

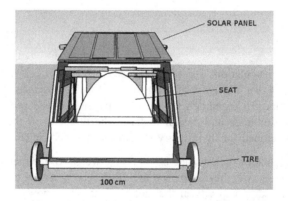

Fig. 2. Front-view of the real size 3D prototype

A horsepower equals 33,000 foot-pounds per minute (4,562.41 kg/m); I.e. the energy required to move an object with a weight in pounds (or kilograms) along a distance of feet (or meters) within one minute.

To estimate the power is necessary to know the work done, for which the following formulas were used:

$$F = P = m * g, \text{ m weight and g gravity} \tag{4}$$

$$W = f * e, \text{ e space} \tag{5}$$

$$P = W/t, \text{ t time} \tag{6}$$

The weight of the prototype vehicle is 90 kg and a passenger of about 160 kg, in total should move 250 kg, what takes you to travel 3 m in a time of 15 s?

$$F = P = 250 * 9.8 = 2450 \, N \tag{7}$$

$$W = 2450 * 3 = 7350 \, J \tag{8}$$

$$P = \frac{7350}{15} = 490 \, W \tag{9}$$

$$HP = \frac{0.00134 * 490}{1 \, \text{Watt}} = 0.6566 \, hp \tag{10}$$

It was considered a 1 HP motor for the pilot tests because according to the formulas was a suitable power. However, there are also other factors such as wind speed, friction, among others.

The battery power of approximately 15 min [6], under normal conditions. The photovoltaic panels we use are 100 W per panel, and we used a total of 2 panels which generate in the tests approximately 180 W, Fig. 3 shows the electrical scheme.

- Stage 3: Final selection of materials, after some tests could be determined the structure of the vehicle, batteries, electric motors and vehicle management system design, Arduino sensors.

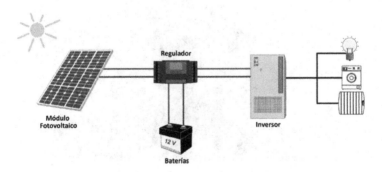

Fig. 3. Electric connections [12].

- Stage 4: Construction of the prototype, at this stage a total of two prototypes were developed. The 1:10 scale prototype of the vehicle for the initial tests and then the prototype #2 scale 1:1. According to specifications of the design and with the materials considered as the ideal ones for the adequate functioning of the prototypes, we proceed to the installation of sensors, batteries, solar panels [5], and others (Figs. 4 and 5).

Fig. 4. Prototype #1 scale 1:10. Top view

Fig. 5. Prototype #1 scale 1:10. Right view

Testing of prototype #1 at 1:10 scale was satisfactory, the prototype #2 was assembled on a 1:1 scale to perform tests on the starting and steering system with body weight plus passenger, engines, sensors, panels and other parts of the experimental vehicle (Fig. 6).

Fig. 6. (a) Protype #2 scale 1:1 start of construction, (b) Protype #2 scale 1:1 final version

- Stage 5: Programming the operation of sensors, when the vehicle prototype was ready, the Arduino program was carried out, allowing the sensors to operate according to the objectives set out in the proposal, a fragment of the code used in the prototype

```
#include <Arduino.h>
#define Pecho 3
#define Ptrig 4
#define Pecho2 7
#define Ptrig2 8
#define Pecho3 10
#define Ptrig3 11
class controlSensores {
  private:
  public:
    long duracion, distancia, distancia2, distancia3;
    void configure() {
Serial.begin (9600);         // inicializa el puerto seria
a 9600 baudios
pinMode(Pecho, INPUT);// define el pin 6 como entrada
pinMode(Ptrig, OUTPUT);     // define el pin 7 como salida
pinMode(Pecho2, INPUT); // define el pin 6 como entrada
pinMode(Ptrig2, OUTPUT); // define el pin 7 como salida
pinMode(Pecho3, INPUT); // define el pin 6 como entrada
pinMode(Ptrig3, OUTPUT); // define el pin 7 como salida
    }
void sensorFrontal() {
  digitalWrite(Ptrig, LOW);
  delayMicroseconds(2);
  digitalWrite(Ptrig, HIGH); // pulso de triger por 10ms
  delayMicroseconds(10);
  digitalWrite(Ptrig, LOW);
  duracion = pulseIn(Pecho, HIGH);
  distancia = (duracion / 2) / 29;
 }

void sensorDerecho() {
  digitalWrite(Ptrig2, LOW);
  delayMicroseconds(2);
  digitalWrite(Ptrig2, HIGH); // pulso de triger por 10ms
  delayMicroseconds(10);
  digitalWrite(Ptrig2, LOW);
  duracion = pulseIn(Pecho2, HIGH);
  distancia2 = (duracion / 2) / 29;
    }
void sensorIzq() {
  digitalWrite(Ptrig3, LOW);
  delayMicroseconds(2);
  digitalWrite(Ptrig3, HIGH); // pulso triger por 10ms
  delayMicroseconds(10);
  digitalWrite(Ptrig3, LOW);
  duracion = pulseIn(Pecho3, HIGH);
  distancia3 = (duracion / 2) / 29;
    }

};
```

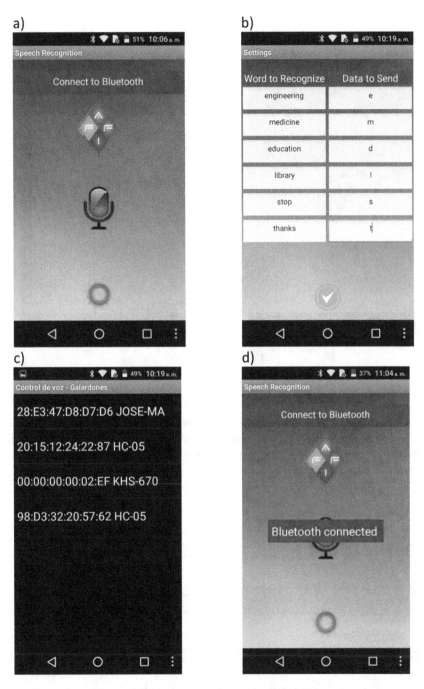

Fig. 7. Screenshots of the Android application. (a) Home screen, (b) Voice and data command configuration screen to be sent, (c) Bluetooth device selection screen, (d) Voice command reception screen, (e) Screen with the successful detection of a voice command configured, (f) Non-detection screen of a configured voice command.

e)

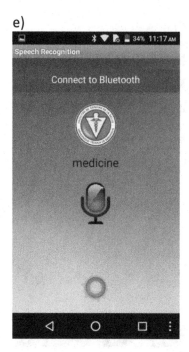

f)

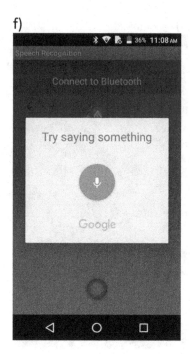

Fig. 7. (*continued*)

3.3 Android Application

Figure 7 shows the screens of the mobile application developed to control the Arduino from a touch device, a friendly, not complicated and easy to use interface was applied.

On the internet, there are numerous free tools to create Android applications in an easy and fast way, for the development of the program was used MIT AppInventor, in Fig. 8 it is possible to observe a code fragment of it.

```
when reconocimiento .Click
do   call SpeechRecognizer1 .GetText

when ListPicker1 .AfterPicking
do   set ListPicker1 . Selection . to   call BluetoothClient1 .Connect
                                                        address  ListPicker1 . Selection .

when ListPicker1 .BeforePicking
do   set ListPicker1 . Elements . to   BluetoothClient1 . AddressesAndNames .
```

Fig. 8. Android application code

- Stage 6: Tests and readjustments, the required tests were carried out to confirm that the prototype of the suggested vehicle works as intended, tests were conducted on the campus of the Technical University of Babahoyo, and the required adjustments were made as to the operation of sensors of Arduino and boot system.

3.4 Functionality Test

Four defined trajectories were generated within the university grounds by which the experimental vehicle was mobilized. The initial position was always the entry #2 of the U.T.B., and the destination depended on the voice command issued by the passenger. When the vehicle arrives at the destination waits about 3 min and then returns to the start of the track.

Two types of tests were performed to verify the autonomy time of the experimental vehicle: (a) During the day when the solar panel receives constant light and (b) at night where we do not have sunlight. The tests allow us to know the actual operating time of the vehicle when it is receiving solar energy from the environment and when there is no solar energy.

Figure 9 shows the result of the tests performed during the day when the vehicle receives solar energy, and the battery performs the dynamical charge and discharge cycles depending on the intensity of the solar rays and the voltage that the vehicle consumes during the travel. The tests were carried out on flat terrain when we find ourselves in the coastal zone or coast the terrain does not present significant inclinations.

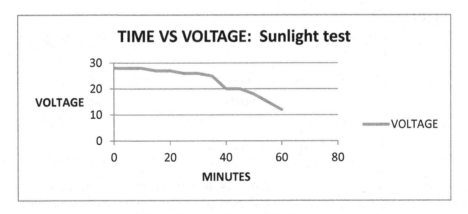

Fig. 9. Time vs Voltage. Sunlight test

In this test it was observed that the voltage slowly falls during vehicle operation and that it is possible to travel approximately 30 km continuously until the voltage is insufficient to move the car approximately after the first hour of the experiment, reaching speeds of up to 8 km/h.

The second test performed at night, shown in Fig. 10, the solar panel was deactivated and only worked with the voltage stored in the batteries.

Fig. 10. Testing at night

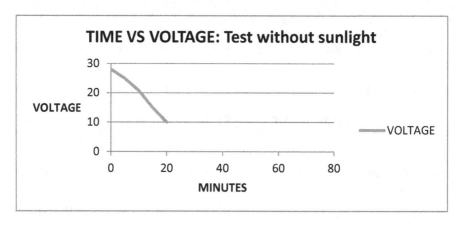

Fig. 11. Time vs Voltage. Test without sunlight

The battery discharge was performed in less time than in the first test, and at about the 20th min the motors stopped working due to the insufficiency of voltage, as can be seen in Fig. 11.

4   Results and Discussion

The solar panels generate approximately a total of 180 W which gives us an average operating time of 60 min when there is sunlight and 20 min at night, reached speeds up to 8 km/h on flat surfaces. For tests, google voice recognition was used. Thanks to its efficiency it is possible to recognize the voice commands of any person with a clear diction and not limited to a single defined speaker. The Arduino voice sensor sometimes did not recognize voices with different accents. Better performance was obtained with google voice recognition. The design and construction of a self-driving vehicle with renewable and non-polluting energy were constructed from creating a lightweight, economical transport that works with zero emission of pollutants for the environment and using computer tools that allow its easy driving, especially for people with motor disabilities. They are the major beneficiaries of this project because they can use this prototype vehicle to get from one place to another on the university campus easily and free of charge. However, the weight of the prototype at the end was greater than initially expected and it was necessary to change the drag motor to one of a higher power. As a future improvement, this research proposes changes in structural aspects to reduce the weight of the body with the objective to achieve higher performance of motors and batteries.

5 Conclusions

The construction of a low-cost self-driving solar vehicle as presented in this project would provide a cheap solution for the mobilization of people with motor disabilities. It also becomes a business opportunity for entrepreneurs that would contribute to improving the environment with high potential at the Latin American and world level a benchmark of sustainable mobility for the country. As a result of the execution of this project, it is hoped to achieve an improvement in the mobilization of people with some disability, in gestation or tourists who visit the Technical University of Babahoyo and using renewable energy takes care of the environment constituting a clear contribution to preventing global warming. During the realization of the tests, the performance of the self-driven vehicle was acceptable, and the operation of the solar panels demonstrated a high degree of reliability. The proposed prototype can be configured to operate within facilities of factories, shopping centers, industries or any company that has its departments located at great distances. Moreover, in a shopping center, it facilitates users can quickly reach the desired site or to mobilize merchandise from one place to another automatically and safely.

Acknowledgements. We would like to thank the Technical University of Babahoyo that supported this project.

References

1. Del Pilar Carreño Aguillón, E., Melo, V., Alfonso, E., Ingrid, L.A.: Diseño y fabricación de un vehículo autónomo impulsado por energía solar. Tecnura **16**, 91–106 (2012)
2. Méndez, J., García, R.: Energía solar fotovoltaica. Fundación Confemetal, Madrid (2007)
3. Roldán, J.: Instalaciones solares fotovoltaicas, pp. 27–28 (2010)
4. Rossi, S., Spina, M., Benger, F., De La Vega, R., Leegstra, R., Santillán, G.: Pampa solar: un proyecto multidisciplinario para la construcción de un vehículo solar. Ciencia, docencia y tecnología (48), 225–249 (2014). http://www.scielo.org.ar/scielo.php?script=sci_arttext&pid=s1851-17162014000100010&lng=es&tlng=es. Recuperado en 09 de junio de 2017

5. Tamajón-Reyes, C.H., Quevedo-Lora, F.R.: Estudio del impacto ambiental de un colector solar de polipropileno. Ciencia en su pc, octubre–diciembre, pp. 53–66 (2007)
6. Yro, H.: Análisis de las componentes armónicas de los inversores fotovoltaicos de conexión a red. Universidad Carlos III de Madrid, España (2009)
7. Harper, G.: El libro práctico de los generadores, transformadores y motores eléctricos. Limusa/Grupo Noriega Editores, México, pp. 8–9 (2000)
8. Quinteros Jaramillo, G.R., Ulloa Toscano, L.F.: Diseño e implementación de un vehículo de transporte giroscópico eléctrico Sedway, con auto balanceo controlado por un sistema embebido con arquitectura ARM (Bachelor's thesis) (2016)
9. Dworsky, M.E.O.: Diseño y Construcción de Conversor DC-DC para Control de Ultracapacitores en Vehículo Eléctrico (Doctoral dissertation, Tesis para obtener el título de Ingeniero Civil Industrial con Diploma en Ingeniería) (2002)
10. Oxlade, C.: Solar Power. Raintree, London (2012)
11. Pedrera, A.: Arduino para principiantes/Arduino for beginners. Createspace Independent P, S.l (2017)
12. Cenit Solar: Fotovoltaica aislada. España (2017). http://www.cenitsolar.com/imagenes/esquema_aislada.jpg. Recuperado en junio 10 de 2017
13. Evoleo y su vehículo solar Mö. http://www.evovelo.com/. Recuperado en junio 10 de 2017

A Kinect-Based Gesture Recognition Approach for the Design of an Interactive Tourism Guide Application

Diana Minda Gilces$^{(\boxtimes)}$ (iD) and Kevin Matamoros Torres (iD)

Universidad de Guayaquil, Guayaquil, Ecuador
{diana.mindag,kevinmatamorost}@ug.edu.ec

Abstract. Emerging technologies have revolutionized industrial and economic processes in the present days, tourism is no exception. For the modern tourist, access to readily available information about destinations they visit has become a necessity. To remain competitive cities must provide their visitors with interactive tools, which allow them to gain insight of their surroundings so that they feel confident enough to explore points of interest. This article proposes the design of an interactive tourism visitor guide that recognizes gesture commands to display significant information regarding shopping centers, restaurants, hotels and landmarks in the city of Guayaquil, Ecuador. To achieve this objective, a Kinect based natural user interface is deployed to allow tourist to control the tourism guide with the movements of their hands to preview images, data, and maps of how to reach touristic locations in the city. Integration with Kinect is handled through the deployment of a C# software based on the Microsoft Kinect Software Development Kit and Windows Presentation Foundation. The interface recognizes two main gestures when browsing the guide: push-to-press and grip-to-pan. Preliminary results demonstrate that the quality of interaction and overall user experience of the application allows for implementations in a real-world setting to reinforce local and international tourism.

Keywords: Tourism guide · Kinect · Gesture recognition · Natural user interface
Application

1 Introduction

Tourism is an industry that has undergone continued growth and diversification and is currently a key driver for the socio-economic progress of all nations. In Ecuador, there exist 25,672 tourist establishments, which generate at least 1.8 million dollars on a daily basis. International tourism contributes 2% of GDP to the national economy directly, and in full with 5.1%. For that matter, the number of jobs related to tourism, including housing and food services grew by a 12.4% during the year 2016. During the present year, between January and July, Ecuador has received 914,477 foreigners; this represents an increase of 9.3% in international tourism with respect to the same period last year [1]. Guayaquil has remained the leading touristic destination for years 2014–2016 as shown in Table 1. As with many other sectors, the use of information technology enhances the

M. Botto-Tobar et al. (Eds.): CITT 2017, CCIS 798, pp. 115–129, 2018.
https://doi.org/10.1007/978-3-319-72727-1_9

growth and progress of tourism. Currently, Ecuador advertises touristic information of its cities internationally, through web sites or mobile applications. However, once the tourists arrive at their destination, they face the trouble of finding touristic establishments and landmarks, due to the lack of touristic signage and posts that ease tourists' mobility and knowledge of the places they visit.

Table 1. Number of foreign tourists in the country's most visited cities

Head of migration	2014	2015	2016
Guayaquil	548,470	1,739,662	1,965,818
Quito	509,712	562,877	636,051
Manta	4,032	4,946	5,440
Others	20,7455	9,854,941	10,840,435
Total	**1,269,675**	**12,162,426**	**13,447,744**

Contemporary research in information technology focuses on human-computer interaction (HCI); specifically in the implementation of human-focused computer environments [2]. For a long time, the only available alternatives for user interaction with a computer were traditional user interfaces such as a keyboard or a mouse. The rise of touch screens in the mobile devices sector produced a shift in the way users interact with computers, communication, and home entertainment equipment. Manufactures place greater importance in providing immerse experience in the control of devices allowing users to operate their gadgets with simple motions and gestures through the implementation of natural user interfaces (NUIs). A natural user interface is a system operated through intuitive motions related to natural human behavior that creates a seamless human-computer interaction [3].

This paper proposes a hand gesture recognition approach that facilitates the design of an interactive tourism guide application without any specific NUI knowledge. The general objective of this study is to develop the prototype of an interactive tourism guide that receives gesture commands as an input to retrieve accurate information regarding hotels, restaurants, shopping centers and landmarks of the city of Guayaquil. The project aims to (1) design a system architecture to deploy a simple natural user interface, (2) to develop a navigation system that uses hand gestures to provide human-computer interaction and (3) to test the deployment of the prototype regarding User Acceptability Tests.

1.1 Related Work

Gesture recognition through visual and depth data is an active research topic in computer science [4]. An increasing number of devices built with natural user interfaces accept input in the form of taps, swipes, hand and arm motions, and other types of body movement [5]. Video game consoles were the pioneers in adopting the use of natural user interfaces to improve the user experience. The recent spreading of advanced controllers, initially designed for consoles and home entertainment systems, has been rapidly followed by the release of third-party PC drivers and Software Development Kits (SDKs) suitable for implementing new types of gesture-based natural user interfaces [6].

An example is the Kinect sensor for Xbox 360. After Microsoft Kinect granted access to its SDK, the device has been widely used to develop a large number of innovative applications that suit purposes different from gaming.

Alternative uses of the Kinect technology range from manipulating images via gestures during surgery [7], generating high-quality augmented anatomical overlays [8], translation of sign language [9] and controlling CAD systems [10] through NUIs. However, there has been limited investigation regarding Kinect in the tourism domain. Some examples include REXplorer, [11] a game that combines education and entertainment to help visitors engage with the history and culture of their destination through location-based gameplay. Similarly [12] presents HT3DViewer, an application for heritage tourism that helps people to outlook the heritages through their computer in the realistic view, controlled by their hand's gestures instead of using mouse or keyboard. A more elaborated application is shown in [2] where 3-D (three-dimensional) virtual globes such as Google Earth, Bing Maps 3D, and NASA World Wind are controlled through a natural user interface to navigate through diverse landscapes. Most of the gesture recognition approaches (i.e. [7–10]) rely on hand-tracking mechanisms for user interaction.

In contrast to [11, 12] the gesture recognition approach in this paper is focused on providing current information rather than historical background, to improve touristic planning and experience in a specific city, which also makes it different from [2] which presents all world maps. Our proposal aims at providing a smaller number of gestures to go beyond the learnability obtainable with previous approaches [7, 9, 11, 12] and improving the recognition accuracy at the same time.

2   Kinect Overview

Kinect [13] is a game controller technology introduced by Microsoft in November 2010, used within the Xbox 360 platform. It allows player interaction with the console through a natural user interface, using gestures, spoken commands or presented objects and images.

The Kinect sensor consists of a horizontal bar approximately 23 cm connected to a small circular base with a pivot-type hinge axis. Regarding hardware, it consists of an infrared emitter, a color sensor, an IR depth sensor a four-microphone array and a custom proprietary processor that runs the patented software, which provides motion capture, real-time 3D body, facial and voice recognition capabilities. The IR depth sensor is an infrared projector with a monochrome CMOS sensor that allows Kinect to see the room in which it is in 3D under any ambient light condition. Depth detection range is adjustable thanks to internal Kinect software that automatically calibrates the sensor. Figure 1 shows the Kinect sensor's internal components. The Kinect version to be used in this proposal is Kinect v1. Table 2 presents a summary of the device's technical specifications as studied in [2, 6, 13].

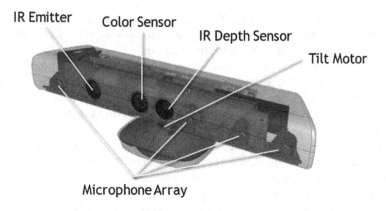

Fig. 1. Kinect sensor architecture

Table 2. Kinect v1 rundown

Kinect v1.0	
Video	640 × 480 @30 fps - 1280 × 960 @12 fps
Depth	320 × 240, 640 × 480
Method to calculate depth of objects in scene	Structured light
Distance	1 m to 1.20 m interaction 1.20 to 1.80 m without interaction
The number of skeletons tracked	2
The number of joints tracked	20
Tilt motor	Can be graduated between +27° and −27°
USB	2.0
Operating system	Windows 7 or higher
SDKs available	Kinect for Windows SDK v1.8 OpenNI v2.2

3 Architectural Design

The central element in the proposed solution is the Kinect sensor, so the architectural design focuses on determining and gathering hardware and software components for which integration to the Kinect device is feasible. A product backlog, consisting of a user-centric list of things to do within the project [14] is created to organize user stories into sprints that take similar amounts of time and effort to complete. Table 3 shows the product backlog with the five user stories required for the execution of this project organized into three sprints. Notice that the minimum time set for each sprint s 14 days and the maximum 25 days. Each one consists of user stories that add up to a similar estimate of time or effort.

Table 3. Product backlog

No.	User stories	Estimate (days)	Sprint backlog
1	Select hardware and software components	5	01
2	Design the navigation system	20	
3	Code the proposed NUI design	25	02
4	Map scrolling	7	03
5	User Quality Testing	7	

For the sprint 01 dealing with the selection of hardware and software components, study of related work [2, 4, 13] determines that the prototype's development requires the Kinect SDK, a free software package that enables developers to create applications that support gesture and voice recognition [13]. The software automatically detects the 3D location of 20 joints for two people. No accessories are required to identify joint locations, document [15] describes the software's algorithm. The Kinect SDK runs over a native operating system; it is not possible to execute it in a virtual machine. Based on the Kinect rundown in Table 2 and research [2, 4, 12] components in Table 4 have been selected and assembled as shown in Fig. 2.

Table 4. Selected software and hardware components

Components		
Hardware	Kinect SDK	
	Element	Description
Kinect device for Xbox 360	Visual Studio	Integrated development environment for Windows operating systems. Supports multiple programming languages such as C++, C#, Visual Basic .NET, and Java programming language
Dual core computer, 2.66 GHz or higher	C#	Object-Oriented Programming Language developed and standardized by Microsoft as part of its .NET platform
Kinect PC adapter		
Graphics card that supports Microsoft DirectX 9.0c	WPF (Windows Presentation Foundation)	Develop visually appealing applications with interaction facilities including animation, video, audio, documents, navigation or 3D graphics

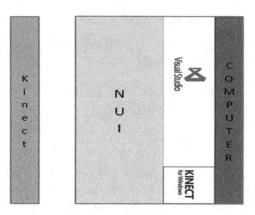

Fig. 2. Project architecture

The Kinect can detect up to 6 skeletons but only tracks a maximum of 2 skeletons [13]. The gesture recognition approach is designed to allow only one person at a time to interact with the system. If two people are detected, the one that uses the predefined gestures for interaction is preferred and tracked. Following height and depth parameters in [13] that prove successful for gaming purposes and applications in [7–10] place the Kinect in front of the computer; a height of 0.85 m from the floor and a depth of approximately 1 m to 1.20 m is required.

An initial user study was conducted through short contextual interviews in the airport of the city and other points of interest such as the Malecon 2000, to determine the kind of information and features that tourists wish an interactive tourism guide to have. According to the survey results, which include a total of one hundred interviews, tourists expect the application to provide an easy to use interface, and to present reliable data that can be retrieved quickly. These characteristics are taken into account for completion of the other activities in the sprints.

4   Gestures Recognition

The development of a basic navigation system that uses hand gestures recognition relies on determining the bridge in communication between the humans to perform gestures and then, translate these gestures to a human-computer communication so that they can be expressed naturally and remembered easily [5, 10]. Determining a set of gestures to define an action is a complicated task because there are many different ways to say something depending on the context, for example, the language and culture of the people [4, 10].

Also, not all gestures are identified or remembered, according to a study performed by George A. Miller in 1955, the ability of humans to store data in short-term memory is seven ±2, meaning that only between five and nine elements are retained for short periods. Based on [10], one of the principal characteristics to be implemented in the design of the gesture recognition interface is that the number of gestures used by the application are two or more, but do not exceed nine.

Another fundamental aspect to consider is that the gestures are not misread by the system; the application must be able to distinguish movements that represent a gesture from the movements that do not. Moreover, the system cannot perform something that has not referred to do in the development of the tasks. The software implements elements in the Microsoft.Kinect.Toolkit.Controls library [12], which contain the skeletal tracking features, and Windows Presentation Foundation controls for Kinect gesture-based interactions designed for hands-free control of applications [2, 3, 15].

4.1 Kinect Interaction Module

The KinectInteraction Module in the SDK uses joint information from the Kinect sensor to differentiate gestures entered by a user from other gestures [2]. Controls that provide Kinect Interactions are grouped into the Microsoft.Kinect.Toolkit.Controls library. For KinectInteraction to extract joint information, the KinectSensorChooser control must first detect the status of the attached Kinect sensor and define the screen area in which physical human interaction is sensed. The KinectSensorChooser command informs the user if the sensor is unplugged, plugged into the wrong USB port, or if they need to check the power supply.

The KinectRegion provides a canvas for other KinectInteraction Controls; the construction of the C#/WPF application begins when the KinectRegion command defines the screen area where interactive elements are placed for the user to manipulate; this command also provides the functionality to display and move the hand cursor. A Kinect region must be associated with a Kinect sensor to enable Kinect Interaction. An application can have multiple KinectRegions, but they cannot be nested [15]. The KinectInteraction module loads human hand data using the KinectSensorChooserUI and

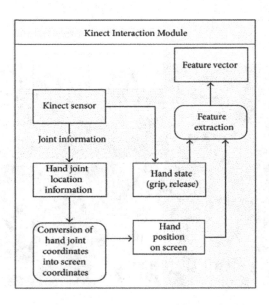

Fig. 3. Kinect interaction module data flow

converts hand coordinates into screen coordinates. These coordinates are compared with the established Kinect Region to obtain a feature vector that represents the trajectory of the hand [13, 15]. Figure 3 shows the KinectInteraction Module data flow.

The natural user interface designed for this application incorporates two types of gestures: "push-to-press" (Fig. 4), used to identify a pressed button through a human gesture and "grip-to-pan" (Fig. 5), which is used to drag or move any controls in the scroll viewer. The KinectInteraction controls used to implement these two hand gestures within the code are the Kinect Cursor KinectTileButton, KinectCircleButton, and KinectScroll viewer.

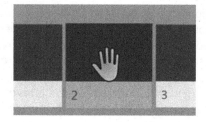
Fig. 4. Push-to-press gesture

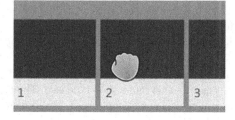
Fig. 5. Grip to pan gesture

5   Navigation and Information Retrieval

The tourist can browse through four different tourist establishment categories; hotels, landmarks, restaurants and shopping centers. Therefore the graphical interface is organized into four screens: a home page, an options page, a scroll view page and a descriptions page.

Fig. 6. Home page

The home page (Fig. 6) is the primary menu and is the first screen to be shown; it allows the user to select the language while showing a video of the city of Guayaquil. The tourist can choose to view the content in Spanish or English by pressing the KinectCircleButtons and starts running the application by pressing the KinectTileButton on the screen.

Internally, the application consists of a.xaml.cs file which contains code that provides the functionality for the.xaml file which is used to display content stored in a project folder created upon starting the development. This folder can be later located anywhere in the computer or an external drive and instanced in the code through XAML – WPF URIs.[1] The project folder contains subfolders for each of the images, text, video and other resources to be referenced through the.xaml.cs file. The code references each of the categories within the code as a level, and each level points to a different subfolder within the project folder to retrieve information.

Navigation through the application consists of the system detecting grip-to-pan gesture to scroll through content and the push-to-press to press buttons to modify the information level content to display. In turn, the following steps summarize the navigation for the proposed solution:

1. The user positions themselves in front of the Kinect device.
2. Kinect senses the presence of a person and the screen displays the home page (level 0).
3. The system can distinguish two hand gestures: an open hand or a closed hand.
   a. An open hand allows the user to push-to-press an item in the menu. (Select a new level)
      i. A pressed button feedbacks the user with the corresponding level screen and its data.
   b. A close hand allows the user to grip-to-pan (scroll) through items in the level menu.
4. Operation continues until the Kinect sensor no longer detects the presence of a user.
   a. The application goes back to level 0 if it does not sense a user.

Information is retrieved from the folders only when the push-to-press gesture is used to press either the KinectTile or KinectCircle buttons. Figure 7 provides a flow chart of the workflow of the application retrieving content as the user browses through each of the screens. The code uses a case structure to select content for the corresponding category by comparing it to a string stored in button.Label.Equals when the push-to-press gesture is detected. A level 0 instructs the application to display content on the home page. The user can use push-to-press gesture to switch to level 1. Level 1 retrieves the options page (Figure TAL) that contains four KinectTileButtons to allow the user to choose whether to search for hotels, landmarks, restaurants or malls.

---

[1] Uniform Resource Identifier (URI) is a string of characters used to identify a resource.

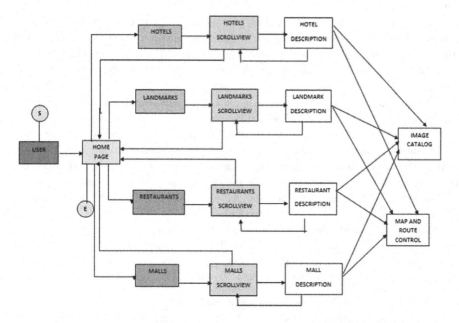

Fig. 7. Application workflow

Once a category is selected, the scroll view page is displayed. Within this screen, the user may use the grip-to-pan gesture to browse through the different touristic establishments for the selected category. Figure 8 shows the grip-to-pan gesture being used in the scroll view page for the hotel's category. Notice that besides the scroll on the page, two KinectCircleButtons are included. The home button, which returns the system to level 0 and the back arrow button, which if pushed-to-press sets the level variable to a

Fig. 8. Scroll view page

value of 2 and instructs the application to display the previous screen. If the push-to-press gesture is used to select one of the establishments, the descriptions page Fig. 9 is retrieved.

Fig. 9. Description page

The grip-to-pan gesture can be used to read through the establishment's information details. The push-to-press gesture allows the user to press the image on the left side of the screen, to view more of the touristic establishment photos. This feature is the result of setting the level to a value of 3, which displays a mosaic of images for the selected category. When the user picks a new image, the level variable holds a value of 4. Level 4 is also used to disable maps and clear routes within the code.

The Bing maps included in the description page resemble those in [2], the added value of this proposal it that it shows the map and the route from the tourist landmark towards the touristic establishment that the tourist is browsing. Observe in Fig. 10 the

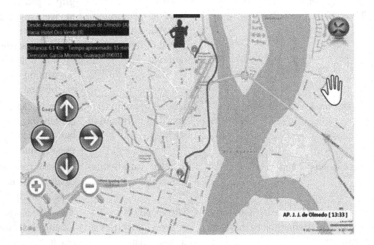

Fig. 10. Map

selected map in fullscreen, detecting the skeleton and the hand gestures. Push-to-press can be used to select the buttons to move the map, the same can be achieved more precisely with the grip-to-pan gesture. The KinectCircleButton displaying the X allows the user to go back to the description page.

If at any point the contents of the application should be edited, the code must undergo changes. Files in the project folder, XAML – WPF URI references, as well as some button.Labels in the programming would require modification.

6   User Acceptability Tests

Evaluation of the prototype was carried out with 50 people of which 30 were men and 20 women, between 20 and 50 years old, with various economic and cultural backgrounds. Participants validated the tourism guide application through six use case test

Table 5. User AcceptanceTests

Test no	Description	Criteria to be tested	Expected result
1	Select the English Language to view content	Comprehensible interface Ease of operation	Information displayed in English
2	Choose a category from which to get establishment info	Comprehensible interface Ease of operation	The user can select between hotels, restaurants, landmarks, and malls using the push to press gesture
3	Browse through the content for each of the establishments Then select a new category	Comprehensible interface Ease of operation Reliable data Speed of information retrieval	The user can use the grip to pan gesture to navigate through the scroll view and arrows The user uses push to press to find the description of each establishment
4	Switch the Language to Spanish	Ease of operation Speed of information retrieval	The user can change the language using the buttons and the push to press gesture
5	Repeat steps 2 and 3	Speed of information retrieval	The user can navigate easily. Content appears in Spanish
6	Use the map feature to display the route from destination to tourist establishment	The speed of information retrieval Reliable data	The user can get reliable data on how to reach the tourist establishment

and answered a set of 8 questions regarding the experience of using the natural user interface for human-computer communication.

The questions evaluated four criteria: a comprehensible interface, ease of operation, reliable data and speed of information retrieval. These standards were selected based on the initial user study described in Sect. 3: Architectural Design. Each criterion was rated using the following scale; a 0 indicates that the application does not meet the requirements at any level, a value of 1 suggests a poor fulfillment of the specification, and a 2 evidences an attained criterion.

Table 5 lists each of the user acceptance cases. It shows the test description along with the criteria to be tested within each case and the expected result. Evaluation involved testing features such as setting the language to display the contents choosing the establishment categories (push-to-press gesture), and browsing through information (grip-to-pan) and maps (push-to-press and grip-to-pan).

Results for each of the user acceptance test expressed as percentages appear in Table 6. Notice that all of the four criteria score above 80% success rate, proving that the outcome of the user acceptance tests highly resembled and matched the user expectations. The Kinect-based gesture recognition approach for the design of an interactive tourism guide application is feasible and proves adequate; its natural user interface for hand tracking and gesture recognition in the deployment of an interactive tourism guide application is comprehensible, provides an easy way to navigate through the content, and shows reliable data in a moderate amount of time.

Table 6. Evaluation of results

Outcome	Maximum weighted score per survey	Total score per survey	Success %
Comprehensible interface	6	6	100
Ease of operation	8	8	100
Reliable data	4	4	100
Speed of information retrieval	8	7	87.5

7 Conclusions

This paper proposes a Kinect-based gesture recognition approach for the design of an interactive tourism guide application. The project fulfilled all three of the objectives: (1) sketch a system architecture to deploy a simple natural user interface, (2) to develop a navigation system that uses hand gestures to provide human-computer interaction and (3) to test the deployment of the prototype regarding User Acceptability Tests. A basic navigation system using the push-to-press and grip-to-pan hand gestures for provide human-computer interaction was successfully implemented within the architectural design, by using controls from the Kinect Interaction Module together with C# and WPF. It is stressed that the natural user interface developed for this application is designed with no prior NUI design expertise, and is deployed exclusively through C#

programming knowledge and the Kinect Software Development Kit. Still, it proves simple and easy to use as demonstrated by results of the preliminary user acceptance tests; confirming the viability of combining C# programming and the Kinect technology implementing a hand tracking navigation system based on the KinectInteraction Module. The implementation of this application in the city of Guayaquil represents an opportunity to improve the touristic experience in the whole country. The prototype can be easily adjusted so that the content provides information on other cities.

8   Future Work

We recommend that further development of this project considers updating the Kinect sensor version as well as the SDK. If so, the application can include more input gestures (as long as the number of gestures does not exceed nine), e.g., wave a hand to navigate the system. Also, it is important that the extension of this project incorporates user profiles. For instance, it is convenient that later versions allows an administrator to modify the application content without the need to program, but use it as a content management system instead, where images and other resources are uploaded without the need to edit code references, doing so would represent a milestone to deploy the tourism guide application in other cities in the Ecuadorian territory.

References

1. Ministerio De Turismo Ecuador, Ecuador 2016 Investment Summit, Quito (2016). http://www.proecuador.gob.ec. Accessed 20 Mar 2017
2. Cho, K., et al.: Development of a hand gestures SDK for NUI-based applications. Math. Probl. Eng. **2015**, 10 (2015). Hindawi Publishing Corporation, Article no. 212639
3. Valentino, F., Domenico, P.: Using Kinect for hand tracking and rendering in wearable haptics. In: IEEE World Haptics Conference, 21–24 June 2011, Istanbul, Turkey (2011)
4. Moya, J.M., de Espinosa, A.M., Araujo, Á., de Goyeneche, J.M., Vallejo, J.C.: Low-cost gesture-based interaction for intelligent environments. In: Omatu, S., Rocha, M.P., Bravo, J., Fernández, F., Corchado, E., Bustillo, A., Corchado, J.M. (eds.) IWANN 2009. LNCS, vol. 5518, pp. 752–755. Springer, Heidelberg (2009). https://doi.org/10.1007/978-3-642-02481-8_114
5. Grazia, C., Atletico, C., Guaragnella, C., D'Orazio, T.: A Kinect-based gesture recognition approach for a natural human-robot interface. Int. J. Adv. Robot. Syst. **12**, 22 (2014). https://doi.org/10.5772/59974
6. Ken, S., Jeff, S.: The Definitive Guide to Scrum: The Rules of the Game. Scrum.Org and Scrum Inc. (2013)
7. Davudinasab, A.: Kinect Sensor. Amirkabir University of Technology, Tehran (2014)
8. JenChanga, Y.: A Kinect-based system for physical rehabilitation: a pilot study for young adults with motor disabilities. Res. Dev. Disabil. **32**(6), 2566–2570 (2011)
9. Algar, D.: Insole modeling using Kinect 3D. Chalmers University of Technology Division of Signal Processing and Biomedical Engineering, Department of Signals and Systems, Goteborg (2013)
10. Yang, H.D.: Sign language recognition with the kinect sensor based on conditional random fields. Sensors **15**, 135–147 (2015)

11. Wipfli, R.: Gesture-controlled image management for operating room: a randomized crossover study to compare interaction using gestures, mouse, and third person relaying. PLoS One **11**(4), e0153596 (2016)
12. Meng, M.: Kinect for interactive AR anatomy learning. IEEE Explore, Adelaide (2013)
13. Zhou, Z., et al.: Image-based clothes animation for virtual fitting. SIGASIA, Singapore (2011)
14. Shotton, J., et al.: Real-time human pose recognition in parts from single depth. In: Proceedings of the 2011 IEEE Conference on Computer Vision and Pattern Recognition, pp. 1297–1304 (2011)
15. Microsoft, KinectInteraction Controls. https://msdn.microsoft.com/en-us/library/dn188674.aspx. Accessed 1 May 2017

An Agent-Based Model for Game Development

Alejandro Garcés-Calvelo[1] , Aldo Garcés-Matilla[2(✉)] ,
and Alejandro Pacheco-Morales[2]

[1] Institute of New Imaging Technologies, Universitat Jaume I,
Castellón de la Plana, Spain
agarcesc62@gmail.com
[2] Department of Computer Science, University of Oriente,
Santiago de Cuba, Cuba
{aldo,apacheco}@uo.edu.cu

Abstract. In this paper we describe a new agent-based model for games development. This model has the advantage that it allows both high- and low-level behavior specifications. These methods reduce the gap between abstract specification and system implementation. The use of the model is demonstrated with a real-world game example. The proposed results have been used for the development of the GAMESONOMY platform. GAMESONOMY is a visual tool to create multiuser games (including serious games) in the cloud. Also, there is a large class of systems with reactive components that can benefit from our model; for example, e-learning environments, monitoring and control systems, telecommuting services and e-commerce systems.

Keywords: Software agents · Software methodologies
Agent-Oriented Software Engineering · Games

1 Introduction

Abstraction has always been an object of study of Computer Science. The evolution of programming models has been mainly related to the level of abstraction introduced by the different paradigms. Computer systems allow the creation, manipulation and reasoning about abstractions. Abstraction methods are essential in the models definition, designs and appropriate implementations for handle the complexity inherent in software development [1].

Game systems have also evolved from single-processor centralized computing towards distributed computing over wide-area networks and the Internet. Many researchers have developed techniques for the design and implementation of games; however, the existing approaches cannot fully catch up the increasing complexity of modern Virtual Environments applications [2].

In these systems agents have become the choice of paradigm for ubiquitous programming [1]. Agents and Multi Agent Systems (MASs), other than a technology, represent a brand new paradigm for software development [3]. This paradigm allows a natural specification of modular and distributed systems.

© Springer International Publishing AG 2018
M. Botto-Tobar et al. (Eds.): CITT 2017, CCIS 798, pp. 130–144, 2018.
https://doi.org/10.1007/978-3-319-72727-1_10

A lot of wide-ranging methodologies for the development of MAS have been proposed. Gaia [4], MAS-CommonKADS [5], MaSE [6] and Ingenias [7] are examples of them. These methodologies include notations, methods and techniques to guide the development process of MASs.

However, the agent paradigm is not frequently used for the development of real-world applications. As pointed out Winikoff [8] "too long time, the agent community has been trying to tell outsiders a story based on words such as 'agents' and 'autonomy'. Nevertheless, we do not present a coherent story. We do not agree ourselves in the agent concept. Also, autonomy can be a scary concept, evoking AI notions of rampant robots. We have been occupying in the development of complex theories, which generally are useless for the implementation of real-world applications".

These issues limit the development of simple practical prototypes of MASs. To address this problem, we propose a new formal model for the specification of Multi-Agent system, which has the following features:

- The three main concepts in our model are the environment, roles and agents. Multi-agent systems are made of simple components whose abstract representations are agents. They encapsulate complex behavior and communication protocols. Roles describe the behaviors of the actors in the systems. The environment contains information resources, which are used by agents.
- We impose a static organizational structure. Roles and relationships do not change during execution time. Their skills and services are static.
- Agents implement a unique role. They are homogeneous, because all agents are supported by the same language and execution platform. Our model of MAS focuses on a class of software agents: the stationary agents. These software agents execute only on the system on which it begins the execution; they may typically use communication mechanisms such as remote procedure calling and shared memory. A stationary agent is implemented as a code component and a state component. Furthermore, agents need an execution environment at all involved computers.
- There is a centralized mechanism that creates, activates, shuts down and removes the agents of the system. It manages all global resources and interaction protocols of the application.

System in this restrictive class of MASs are called Moderately Open Multi-Agent Systems for Games (G-MOMASs). This class of MASs provides a new model for software component (agent) definition and implementation. The features just described may seem unsuited for large-scale agent communities with high pro-activity. However, there is a large class of systems that can benefit from our model, especially the game technology. The main contribution of this model is that it reduces the gap between abstract specification and system implementation.

We describe and demonstrate the use of our model with two real-world application examples. The first example implements the very simple game Pong. We use it throughout the paper to illustrate the features of our model. Additionally, we describe the whole specification process by means of another game. These examples show how our results can be applied to the design and construction of games.

2 Related Works

In the last decades, the games technology has reached an extraordinary development. This kind of entertainment software is causing many advances in certain technologies, such as the computer Graphics, simulation, Artificial Intelligence (AI), distributed systems and Graphical User Interfaces (GUI). These advances are going beyond the world of the entertainment; and they are propitiating a revolution in the development of Virtual Environments (VEs) in the network with many applications for the education, communications, commerce, etc. [9–11].

Although the visualization techniques represent the essential task for all interactive systems, the game development must consider several semantic problems. In the last decade, numerous papers on modeling techniques to incorporate extra design information in the representation of objects have been presented [12]. The main goal of these works has been to provide of meaning to objects in the virtual world, by including semantic information in their representations; and a lot of them are aimed at defining life-like behavior for virtual objects [13].

Users are not the only living objects inside a game. Non-Player Characters (NPCs) also co-exist with regular users, and they need their own social behavior. There are the avatars, which are the representations of both users and NPCs in the virtual world. However, there is a main difference between these kinds of avatar: the NPC-avatars are not controlled by the actions of the players [14]. Thus, besides of the basic geometric model of these objects, we should add substantial amount of knowledge about itself and its surroundings.

Many methods have been developed for the implementation of Artificial Intelligence (AI) into games [15]. At a semantic level, game intelligence implementations are highly dependent on the application domain. In most cases intelligence has been specified using AI techniques embedded in the Virtual Reality system [16]. However, this prevents changing or removing faulty intelligence.

Alternatively, AI can be programmed using a multi-layer approach, which includes a more abstract layer to introduce intelligent behaviors in games [17]. This layer use communication protocols to interact with the game engine. In this approach, the multi-agent systems become one choice.

In Several works (for example, [17, 18]) have incorporated different types of middleware to connect the agents in the MAS with its realizations in the game engine. However, they are based on informal models, which do not facilities the modelling and verification of system requirements.

We have proposed [19] a model and development framework to introduce non-player characters in virtual environments using multi-layer approach. Our method [19] incorporates an abstract layer which implements a Moderately Open Multi-Agent System (MOMAS) [1].

There are both game and agent technologies. However, the combination of these technologies is not a trivial task. This introduces conceptual and technical problems. Both technologies have different levels of abstraction. The game engines work with representations of low-level data for virtual environments and characters. In contrast, MOMAS technology is useful to describe high-level semantic concepts, which are defined for the perception of the environment and the related behaviors. The separation of the abstract layer (MOMAS) and the low-level layer (controlled by the games engine) requires heterogeneous concepts and techniques that hinder the development process [20]. The combination of these two types of specialized software introduces some complex questions to software engineering.

To address these problems many authors have proposed practical agent-oriented methods and tools for game development [21]. However, they are based on informal models, which difficult the modeling and verification of system requirements; or they do not propose a homogeneous development process for the design and implementation of all game components.

There is a good reason to use informal approaches: the utilization of existing formal methods [22] to reasoning about the MAS systems is extremely complex. They are based on extensions of high-level model that maintain the artifacts and limitations of those models. Or they introduce formalisms that are too abstract for production-strength implementations. Therefore, we claim for the development of new formal models from a practical point of view.

In this work we propose a new model for games development. It specifies all structural individuals in a game by means of a unique software component. This new model is based on a constructive approach of role concept. The main idea is to define a new type of role, which is useful to specify both the user and NPCs behaviors. Also, it allows incorporate intelligence into actor definition. In this model all actors (players and NPCs) are defined by agents. Each agent accomplishes a role. The whole development process, from the modeling to implementation, is performed by refining the roles step by step. The roles are the highest abstraction concepts in our theory. They define information resources, properties and behavior that agents may perform during the execution of the game [20].

3   An Application to Game Specification

In this paper, we use a simple game to show how our model can be applied. This is the well-known 2-D Game Pong. It consists of a single scene, which contains a small number of actors (see Fig. 1). There are two types of actors: CPU-controlled actors and user-controlled actors.

Fig. 1. A screenshot of the 2-D Game Pong.

At least there is a user-controlled actor, which should handle an in-game paddle by moving it vertically across the left side of the screen (see Fig. 1); then he can play against either a CPU-controlled actor or another user-controlled actor controlling a second paddle on the opposing side. Also, we have others CPU-controlled actors: for example, two final walls, two lateral walls and the ball, among others. They can be grouped by the played roles.

For instance, the two final walls have the same role. The main attributes of each final wall are the position, and its width and height. The role behavior is simply to wait for a collision with the ball; then there must display the new score (increased by one) of the opposite player.

This game is well defined; agents and communication protocols are static; and control is centralized based on global goals and responsibilities. These features support system specification using our model. So, we use it as an example application.

4 Foundations of G-MOMAS Model

To describe the behavior of a system, we must know its organization: the location for its components (the spatial-static-structural behavior) and their performances and interactions (the temporal-dynamical-functional behavior). In G-MOMAS technology, multi-agent systems are made of simple components whose representations are agents. They encapsulate complex behavior and communication protocols, which are predetermined by means of roles definition. Also, agents interact with the environment through the global information resources. The model allows fast specification of agent-based systems in an incremental process based on roles.

4.1 A Conceptual Framework

We describe how to organize agents in communities and how to architect a G-MOMAS (see Fig. 2) using fast prototyping. Our programming environment allows prototyping G-MOMAS with the above architecture. Such systems run on homogenous distributed operating platforms, each associated with a server.

Applications have a static structure since roles and their relationships do not change during execution. Services provided by the agents are also static. Agents are clustered into communities called *packages*. A *management module* within the MAS handles the life cycle of packages and agents, their communication, and the social state's public information. This module is a special agent that interfaces between the *social state*, the agents and the *user* in charge of running the system. It has tools for language interpretation, message routing and information management. It can share a platform with a package or it can run on an independent platform in a separate server [19].

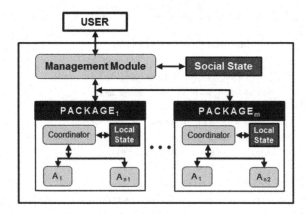

Fig. 2. Architecture of a multi-agent system in our model for games

Agent Communities

Agents in our environment are clustered into packages, each managed by an agent (community *coordinator*). The coordinator handles intra-community communication channels and protocols as well as communication between the communities and the system's management module. Also, it handles the management of the local state. A coordinator is created each time that a new package is declared. The social world includes all packages handled by the management module.

Social State

Let $R = \{r_1, ..., r_n\}$ and V be the set of role identifiers and the S-set of variables, respectively. The social state is a 6-tuple <L, P, A, M, V, K> where:

(a) $L \subseteq R = \{\rho_1, \rho_2, ...\}$ is the set of defined roles for a game, which are available to implement the agents in MAS

(b) $P = \{P_1, P_2, ...\}$ is the set of packages to cluster the communities of agents.

(c) $A = \{a_1, a_2, ...\} \subseteq A$ is a L-set of agents in the system.

(d) M: $A \rightarrow P$ is a function that maps each agent in system with a unique package.

(e) V is a S-set of global variables of the system such that $V_s \subseteq V_s$. It includes common parameters and process descriptions, among others. Some agents can be authorized to add, update and remove global variables.

(f) K is the global knowledge, which contains laws and social experiences. Social experiences are defined by means of set Pg of Horn clauses (we use a Prolog style); we communicate with a logic program using queries like: $?P(T_1, T_2, ..., T_n)$ where P is a predicate and $T_1, T_2, ..., T_n$ are terms (as they are define in standard logic programming). Social laws must contain at least the two following sets:

C(L) is the set of constraints that affect role assignment.

C(V) is the set of constraints on the global variables of the social state.

Example 1. Specification of the social state for game Pong.

```
L= {SCORE_ROLE, FBORDER_ROLE, BALL_ROLE, ...}
P={SCENE}
A={{left_score_ag, right_score_ag}SCORE_ROLE,
   {left_border_ag, right_border_ag}FBORDER_ROLE ,
   {ball_ag}BALL_ROLE , ...}
M: A → P , such that for all a ∈ A, M(a)=SCENE.
V={{ball_def_velocity, ball_radius, ...}NATURAL , {ball_pos, ...}POSITION
   { maxscore, left_points, right_points}SCORE , ...}
K={Pg, C(L), C(V)}, where:
   Pg is defined by:
       finish_game :- left_points == maxscore.
       finish_game :- right_points == maxscore.
   C(L)={ |ASCORE_ROLE|= 2, |AFBORDER_ROLE|= 2, |ABALL_ROLE|= 1, ...}
   C(V)={ball_def_velocity > 0 ,
          left_points ≥ 0 ∧ left_points < maxscore ,
          right_points ≥ 0 ∧ right_points < maxscore , ...}
```

4.2 Intelligent Agents

Abstraction is a basic tool for handling complexity. It formalizes the essential features of an entity setting it apart from the other entities in a close environment. We propose an agent definition based on concepts and methodologies of the Agent-Oriented Software Engineering (AOSE). Specifically, our definition redefines MOMAS approach [1] to allow prototyping of games.

The two main concepts in G-MOMAS model are: Roles and Agents. Roles are the basic modeling structure. Agents are personalized implementation of roles. The whole development process, from the modeling to implementation, is performed by refining the roles step by step.

Roles

A role represents a set of responsibilities, tasks, permissions and services that model a purpose. Roles are specified using entities like attributes, social experience, activities needed for the purpose of the roles and services.

Let $R = \{r_1, ..., r_n\}$ and $\Sigma = <S, P, F>$ be a set of role identifiers and a signature, respectively; then we denote by Δ, T and G to the $S^* \times S$ – sets of operators symbols, task and services, respectively. The collection of sets $\{\Delta, T, G\}$ is pairwise disjoint. In Δ we have two distinguished elements: SKIP and BREAK operators, which are used to denote the identity and interruption of control flow, respectively. Also, we consider the S–set of attributes symbols Y (where, $Y^* \cap V^* = \emptyset$).

Let A, V and Y a set of agent identifiers and two S – sets of variables and attributes, respectively. The set of operators (or statements) $\Gamma(\Sigma[A, V, Y])$ for a signature $\Sigma = <S, P, F>$ and the sets A, V and Y is defined recursively as below:

(a) $f(e_1, ..., e_n) \in \Gamma((\Sigma[A, V, Y])$ if $f \in F_{w1\times...\times wn,s} \cup G_{w1\times...\times wn,s}$ and $e_i \in Term_{wi}(\Sigma[V \cup^s Y]))$ for each $i(1 \leq i \leq n)$.

(b) $\delta(e_1,..., e_n) \in \Gamma((\Sigma[A, V, Y]))$ if $\delta \in \Delta_{w1\times...\times wn,s}$ and $e_i \in Term_{wi}(\Sigma[V \cup^s Y])$ for each $i(1 \leq i \leq n)$.

(c) $r::O(e_1,..., e_n) \in \Gamma((\Sigma[A, V, Y]$ if $r \in R$ and $O \in (T_{w1\times...\times wn,s} \cup G_{w1\times...\times wn,s})$ such that for each i $(1 \leq i \leq n)$, $e_i \in Term_{wi}(\Sigma[V \cup^s Y])$.

(d) $a1 \sim \blacklozenge a2 \gg r::O(e_1,..., e_n) \in \Gamma((\Sigma[A, V, Y]$ if $a_1, a_2 \in A$ and $r \in R$ and $O \in G_{w1\times...\times wn,s}$ such that for each i $(1 \leq i \leq n)$, $e_i \in Term_{wi}(\Sigma[V \cup^s Y])$.

(e) Let B, S_1 and S_2 be a formula and two operators $(S_1, S_2 \in \Gamma(\Sigma[A, V, Y]))$, respectively; then the expressions $S_1 \cdot S_2, S_1||S_2$ and $B:S_1|S_2$ are operators too. More precisely, $S_1 \bullet S_2 \in \Gamma(\Sigma[A, V, Y])$, $S_1||S_2 \in \Gamma(\Sigma[A, V, Y])$ and $B:S_1|S_2 \in \Gamma(\Sigma[A, V, Y])$.

(f) The expressions (S) and $(S)^*$ are operators if S is an operator. That is, $(S) \in (\Sigma[V, Y])$ and $(S)^* \in \Gamma(\Sigma[V, Y])$ if $S \in \Gamma(\Sigma[V, Y])$.

(g) Only expressions which can be obtained by finitely many applications of rules a–d are operators for the signature Σ and the S–sets V and Y.

The set of structural operations is denoted by STRs = $\{\cdot, ||, :, |, (\_), (\_)^*\}$; and it satisfies the condition STRs $\cap \Delta = \varnothing$. From a practical point of view, the operation symbols "$\bullet$", "$||$", "$:$", "$|$", "$(\_)$" y $(\_)^*$ denote the statements (like to imperative programming) of sequence, concurrent, conditional, alternative, composition and iteration, respectively.

For all S1, S2, S3 $\in \Gamma((\Sigma[A, V, Y]))$, we require the followings properties on STRs:

[Associability of "$\bullet$"]: $S_1 \bullet (S_2 \bullet S_3) = (S_1 \bullet S_2) \bullet S_3$
[Associability of "$||$"]: $S_1||(S_2||S_3) = (S_1||S_2)||S_3$
[Commutability of "$||$"]: $S_1||S_2 = S_2||S_1$
[SKIP is an identity element with respect to "$||$"]: $SKIP||S_1 = S_1||SKIP = S_1$
[SKIP is an identity element with respect to "$\bullet$"]: $SKIP.S_1 = S_1 \bullet SKIP = S_1$
[BREAK is a zero element with respect to "$||$"]: $BREAK||S_1 = S_1||BREAK = BREAK$
[BREAK is a left-zero element with respect to "$\bullet$"]: $BREAK.S_1 = BREAK$

Remark: From an operational point of view, $S_1 \bullet BREAK$ is not necessarily equal to BREAK.

Definition 5 (Role). *For an Σ-algebra $\Psi[\Sigma] = <D^\Psi, P^\Psi, F^\Psi>$ of the signature $\Sigma = <S, P, F>$, a set A of agent identifiers and the S-sets V and Y of variables and attributes, respectively, we define a role ρ by a 10-tuple $\rho = <R, M, X, \phi, T, G, \eta, H, C, h>$ such that:*

(a) $R \in P(R)$
(b) M is a R-set of agent variables, such that $A_r \subseteq A)$.

(c) X is a R–set, which satisfies the following condition: for all r ∈ R, if x ∈ X_r then there exist s ∈ S such that x ∈ Y_s

(d) φ is a R-set of sets of Horn clauses. That is, for all r ∈ R, $φ_r$ is a set of Horn clauses (or more precisely, a logic program in the Prolog style)

(e) T and G are two R-sets such that:
  i. *T ∩ G = ∅*
  ii. *For all r ∈ R, T_r ⊆ ∪T × V * × Form(Σ[V *∪ X_r]) × Γ(Σ[A, V, X_r])*
  iii. *For all r ∈ R, G_r ⊆ ∪G × V * × Form(Σ[V *∪ X_r]) × Γ(Σ[A, V, X_r])*

(f) η is a R-set of permissions, such that for all r ∈ R, $η_r$ ⊆ G_r × P(L), where L is the set of defined roles in the social state (see Sect. 4.2).

(g) H is a R-set of liveness properties, such that for all r ∈ R, H_r ⊆ ∪T × V * × Γ(Σ[A, V, X])

(h) C is a R-set of safety properties, such that for all r ∈ R, C_r ⊆ Form(Σ[V ∪ X_r])

(i) *h is the lifecycle of the role ρ, such that h ∈ Γ(Σ[A, V, X_r])*

Roles are the higher-level concepts for the definition of abstractions in G-MOMAS. They define information resources, properties and behaviors that each agent will play in the system. Without loss of generality, we assume that each agent in the system plays a unique role, which can be basic or compound. The basic roles are defined by means of a single role. A compound role defines an aggregation of two or more basic roles. In this section, we define a typical function for role composition.

If we compare our model with OOP (if it is possible), then a role corresponds to a proactive objects class; and an agent is an instance of one of these classes. Therefore, a role should contain both data components and dynamic behavior. The dynamic behavior is defined by a set of internal and external functions, which establish the performance for the actors with this role.

The data components are defined using two different types of dynamic information resources: attributes and declarative knowledge. For each role r in *R*, the set of attributes X_r describes a set of variables using the principles of imperative programming. There is a unique sort in the signature for each attribute of a role. The declarative knowledge $φ_r$ is defined by a set of Horn clauses. This preliminary knowledge is common to all agents with this role, but it can be modified at some stage in the life of the agents.

To describe an internal functionality of the role behavior we defined two function types: the lifecycle *h* (or liveness property) and a set of own tasks (or activities) *T*. The life cycle is a distinguished task, which is determined by a valid operator in our model. This overall behavior is interrupted at any stage where the safe conditions (in *C*) cannot be verified. Each task is composed for a function and an associated assertion. This assertion describes the consistence conditions for execution of the function.

The communication mechanisms in G-MOMAS model are message passing and shared memory. The shared-memory communication in agent communities supports global access to the information resources into social state (see Sect. 4.2).

The message passing is a main mechanism for direct communications among agents. This kind of interaction must be modeled in the role definition by means of the external functionality (role services) and messages in the corresponding roles. The external functionality of roles describes the offered services by its agents, which may be requested by some agent. Unlike OOP methods, services have a behavior limited by the features of the requesting agent. Classified information, for example, must not be provided to most requesting agents. The use of any service is restricted by means of η. This role component defines the client-server relation among roles.

Messages in a role definition have the following components: The *sender* is the agent that initializes the communication.

- The *receiver* is the called agent by the sender.
- The component *ρ::content* defines the used protocol in the communication. The role ρ corresponds to one of the roles of the receiver agent. The *content* requests a service of this role.

To simplify we use the following notation: *sender ∼ >receiver>>ρ::content*. Also, we may write *reciever>>p::content* when its interpretation is obvious. There is a public interaction protocol that all the agents follow. This protocol is implemented by the G-MOMAS management module (see Sect. 4.2) which guarantees compliance for all the agents.

To create a role ρ we use the symbol "$\Leftarrow$"; that is: $\rho \Leftarrow <R, M, X, \phi, T, G, \eta, L, C, h>$, where $R, M, X, \phi, T, G, \eta, L, C, y, h$ must satisfy the conditions that we have imposed in Definition 5.

Example 2. A specification of one roles for the game Pong.

```
Role SCORE_ROLE⇐< R, A, X, φ, T, G, η, H, C, h>

R={SCORE_ROLE}
M={∅_SCORE_ROLE}
X={{{value}_SCORE ,{s_pos}_POSITION}_SCORE_ROLE }
φ=∅
T and G are the following R-sets:
  T={{<display_task,<>,{value≥0∧value≤maxscore},diplay(value,s_pos)>}_SCORE_ROLE}
  G={{<inc_service>,<i>,{maxscore - value ≥ i},
        inc(value,i) • SCORE_ROLE::display_task()>}_SCORE_ROLE}
η={{<inc, FBORDER_ROLE>}_SCORE_ROLE }
H={{< score_role_handler, < >,
      value:=0 • (value=maxscore: prints('END') •BREAK | display_task())*
      >}_SCORE_ROLE}
C ={ {value ≥ 0 ∧ value ≤ maxscore}_SCORE_ROLE }
h= score_role_handler()
```

Definition 6 (Basic Composition of Roles). *Let* $\rho_1 = <R^1, M^1, X^1, \phi^1, T^1, G^1, \eta^1, L^1, C^1, h^1 >$ *and* $\rho_2 = <R^2, M^1, X^2, \phi^2, T^2, G^2, \eta^2, L^2, C^2, h^2 >$ *be two roles. We define the composition of roles* ρ_1 *and* ρ_2 *(denoted by* $\rho_1 \oplus \rho_2$*) as the 10-tupla* $\rho_2 = \rho_1 \oplus \rho_2 = <R, Y, \phi, T, G, \eta, L, C, h >$ *, where:*

(a) $R = R^1 \cup R^2$

(b) $M = M^1 \cup^R M^2$

(c) $X = X^1 \cup^R X^2$

(d) $\phi = \phi_1 \cup^R \phi_2$

(e) $T = T_1 \cup^R T_2$

(f) $G = G_1 \cup^R G_2$

(g) $\eta = \eta_1 \cup^R \eta_2$

(h) $L = L^1 \cup^R L^2$

(i) $C = C_1 \cup^R C_2$

(j) $h = h^1 \| h^2$

Example 3. A basic composition of the SCORE_ROLE and FBORDER_ROLE roles.

```
Role SCORE_FBORDER_ROLE⇐=<R, M, X, φ, T, G, η, H, C, h>=SCORE_ROLE⊕FBORDER_ROLE
```

R={**SCORE_ROLE**,FBORDER_**ROLE** }

A^P={∅$_{SCORE\_ROLE}$,{some_score_agent}$_{FBORDER\_ROLE}$}

X={{{value}$_{SCORE}$,{s_pos}$_{POSITION}$}$_{SCORE\_ROLE}$,
    {{b_pos}$_{POSITION}$,{width,height}$_{NATURAL}$}$_{FBORDER\_ROLE}$ }

ϕ is defined as below:
    collision():- xpos(ball_pos) >= xpos(b_pos).

T={{<display_task,<>,{value≥0∧value≤maxscore},display(value,s_pos)>}$_{SCORE\_ROLE}$,
    ∅$_{FBORDER\_ROLE}$}

G={{<inc_service>,<i>,{maxscore - value ≥ i},
    inc(value, i) • **SCORE_ROLE**::display_task()>}$_{SCORE\_ROLE}$, ∅$_{FBORDER\_ROLE}$}

η={{<inc, FBORDER_ROLE>}$_{SCORE\_ROLE}$, ∅$_{FBORDER\_ROLE}$ }

H={{< score_role_handler, < >,
    value:=0•(value=maxscore: prints('END')•BREAK|display_task())*>}$_{SCORE\_ROLE}$,
    {<fborder_role_handler, < >,
    (? collision():some_score_agent>>SCORE_ROLE::inc(1) | SKIP)*
    >}$_{FBORDER\_ROLE}$}

C={ {value ≥ 0 ∧ value ≤ maxscore}$_{SCORE\_ROLE}$, {true}$_{FBORDER\_ROLE}$ }

h= score_role_handler() ‖ fborder_role_handler()

Lemma 2. *Let $\mathfrak{R}$ be the set of all roles. Then the operation $\oplus$ (basic composition of roles) is a closed binary operation on $\mathfrak{R}$.*

Theorem 1. *Let $\mathfrak{R}$ be the set of all roles. Then the set $\mathfrak{R}$, together with the closed binary operation $\oplus$ (basic composition of roles) is an abelian monoid.*

Mental State

Agents have a mental state that includes data, assertions and goals. It also contains information about how to behave in the presence of changes in the environment. Formally, the mental state of an agent is a 2-tuple $\zeta = <A_\zeta, C_\zeta>$, where A_ζ is an attribute set and C_ζ is a specific experience expressed as a set of formulas. C_ζ includes both facts and rules.

The mental state represents the dynamic behavior of an agent handled by the agent's own procedures. Attributes are private state of the agent and its specific experience is a logic program. Procedures communicate with a logic program using queries like: $?P(T_1, T_2, \ldots, T_n)$ where P is a predicate and $T_1, T_2, \ldots, T_n$ are terms (as they are define in standard logic programing).

Inter-Agent Communication

The communication mechanisms in G-MOMAS model are message passing and shared memory. The message passing is a main mechanism for direct communications among agents. The shared-memory communication in agent communities supports global access to the social state (see Sect. 4.2). Message passing supports asynchronous agent communication and requires input buffers in each agent. There is a public interaction protocol that all the agents follow. This protocol is implemented by the G-MOMAS management module (see Sect. 4.2) which guarantees compliance for all the agents.

Interaction between agents is based on role services (see Sect. 4.2). Messages have the following components:

- The *sender* is the agent that initializes the communication.
- The *receiver* is the called agent by the sender.
- The component *ρ::content* defines the used protocol in the communication. The role ρ corresponds to one of the roles of the receiver agent. The *content* request a service of this role.

4.3 Defining Agents in the G-MOMAS Model

In G-MOMAS technology, multi-agent systems are made of simple components whose abstract representations are agents. They encapsulate complex behavior and communication protocols, which are predetermined by means of roles definition. In Sect. 4.3, we describe rigorously the concepts, principles and methods to create roles that will play the agents in MAS. In this section we introduce the concept of agents, which are specialized instances of defined roles in our model.

Definition 7 (Agent). *For an Σ-algebra $\Psi[\Sigma] = <D^\Psi, P^\Psi, F^\Psi>$ of the signature $\Sigma = <S, P, F>$, a set A of agent identifiers and the S-sets V and Y of variables and attributes, respectively, we define a agent by means of a 4-tuple $\alpha = <\rho, \zeta, \tau, \sigma>$, where:*

(a) ρ *is a role or generic behavior of the agent.*
(b) ζ *is the mental state of the agent, which is a 2-tuple $\zeta = <v, \varphi>$, where:*
  i. v *is a S'-set, which satisfies the followings conditions:*
    - $S' \subseteq S$; *and*
    - *For all $s \in S$, $v_s \subseteq V_s$*

ii. *φ is a specific experience, which is expressed through a set of Horn clauses (in this case, we also use a Prolog style).*

(c) τ is a set of private functions (or tasks) on the mental state. That is:: $\tau \subseteq \cup\, T \times V^* \times \text{Form}(\Sigma[V]) \times \Gamma(\Sigma[A, V, \emptyset])$

(d) σ is the agent lifecycle, such that $h \in \cup\, T \times V^* \times \text{Form}(\Sigma[V]) \times \Gamma(\Sigma[A, V, \emptyset])$.

From Definition 7, agents have two states: a *concrete state* and an *abstract state*. The abstract state is static and common to all the agents with a same role. The concrete state is time-dependent and specific to the *mental state* of each agent that includes data, assertions and goals. It also contains customized tasks and information about how to behave in the presence of changes in the environment.

The mental state represents the dynamic behavior of an agent handled by the agent's own procedures. Attributes belong to private state of the agent; and its specific experience is a logic program. Operators communicate with a logic program using queries like in the logic programming.

Example 4. A specification of the left_border_ag and right_score_ag agents.

Agent left_border_ag=$\langle \rho, \zeta, \tau, \sigma \rangle$
ρ=FBORDER_**ROLE**[some_score_agent←right_score_ag]   ζ=$\langle$v, φ$\rangle$,such that φ=∅ and v={{p}$_{\text{POSITION}}$,{x,y}$_{\text{NATURAL}}$} is a S′-set, where   S′= {NATURAL, POSITION}   σ=FBORDER_**ROLE**::init_border($\langle$0,0$\rangle$,10,320)•FBORDER_**ROLE**::h
Agent right_score_ag
ρ= SCORE_ROLE ζ=$\langle$ v, φ $\rangle$, such that v=∅ and φ=∅ σ=SCORE_**ROLE**::h

In the example 4, we have denoted a syntactic substitution by means of the expression FBORDER_**ROLE**[some_score_agent←right_score_ag].

5 Conclusions

In this work we defined a new model of MASs for games development, which is based on MOMAS approach. It has been called G-MOMAS (Moderately Open Multi-Agent System for Games) model; and it redefines the role concept in MOMAS model.

The main idea is to define a new type of role, which is useful to specify both the user and NPCs behaviors in the games. Also, it allows incorporate intelligence into actor definition. In G-MOMAS systems all actors (players and NPCs) are defined by agents. Each agent accomplishes a role. The whole development process, from the modeling to implementation, is performed by refining the roles step by step.

We define an algebraic structure with a set of primitive roles. A composition operation to create more complex roles is introduced. Each agent in the game has a unique role. We have verified that the set of roles with the basic composition operation is a monoid. Produced Games by means of G-MOMAS model are substructures of this monoid. From our theory, we can demonstrate the consistence of the implemented games. Also, other properties semantic can be proved; for example, inclusion and equivalence of games, among others.

We describe and demonstrate the use of our model with a real-world application example. It implements the very simple game Pong. We use it throughout the paper to illustrate the features of our model. It shows how our work can be applied to the design and construction of games.

These results are some of the most important consequences of our work. They have been used in the development of GAMESONOMY platform. GAMESONOMY is a visual tool to create multiuser games (including serious games) in the cloud.

References

1. Garcés, A., Quirós, R., Chover, M., Camahort, E.: Implementing moderately open agent-based systems. In: Proceedings of IADIS International Conference WWW/Internet 2006, Murcia, España (2006)
2. Smelik, R.M., Tutenel, T., Bidarra, R., Benes, B.: A survey on procedural modelling for virtual worlds. Comput. Graph. Forum 33(6), 31–50 (2014)
3. Zambonelli, F., Jennings, N., Wooldridge, M.: Developing multi-agent systems: the Gaia methodology. ACM Trans. Softw. Eng. Methodol. 12(3), 317–370 (2003)
4. Wooldridge, M., Jennings, N., Kinny, D.: The Gaia methodology for agent-oriented analysis and design. Auton. Agents Multi-Agent Syst. 3(3), 285–312 (2000)
5. Iglesias, C.A., Garijo, M., González, J.C., Velasco, J.R.: Analysis and design of multiagent systems using MAS-CommonKADS. In: Singh, M.P., Rao, A., Wooldridge, M.J. (eds.) ATAL 1997. LNCS, vol. 1365, pp. 313–327. Springer, Heidelberg (1998). https://doi.org/10.1007/BFb0026768
6. DeLoach, S.A.: Analysis and design using MaSE and agentTool. In: Proceedings of the 12th Midwest Artificial Intelligence and Cognitive Science Conference (MAICS 2001) (2001)
7. G Group: INGENIAS (2009). http://grasia.fdi.ucm.es/ingenias/
8. Winikoff, M.: Future directions for agent-based software engineering. Int. J. Agent Oriented Softw. Eng. 3(4), 402–410 (2009)
9. Remolar, I., Garcés, A., Rebollo, C., Chover, M., Quirós, R., Gumbau, J.: Developing a virtual trade fair using an agent-oriented approach. Multimedia Tools Appl. 74(13), 4561–4582 (2015). Springer
10. McCreery, M.P., Vallett, D.B., Clark, C.: Social interaction in a virtual environment: examining socio-spatial interactivity and social presence using behavioral analytics. Comput. Hum. Behav. 51, 203–206 (2015)
11. Lau, K.W., Lee, P.Y.: The use of virtual reality for creating unusual environmental stimulation to motivate students to explore creative ideas. Interact. Learn. Environ. 23(1), 3–18 (2015)
12. Kessing, J., Tutenel, T., Bidarra, R.: Designing semantic game worlds. In: Proceedings of the Third Workshop on Procedural Content Generation in Games (PCG 2012), Raleigh, NC, USA (2012)
13. Tutenel, R., Bidarra, R., Smelik, R.M., De Kraker, K.J.: The role of semantics in games and simulations. Comput. Entertain. (CIE) 6(4) (2008). ACM

14. Aranda, G., Carrascosa, C., Botti, V.: Characterizing massively multiplayer online games as multi-agent systems. In: Corchado, E., Abraham, A., Pedrycz, W. (eds.) HAIS 2008. LNCS (LNAI), vol. 5271, pp. 507–514. Springer, Heidelberg (2008). https://doi.org/10.1007/978-3-540-87656-4_63

15. Chalkiadakis, G., Elkind, E., Wooldridge, M.: Computational aspects of cooperative game theory. Synth. Lect. Artif. Intell. Mach. Learn. 5(6), 1–168 (2011)

16. Bryant, B.D.: Evolving visibly intelligent behavior for embedded game agents. University of Texas at Austin (2006)

17. Aranda, G., Trescak, T., Esteva, M., Rodriguez, I., Carrascosa, C.: Massively multiplayer online games developed with agents. In: Pan, Z., Cheok, A.D., Müller, W., Chang, M., Zhang, M. (eds.) Transactions on Edutainment VII. LNCS, vol. 7145, pp. 129–138. Springer, Heidelberg (2012). https://doi.org/10.1007/978-3-642-29050-3_12

18. van Oijen, J., Vanhée, L., Dignum, F.: CIGA: a middleware for intelligent agents in virtual environments. In: Beer, M., Brom, C., Dignum, F., Soo, V.-W. (eds.) AEGS 2011. LNCS (LNAI), vol. 7471, pp. 22–37. Springer, Heidelberg (2012). https://doi.org/10.1007/978-3-642-32326-3_2

19. Garcés, A., Quirós, R., Chover, M., Camahort, E.: Implementing virtual agents: a HABA-based approach. Int. J. Multimedia Appl. (IJMA) 2(4), 1–15 (2010)

20. Garces, A., Chover, M., Garcés-Matilla, A., Pacheco-Morales, A.: Design and implementation of games using moderately open multi-agent systems. In: Proceedings of the IADIS International Conference Game and Entertainment Technologies 2012, Lisbon, Portugal (2012)

21. Aranda, G., Botti, V., Carrascosa, C.: MMOG based on MAS: the MMOG layer. In: 8th International Conference on Autonomous Agents and Multiagent Systems, AAMAS 2009, Budapest, Hungary (2009)

22. Dennis, L.A., Fisher, M.: Programming verifiable heterogeneous agent systems. In: Hindriks, K.V., Pokahr, A., Sardina, S. (eds.) ProMAS 2008. LNCS (LNAI), vol. 5442, pp. 40–55. Springer, Heidelberg (2009). https://doi.org/10.1007/978-3-642-03278-3_3

Analysis of Transport Logistics Costs in Supply Chain Management by Applying Fuzzy Logic

Alfonso A. Guijarro-Rodríguez[1(✉)], Lorenzo J. Cevallos-Torres[1],
Edison R. Valencia-Nuñez[2], Alexandra M. Wilches-Medina[3],
and Vicente A. Correa-Barrera[1]

[1] Faculty of Mathematical and Physical Sciences,
University of Guayaquil, Guayaquil, Ecuador
{alfonso.guijarror, lorenzo.cevallost,
armando.correab}@ug.edu.ec
[2] Accounting and Auditing Career,
University Technique of Ambato, Ambato, Ecuador
edisonrvalencia@uta.edu.ec
[3] Faculty of Administrative Sciences,
University of Guayaquil, Guayaquil, Ecuador
alexandra.wilchesme@ug.edu.ec

Abstract. Supply chain management is one of the main concerns of the companies, due to the expected conditions of the markets, have become factors generating risk causing, uncertainty in the process of delivery of goods associated with transportation. Several studies suggest that the main components of delivery correspond to its quality and timeliness. Other works of estimation of commissions give relevance to the application of tariffs previously established. In this way, the beginning of the use of methodologies focused on the systematization and in the obtaining of estimates of tariffs by means of transport is described. In this paper we study the possibility of establishing, through a computational analysis, whether the variables: Service Provision, Condition of the goods and Time of Delivery, have any influence on the freight rate, we will do this analysis using techniques developed with fuzzy logic. As a result of this work, it was demonstrated that transport rates are estimated more reasonably in terms of the constant improvement in the service. Finally, these results were obtained from MATLAB's fuzzy logic module.

Keywords: Supply chain · Costs per transport · Fuzzy logic · Logistics
Inference systems

1 Introduction

Logistics is responsible for managing the flow of materials as the main hub of the customer's value proposition: procurement, production, and distribution [1–3]. For this reason, institutions seek to improve logistics processes by reducing costs and diminishing errors [4, 5].

The delivery of goods and services from the distribution centers to the customers, is a challenge. When there are eventualities in the process of delivering the goods,

© Springer International Publishing AG 2018
M. Botto-Tobar et al. (Eds.): CITT 2017, CCIS 798, pp. 145–159, 2018.
https://doi.org/10.1007/978-3-319-72727-1_11

situations arise that affect said process and directly lead to a decrease in the quality of the service offered by the company.

Works performed to improve delivery operations in organizations suggest optimizing cost management with traditional mathematical models in order to maintain the Organization's profit margins. Approaches based on linear programming, provide an effective solution for the management of resources that are dedicated to the logistics operation, using variables such as: attention, time, product quality [6].

Another study based on operations research describes the treatment of resources through operative research techniques such as: decision theory and dynamic programming, as mentioned [7].

It is of great importance to have a clear and precise strategy of the offer of services, based on the satisfaction of the client, being; the delivery processes the last step within the sale and the most relevant. Currently, there is a steady increase in the application of less common methodologies; which are based on experiences developed in Artificial Intelligence (AI) [8–10].

Fuzzy logic is an AI methodology that allows the simulation of human reasoning [11]. Diffuse control systems are widely used in different control systems, since an adequate design takes advantage of speed and precision control [12, 13], using mathematical software technological tools, able to infer the actions to perform.

This paper proposes an alternative to the traditional mathematical models applying the analytic hierarchy process (AHP) methodology to correctly estimate the transport tariff, considering the quality parameters of the services offered.

Section 2 shows fuzzy logic techniques, Typical Membership Functions, Sect. 3 Case Study, analysis of logistic costs through the analytic hierarchy process the delivery model, from which the scenario proposed for the study is shown. Henceforth, presents the methodology used in the application of fuzzy Control. Section 4 shows the results obtained having simulated data for the scenario presented. The conclusions are presented in Sect. 5.

2 Fuzzy Logic Techniques

The Fuzzy Logic, in its short time of use, has demonstrated a very stable growth, also solves problems related to uncertainty, using formal methods for the expression of understandable ideas. This technique, initiated by [16], uses ambiguous concepts to reduce the intuitive complexity of a process, so that it can perform control operations, either roughly or heuristically, on non-linear processes or variations over time.

The Fuzzy logic allows the transfer of sophisticated sentences from natural language to a mathematical form, i.e., they give flexibility to modeling using linguistic expressions such as "much", "few", "mild", "severe", "scarce", "sufficient", "hot", "cold", "young". Within diffuse logic, specifically a fuzzy set, we find the so-called membership function of a set, i.e., determining the fact of "belonging to a set", or "not belonging to a set", given a | A On a universe X of the following form: $\mu A: X \rightarrow [0, 1]$, where $\mu A (x) = r$ if r is the degree x belongs to A, whose characteristic will take the values whose set are between $\{0, 1\}$, whereas, if it is fuzzy, it will take them in the closed interval of $[0, 1]$.

If $\mu A\,(x) = 0$ the element does not belong to the set, otherwise if $\mu A\,(x) = 1$ the element does belong totally to the set [17].

2.1   Typical Membership Functions

There are numerous ways to represent a membership function based on linear mathematical models, we have the triangular, trapezoidal and Gaussian functions, which are the most used, as shown in Fig. 1. The membership function of the fuzzy set takes all real values included in the interval [0, 1]. Therefore, the function assigns a degree of membership to a given set of elements and is called the membership function of the fuzzy set.

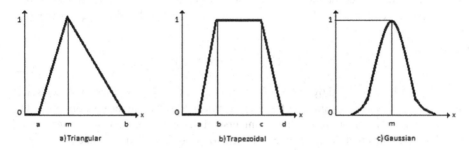

Fig. 1. Membership function based on linear mathematical models

2.2   Triangular Function

Defined by its limits (lower and upper b), and the modal value m, such that a < m < b.

$$\mu(x) = \begin{cases} 0 & \textit{if } x \le a \\ (x-a)/(m-a) & \textit{if } x \in (a,m] \\ (b-x)/(b-m) & \textit{if } x \in (m,b] \\ 0 & \textit{if } x \ge b \end{cases}$$

2.3   Trapezoidal Function

Defined by its limits lesser than a and greater than d, and the limits of its support, b and c, lesser and greater, respectively.

$$\mu(x) = \begin{cases} 0 & \textit{if } x \le a \quad o \quad x \ge d \\ (x-a)/(b-a) & \textit{if } x \in (a,b] \\ 1 & \textit{if } x \in (b,c] \\ (d-x)/(d-c) & \textit{if } x \in (b,d) \end{cases}$$

2.4 Gaussian Function

Defined by its mean value m and the value k > 0, it's the typical Gauss bell. The greater that is k, the narrower the bell.

$$\mu(x) = e^{-k(x-m)^2} \tag{1}$$

2.5 Fuzzy Sets

The fuzzy sets are a collection of elements whose characteristics are defined by linguistic values that have a degree of membership between {0, 1} within a universe of discourse. The notation defined for fuzzy sets is that established by Lofti Zadeh that combines the concepts of logic and sets of Lukasiewicz by defining degrees of membership [18].

$$A = \{(x, u\_A(x))/x \in \cup\} \tag{2}$$

Where A is constituted by the set of ordered pairs (x, u_A (x)), where u_A (x) is the result of the membership function for every element x of the universe of discourse U, where x being an element belonging to universe of discourse, and u is the image of the function that takes real values between [0, 1], where 0 there is no membership of the element to the set and 1 is that it has greater degree of membership.

2.6 Basic Operations Between Fuzzy Sets

The basic operations on fuzzy logic and fuzzy sets are Intersection, Union, and Complement; These operations are performed in the membership function of fuzzy sets [19]. According to the operations of fuzzy sets, the following properties are used (Table 1):

Table 1. Fuzzy set properties

Properties	Definition
Associative	$A \cup (B \cap C) = (A \cup B) \cap C \; A \cup (B \cup C) = (A \cup B) \cup C$
Commutative	$A \cap B = B \cap A \; A \cup B = B \cup A$
Involution	$\overline{A} = A$
Identity	$A \cap X = A \; A \cup \emptyset = A$
Morgan law	$A \cup B = \overline{\overline{A} \cup \overline{B}} = \overline{A} \cup \overline{B}$

2.7   Membership Function Characteristics

Figure 2 shows the Characteristics membership function

$$\text{Core } (A) = \{x \in X / u_A(x) = 1\} \tag{3}$$

$$\text{Border } (A) = \{x \in X / 0 < u_A(x) < 1\} \tag{4}$$

$$\text{Support } (A) = \{x \in X / u_A(x) > 1\} \tag{5}$$

$$\text{Crossing } (A) = \{x \in X / u_A(x) = 0.5\} \tag{6}$$

$$\text{Width } (A) = |x_2 - x_1| \tag{7}$$

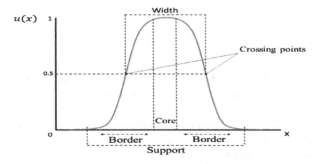

Fig. 2.   Characteristics of the membership function

3   Case Study, Analysis of Logistic Costs Through the Analytic Hierarchy Process (HP)

3.1   Delivery Model

This section presents the scenario for the control of the tariffs for the transporters in charge of the deliveries. See Fig. 3 that represents the delivery of merchandise.

3.2   Structuring the Problem

For the set scenario the following variables are determined:

1. Delivery Service: Corresponds to the quality with which the delivery was made.
2. State of Goods: It shows the state in which the merchandise was delivered.
3. Delivery Time: Determines whether the delivery was made on time or late.

Fig. 3. Delivery scenario

3.3 Methodology

The methodology used to calculate the tariffs was HP, which seeks to determine the appropriate tariff, depending on the proposed scenario considering the weight presented [14].

The HP methodology, assign a level of importance to the criteria and sub-criteria, as shown in Fig. 4. A linguistic scale is given and then taken on a numeric scale on which matrix procedures will be applied.

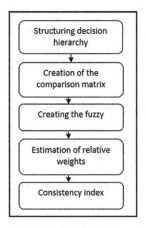

Fig. 4. Steps of the HP methodology

3.4 Creation of the Hierarchical Structure

The level of the hierarchy is established according to the objectives, criteria, and alternatives, as shown in Fig. 5 (Table 2).

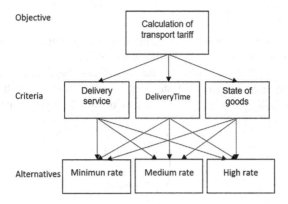

Fig. 5. Hierarchical model of the proposed problem

Table 2. Saaty scale of diffuse values

Scale	Importance	Diffuse scale
1	Equal	1,1,2
3	Moderate	2,3,4
5	Strong	4,5,6
7	Very strong	6,7,8
9	Extremely strong	8,9,9
2,4,6,8	(Omitted values for the sake of simplicity)	

Among the membership functions, we have the triangular functions and the trapezoidal functions among others [12, 15].

3.5   Creation of the Diffuse Matrix for the Criteria

Once the criteria and the alternatives have been defined, a hierarchy is assigned to them, calculating a square matrix called a comparison matrix in pairs (Table 3).

Table 3. Comparison matrix

Criteria	Service deliveries			State of goods			Delivery time		
Service deliveries	1	1	1	1/4	1/3	1/2	1/6	1/5	1/4
State of goods	2	3	4	1	1	1	1/3	1/2	1
Delivery time	4	5	6	1	2	3	1	1	1

3.6   Calculation of Relative Weights

This is performed using the own values method, in which weights are assigned among n alternatives, for which only n − 1 estimates are required.

Once the values of the comparison matrix are calculated, the columns are normalized to 1, dividing each element by the total sum of the columns. The own vector is obtained by calculating the average of each row of the normalized matrix.

$$p = \begin{pmatrix} \frac{1}{n}\sum_1^n a_{1j} \\ \frac{1}{n}\sum_1^n a_{2j} \\ \dots \\ \frac{1}{n}\sum_1^n a_{nj} \end{pmatrix} \tag{8}$$

The priority vector of the criteria is obtained, as expressed in (9)

$$p = \begin{pmatrix} p_{c11} \\ p_{c12} \\ \dots \\ p_{c1n} \end{pmatrix} \tag{9}$$

3.7   Analysis of Results

The HP method allows for measuring the inconsistency and sensitivity of the judgments by calculating the consistency ratio for which the consistency index must first be obtained.

3.8   Calculation of Consistency Index

That measures the consistency of the comparison matrix for which the formula is the following:

$$CI = \frac{\lambda_{max} - n}{n - 1} \tag{10}$$

Where n is the size of the matrix and λ_max is the eigenvalue, which is obtained by multiplying matrices between the elements of the eigenvector and the original matrix, thus obtaining a quotient for each element, which must be added and further divided into n elements.

3.9   Consistency Analysis

This is obtained by dividing the consistency index by an already established random value, which depends on n elements used, it is recommended not to use more than nine elements so that the method can maintain consistency.

$$CR = \frac{IC}{ICA} \qquad (11)$$

Consistency index: n. Max. - n/n − 1
Random index: 0.0525
N: 3
Consistency ratio: 0.1235.

Table 4. Diffusion matrix

Criteria	Delivery service	Delivery time	State of goods
Delivery service	1	4	5
Delivery time	1/4	1	2
State of goods	1/5	1/2	1

Each column of the diffusion matrix is added (Table 4).

Table 5. Sum of the comparison matrix columns

Criteria	Delivery service	Delivery time	State of goods
Delivery service	**1,00**	4,00	5,00
Delivery time	0,25	**1,00**	2,00
State of goods	0,20	0,50	**1,00**
Sum	1,45	5,50	**8,00**

Calculating the values of the comparison matrix, columns normalized to 1, dividing each element of the diffusion matrix, by the sum total of the columns (Table 5).

Table 6. Normalized matrix

0,6897	0,7273	0,6250
0,1724	0,1818	0,2500
0,1379	0,0909	0,1250

The eigenvector is obtained by calculating the average of each row of the normalized matrix (Table 6).

Depending on the priority vector, the weights are assigned for each of the criteria (Tables 7 and 8).

Table 7. Assigned weights

Criteria	Definition	Weights	Vector
SE	Delivery service	WSE	0,68
TE	Delivery time	WTE	0,20
EM	Merchandise status	WEM	0,12

Table 8. Membership function ranks

Variable	Linguistic tag	Rank
Delivery service	Bad	1 5 0
	Good	1 5 5
	Excellent	1 5 10
Merchandise status	Damaged	0 0 1 3
	Good condition	1 9 11 19
Delivery time	Late	0 0 1 1.5
	On time	1 9 11 19

4   Evaluation of Logistic Cost Analysis - Set Method

The results are described graphically. For this, the solution is implemented in MATLAB software, this program has an exclusive module for fuzzy logic, in this case, the solution is implemented by Mandani, because they are trained to make correct decisions based on inaccurate linguistic information, as shown in Figs. 6, 7, 8, 9.

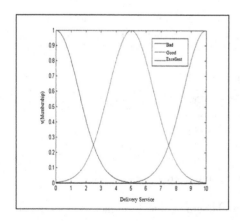

Fig. 6. Diffuse inference model

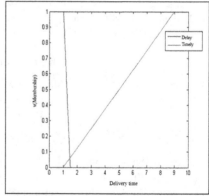

Fig. 7. Membership deliver time

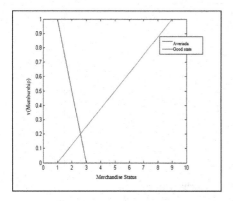
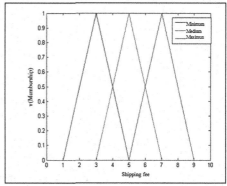

Fig. 8. Condition of merchandise   **Fig. 9.** Shipping fee

The inference is based on the Modus Ponens General model, which is interpreted as the transformation of performance grades. It gives us the weighted functions as shown in Fig. 10.

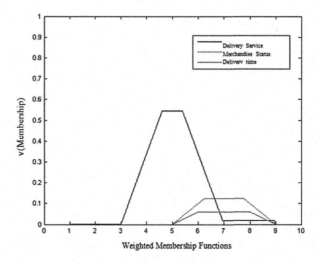

Fig. 10. Functions weighted by HP

Following the resolution of the problem, an inference mechanism is worked out as shown in Fig. 11.

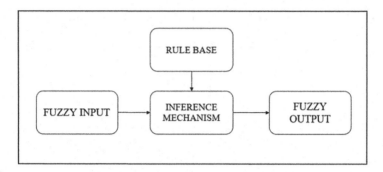

Fig. 11. The inference mechanism

The following two steps are used as part of the inference mechanism:

4.1 Aggregation

It is the union (max) for the output sets referring to the incoming membership functions of Rate Calculation, weighted with their weights and importance level of each variable, as shown in Fig. 12.

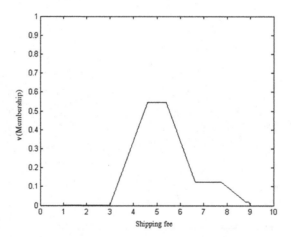

Fig. 12. Aggregation – Maximization

4.2 Defuzzification

For the defuzzification, simple mathematical methods were used as the centroid method whose equation is described below.

Defuzzify using the centroid

Discreetly

$$Centroide = \frac{\sum_{i=0}^{n} f(x)_i x_i}{\sum_{i=0}^{n} f(x)_i} \tag{12}$$

Calculation center of the area, below the union curve of the membership functions, as shown in Fig. 13.

The results show that in the case of a tariff estimated according to an average level of service, with a slightly delayed delivery time, and with an average merchandise condition, a medium transportation rate is generated, as show in Fig. 14. As described in Fig. 13, with a value of 5.34 located by the vertical cut at the height of average and maximum, weighting for the transport tariff.

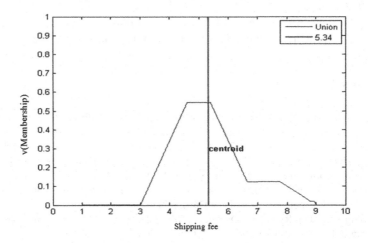

Fig. 13. Applying a centroid

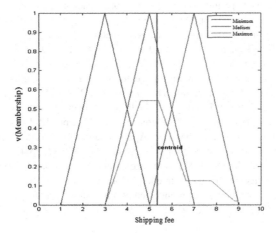

Fig. 14. Study graphic

5 Conclusions

It is perceived throughout this article that a great deal of management commitment is required to achieve an adequate balance between the various logistics costs and the quality of the services provided to the client.

Through the computational analysis carried out on the variables, Service Provision, Merchandise Status, Delivery Time, gave us the result that, these variables Influence the estimation in the transport tariff.

In this process of control of logistics costs, there must be adequate planning of actions leading to the reduction of logistics costs, and to keep them within reasonable limits.

It is proposed a scenario capable of describing how to improve decision making based on fuzzy logic.

Finally, we obtained as results of this study, a diffuse control model, which will automatically determine the fair values to be paid for a transport service.

References

1. Galindo, G., Batta, R.: Review of recent developments in OR/MS research in disaster operations management. Eur. J. Oper. Res. **230**(2), 201–211 (2013)
2. Ganesh, M., Raghunathan, S., Rajendran, C.: The value of information sharing in a multi-product, multi-level supply chain: Impact of product substitution, demand correlation, and partial information sharing. Decis. Support Syst. **102**, 79–94 (2014)
3. Mecozzi, A., Essiambre, R.-J.: Nonlinear Shannon limit in pseudolinear coherent systems. J. Lightwave Technol. **30**(12), 2011–2024 (2012)
4. Kyu Kim, K., Yul Ryoo, S., Dug Jung, M.: Inter-organizational information systems visibility in buyer–supplier relationships. Omega **39**, 667–676 (2011)
5. Dahbi, A., Mouftah, H.T.: Supply chain efficient inventory management as a service offered by a cloud-based platform. In: 2016 IEEE International Conference on Communications (ICC), pp. 1–7 (2016)
6. Sadraddini, S., Belta, C.: Safety control of monotone systems with bounded uncertainties. In: 2016 IEEE 55th Conference on Decision and Control, pp. 4874–4879 (2016)
7. Chai, X., Wang, R.: Research of emergent material dispatching algorithm based on multi-depot and multi-material. Comput. Eng. Appl. **46**, 224–226 (2010)
8. Kouba, N.E.Y, Menaa, M., Hasni, M., Boudour, M.: Optimal load frequency control based on artificial bee colony optimization applied to single, two and multi-area interconnected power systems. In: IEEE Conference Tlemcen, pp. 25–27 (2015)
9. Verma, R., Pal, S., Sathans: Fuzzy gain scheduled automatic generation control of two area multi unit power system. In: IEEE Conference Allahabad, pp. 12–14 (2013)
10. Anastassiou, G.A.: Intelligent Systems: Approximation by Artificial Neural Networks, p. 116. Springer, Heidelberg (2011). https://doi.org/10.1007/978-3-642-21431-8
11. Jain, S.K., Bhargava, A., Pal, R.K.: Three area power system load frequency control using fuzzy logic controller. In: IEEE Conference Indore, pp. 10–12 (2015)
12. Tayeb, E.B.M.: Automation of interconnected power system using fuzzy controller. In: IEEE Conference Pattaya City, pp. 28–30 (2011)

13. Syamala, J., Naidu, I.E.S.: Load frequency control of multi area power systems using PI, PID, and fuzzy logic controlling techniques. Int. J. Innov. Res. Sci. Eng. Technol. **III**, 1285 (2015)
14. Keprate, A., Chandima Ratnayake, R.M.: Determining the degree of fuzziness for fuzzy-AHP methodology used for identifying fatigue critical piping locations for inspection. In: 20th Jubilee IEEE International Conference on Intelligent Engineering Systems, no. 8 (2016)
15. Ismail, J.N., Atlas, H.: A fuzzy logic load frequency controller for power system. In: International Symposium on Mathematical methods in Engineering (2016)
16. Zadeh, L.A.: Fuzzy sets as a basis for theory of possibility. Fuzzy Sets Syst. **1**, 3–28 (1978)
17. Ansari, A., Firuzi, E., Etemadsaeed, L.: Un sistema experto difuso para la clasificación automática de señales sísmicas. Sistemas Expertos con Aplicaciones (2014)
18. Zadeh, L.A.: Fuzzy sets. Inf. Control Fuzzy Sets Syst. **8**, 228–253 (1965)
19. Bede, B.: Mathematics of Fuzzy Sets and Fuzzy Logic (2013)

MSpecFace: A Dataset for Facial Recognition in the Visible, Ultra Violet and Infrared Spectra

Rubén D. Fonnegra(iD), Alexander Molina(iD), Andrés F. Pérez-Zapata(iD),
and Gloria M. Díaz$^{(\boxtimes)}$(iD)

Instituto Tecnológico Metropolitano, Medellín, Colombia
{rubenfonnegra,gloriadiaz}@itm.edu.co,
{alexandermolina94898,andresperez3684}@correo.itm.edu.co
http://www.itm.edu.co/

Abstract. This paper describes the acquisition process and content of a multispectral face database, which can be used to research on face recognition methods dealing with two of the most challenging problems in this area, i.e. partial occlusion and pose variations. Four cameras were synchronized and arranged to simultaneously capture images from visible, thermal, ultraviolet and near-infrared spectra, which had reported promising results for recognizing faces, individually. In order to simulate pose variations, each subject was asked to look forward, up, down, and to the sides, varying the point of view angle. On the other hand, partial occlusion was generated using sunglasses and a paper sheet. Additionally, three lighting changes were also included (halogen, natural and infrared). A total of 306 images were acquired by subject and 31 subjects were recruited. So, the whole database is composed of 9486 images, which are now available to other researchers. Preliminary results showed that spectra variations affect the performance of a deep learning recognition approach. As far as we know, this is the first database of faces including images from those spectra and the other variations simultaneously.

Keywords: Face recognition · Database · Near infrared · Thermal
Occlusion · Pose variations

1 Introduction

Nowadays, biometric recognition systems have been determinant for control access applications, staff control, among others. These applications are based on the use of technological resources for ensuring to find patterns that allow to distinguish uniquely every person. Although several body information such as retina, iris, fingerprints, among others, have been used as biometric data [1,2], facial characteristics are still the most used due to its easy implementation in different environments [3].

Many actual challenges in computer vision for face recognition have been focused on problems such as illumination conditions, pose variations and partial face occlusion [4]. Those have been approached from both computer vision

© Springer International Publishing AG 2018
M. Botto-Tobar et al. (Eds.): CITT 2017, CCIS 798, pp. 160–170, 2018.
https://doi.org/10.1007/978-3-319-72727-1_12

techniques and different spectral analysis such as near infrared - NIR, ultraviolet - UV, thermographic - FIR and visible - VIS. The last one strategy take advantage of the fact that the information in those spectra cannot be easily disturbed [5]. Even though, some works had proposed multimodal information fusion strategies to improve results in face recognition tasks [6]. On the other hand, problems such as the face or head inclination, and occlusion are still open research problems [7].

Despite in the literature have been reported many databases available for developing research on face recognition (See Table 2), neither of them provides simultaneously samples with several variations such as pose, light conditions, occlusion, and spectra acquisition. In this paper, we present a novel - robust database for face recognition research named MSpecFace, which contains data from different participants acquired using different spectral sensors (UV, NIR, FIR y VIS). Additionally, it also contains data with variations in pose (different inclinations to right, left, up and down); and occlusion conditions, which was performed using daily accessories (such as lens, sunglasses and paper leaves covering a face region). Additionally, the MSpecFace also include illumination changes (natural illumination, fluorescent illumination, and infrared illumination). The effect of using the different spectra in a face recognition task was evaluated. For doing so, a deep learning strategy was proposed. Four deep learning models were trained, one for each spectrum. So, we showed that each spectrum provides relevant information for recognition purposes.

This work is organized as follows. In Sect. 2, we present a brief summary of available face databases found in face recognition state-of-the-art. In Sect. 3 main aspects of the database acquisition are presented and its actual content is also described. Then, a simple recognition strategy based on deep learning models is presented in the Sect. 4, which allows to evaluate the effect of using images from different spectra in a face recognition task. Finally, conclusions and future works are presented in Sect. 5.

2   Related Works

At the last few years, face image databases have not been limited to face region capture as inputs to machine learning methods, characterization, among others. This topic has been also oriented to the research of novel techniques and metrics for better describing facial biometrics.

Several proposals such the CASIA database [8] have been developed using high-resolution infrared cameras in order to capture NIR spectra of the face of the participants, considering the absence of illumination. They took images from 197 subjects, with a wide variability of data, where they included the use of lens and sunglasses. It is notable to remark that they only took frontal images.

Other works, likes the IIIT-Delhi Disguise Version 1 face database [9], were designed with the aim of pointing to occlusion problems to identify people with the use of several wearing accessories (such as hats, glasses, wigs, fake beard and mustache, among others). This database contains variations concerning a number of accessories in every participant, which increases the difficulty in face recognition problem. Additionally, the authors extended the dataset including images in NIR spectra.

Other datasets such as CARL database [10], and PUCV-VTF database [11] combine face images in VIS and NIR spectra, where they take frontal pictures from participants. The main advantage of CARL and PUCV-VTF databases is that they include pose variations. However, despite the databases contain similar kind of information, given the environment and acquisition variations between them, it is not suitable to relate them in the same application.

Table 2 summarizes the most relevant available databases reported in the literature for researching in the face recognition area. Note that even when occlusion, pose and illumination variations have been introduced. None of the databases involves those variations in addition of different acquisition spectra.

3   The MSpecFace: A Multi Spectral Database

3.1   Technical Aspects

With the aim of obtaining a database with the required quality image for the task, we decided to use high-resolution cameras to capture every spectrum. For capturing visible spectrum, we used a high-resolution low-cost web camera. For far infrared spectrum, we used a thermographic camera from FLIR, model A655-SC. For near-infrared spectrum, we used a mono sensor Edmund Optics camera with a filter lens of 1000 nm wavelength. Finally, for ultraviolet spectrum, we used a color sensor camera with a filter lens of 400 nm wavelength. Technical information of used cameras is fully described in Table 1.

Table 1. General aspects for used cameras during data acquisition

Model	Sensor	Maximum resolution	Maximum frame rate	Pixel size	Spectra
CMLN-13S2M-CS	Sony ICX445 CCD, 1/3″ Mono	1296 × 964	18 *FPS*	3.75 μm	Near Infrared
CMLN-13S2C-CS	Sony ICX445 CCD, 1/3″ Color	1296 × 964	18 *FPS*	3.75 μm	Ultraviolet
FLIR A655-SC	Vanadium Oxide (VoX) microbolometer	640 × 480	50 *FPS*	17 μm	Termographic (Far Infrared)
QuickCam Connect (E2500)	-	1280 × 960	30 *FPS*	-	Visible

3.2   Acquisition Protocol

With the purpose of obtaining a database for face recognition taking into account occlusion and multispectral analysis, it is required to consider the use of accessories to cover certain face regions (eyes, mouth, head, among others). In this sense, we decided to take samples from participants wearing anything and include

Table 2. Available face databases in the literature

Name	Year	Spectra	Light variations	Pose	Expressions	Accessories	Environment	Subjects	Images
Feret [12]	1997	Visible		1	Neutral, alternative	Glasses	Indoor	Unknown	3816
AR [13]	1998	Visible	Yes	Frontal	smile, anger, scream	Glasses and Scarf	Indoor	126	3000
CAS-PEAL [14]	2004	Visible	Yes	Variations	six expressions	Glasses and hats	Indoor	1040	30781
IRIS [15]	2006	Thermal/Visible	No	Variations	surprised, laughing, angry	No	Indoor	31	8456
IRIS-M3 [16]	2006	Visible/Thermal/Multi spectral	Yes	Frontal	No	No	Indoor/Outdoor	82	2050
BioID [17]	2007	Visible	No	Frontal	Neutral	Glasses	Indoor	23	1521
CBSR NIR [18]	2007	NIR	No	Frontal	No	Glasses	Indoor	197	3940
CASIA-FaceV5 [19]	2010	Visible	Yes	Variations	Neutral/Alternative	Glasses	Indoor	500	2500
WVUM [20]	2010	Visible/NIR	No	Frontal, left, right	No	No	Indoor	50	1250
NVIE [21]	2010	Visible/Thermal	No	Frontal	Neutral/emotion expressions	Glasses	Indoor	100+	
LDHF-DB [22]	2012~	NIR/Visible		Front		0	Indoor/Outdoor	100	Unknown
Carl DB [10]	2013	Visible/NIR/Thermal	Yes	Frontal	Neutral	NO	Indoor	41	7380
NIR-VIS 2.0 [8]	2013	NIR/Visible	Yes	Frontal/Variations	Neutral/Variations	Glasses	Indoor	725	–
Delhi [9]	2013	Visible, Thermal	No	Frontal	Neutral	various disguises	Indoor	75	681
PUCV-VTF [11]	2015	Visible/Thermal	Yes	Frontal	Frown, smile, vowel	Glasses	unknown	76	12160
MSpecFace	**2017**	**NIR, UV, Thermographic, Visible**	**Yes**	**Frontal/Variations**	**Neutral**	**Glasses, Sun Glasses, Artificial Occlusion**	**Indoor**	**31**	**9486**

the use of commonly used accessories, such as glasses, sunglasses (to cover participant's eyes) and scarfs (to cover mouth and nose tip). However, by hygiene issues of many people wearing the same scarf, we better decided to omit the use of scarf and replace it with a simple paper sheet. To sum up, we take images from participants not wearing accessories, wearing different kinds of glasses, different kinds of sunglasses and covering mouth and nose tip with a paper sheet.

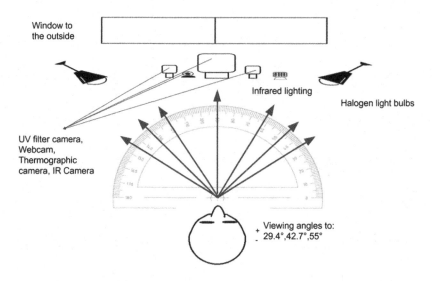

Fig. 1. Diagram with the acquisition protocol, location of devices and capture angles.

Additionally, we considered face inclination for pose estimation. In this sense, we ask the participants to tilt their heads right and left looking points located from different angles ($+-29.4°$, $+-42.7°$ and $55°$ from $90°$ as a reference point), plus we also considered up and down as two more poses. Thus, we acquire images from 9 poses (front, first, second and third angles left; first, second and third angles right; up and down) whilst participants wearing the different accessories (such as glasses, sunglasses, and occlusion) or not (natural). Figure 1 shows a diagram displaying the device distribution (camera, illumination sets) and angles where the participants had to tilt their heads.

To controlling the illumination conditions, we strategically selected a room with a large window ($2 \times 2\,\mathrm{m}^2$) that provided natural illumination, which could be totally obscured using a cover. Additionally, we had professional halogen and infrared illumination sets. For natural illumination (Nat) acquisitions, we locate participants in front of the fully opened window, approximately at $2\,\mathrm{m}$ distance. Due to variance in natural illumination across the day, we considered to take photographies between 9 am and 5 pm, during sunny days. In the case of fluorescent illumination (Fluo), two lamps with diffusers were located on both sides of participants (approximately at $1.5\,\mathrm{m}$), which were turn-on when required. Finally, for infrared illumination (Ifr), we located an infrared lamp in front of

Table 3. Summary of evaluated conditions the database

Modality	Condition	Modality	Condition
Occlusion	None	Spectra	Ultraviolet
	Normal glasses		Near infrared
	Sunglasses		Far Infrared
	Mouth covering		Visible
Illumination	Fluorescent	Pose	Left
	Natural		Right
	Infrared (Thermo and NIR only)		Up
			Down

the participant (circle lamp around the camera), which was turned on when this condition was considered, ensuring the room was completely dark. In this case, accessories were not included due that its use not generates a relevant effect in the images. To sum up, the database contains elements including different aspects described in Table 3.

Finally, because we need to ensure that all images were acquired at the same time, which is difficult to control using the software provided by each camera, we design an API (Application Programming Interface) for triggering the four cameras at the same time. With this API, we ensure the pictures are taken at the same time instant, avoiding time delays in the shots or involuntary movement in the participants. To take the captures, we follow the next steps.

1. We asked participants to look at a corresponding inclination point (front, first, second and third angles left; first, second and third angles right; up and down) and take the picture (for every point of inclination).
2. When finished first step, we ask the participant to wear one accessory (glasses, sunglasses, paper sheet). Then, we repeated the last step. We repeated this step for every different accessory (glasses, sunglasses and paper sheet).
3. When we finished with all accessories, we changed illumination type and repeat step one. We repeated this for every different type of illumination (fluorescent, natural and infrared).

In Fig. 2 is shown the used equipment, cameras setup and scenario during the acquisition stage in an acquisition session.

3.3   Database Description

The database is composed of 31 different subjects (named from S1 to S31). We took samples from four different accessories (natural (P_Nat), glasses (P_LentesVis), sunglasses (P_Lentes) and paper sheet (P_Oclusion)). For every accessory, we separate images captured for every pose (front, first, second and third angles left; first, second and third angles right; up and down). Finally, we

Fig. 2. Acquisition scenario. Left image with natural illumination and right image with artificial illumination.

stored images to the different spectra (NIR, FIR, UV, VIS). Then, we obtained 306 images per subject, where 72 images correspond to every spectrum and 18 correspond to infrared illumination but using each accessory. In total, complete MSpecFace database contains 9486 samples. Random samples taken for one subject are shown in Fig. 3.

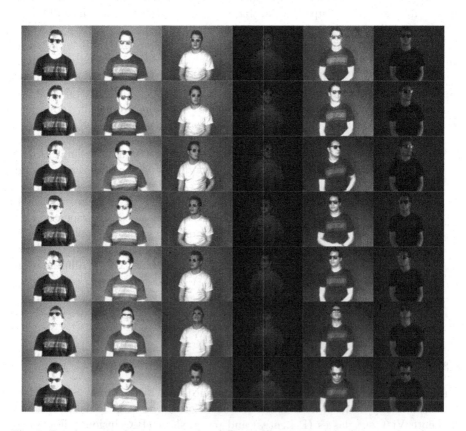

Fig. 3. Random samples images under different illumination conditions taken for one subject from the MSpectra database. (Spectra from left to right: VIS-Nat, VIS-Fluo, NIR-Nat, NIR-Ifr, UV-Nat, UV-Fluo)

4   Initial Evaluation

In this section we present a preliminary evaluation of the MSpecFace database described in Sect. 3.

4.1   Classification Task

With the aim of proving efficiency in the database, we propose a subject recognition task in order to identify every person separately. In this sense, we pretend to achieve a subject recognition for images from different spectra (NIR, VIS, UV). We do not include thermographic spectrum due to information contained in every pixel do not correspond to intensity, but temperature in it. Additionally, we decided not to bias occlusion element and pose variations of subjects. According to this, we gather then 72 images per subject and achieve a total of 2232 images from the database per every spectrum evaluation.

$$Accuracy = \frac{Correct\ predictions\ emotions\ (hits)}{Amount\ of\ samples} \tag{1}$$

4.2   Classification Model

Due to the high performance of Deep learning strategies in computer vision problems during the recent years (such as ImageNet challenge [23]), we decided to implement Convolutional Neural Network (CNN) architecture as classification model. We designed a network consisting of seven convolutional layers with 32, 16, 16, 8, 8, 8 and 16 channels respectively, 3×3 symmetric convolutional filters to non-overlapping regions and Rectified Linear units (RelU) activation functions. After the first, second, third and seven layers we added Max Pooling layers with a pool size regions of 2×2. The output of convolutional layers is then flattened, and connected to a densely connected network in order to discriminate classes. The Dense network included two layers, first with 1500 neurons and second with 1000 neurons. They included both, RelU activation functions. To prevent overfitting, a dropout of 0.5 was used after first and second convolutional layers; and last perceptron layer as well. The learning rate was set on 0.00005, and weights initialization in layers used was Glorot (or Xavier) uniform distribution. Besides, we selected Adaptive Moment Estimation (Adam) optimizer [24] as the optimization algorithm for gradients in the network, due to its momentum based learning algorithm, for adaptive single parameter tuning considering gradients initialization and small decaying rates. These characteristics significantly improve parameters optimization and increase accuracy to avoid divergence during the training stage. Parameters for Adam optimizer were selected as author provided in the original paper. For training stage, we used 5 fold cross validation algorithm. We selected 80% percent of the dataset for training and 20% for testing. The training data was fed to the network through batches of 10 images across 50 epochs. The validation data were used to validate the model and calculate accuracy (Eq. 1).

4.3 Experimental Setup

For training the learning model, we used a Quadro K4000 GPU with 3 GB of RAM in an Ubuntu Gnome 16.04 platform. For the model implementation, we used TensorFlow version 1.1.0, along with Keras 2.0.4. For GPU implementation we used NVIDIA CUDA 7.5 along with cuDNN 5.1. We also required Scipy 0.19.0 for uploading files and additional dependencies.

4.4 Preliminary Results

For proposed strategy described in Subsect. 4.2, we estimate accuracy for all cases. The obtained results are displayed in Table 4. Obtained accuracies for the database shown effectiveness in classification task, besides significant differences for spectral information.

Table 4. Obtained results for classification model

Spectrum	Accuracy
NIR	0.9354
VIS	0.9637
FUV	0.9789

4.5 Advantages and Limitations

Although MSpecFace includes a limited amount of subjects, we considered several needs according to face recognition the state of the art (occlusion, pose estimation and illumination conditions). Thus, considering a number of available samples, conditions, and spectra taken into account during database acquisition, the MSpecFace can be versatile for carrying out unimodal and multimodal information fusion in biometric recognition systems. Besides, the MSpecFace database has been carefully taken with professional equipment developed to visual identification. This is reflected in the obtained results for the classification model, where we demonstrate that MSpecFace could obtain suitable conclusions for other experiments aiming to investigate problems related to mentioned topics.

On the other hand, as was before mentioned, the main disadvantage of MSpecFace lies in the amount of subjects. Additionally, we have to mentioned that it was acquired in fully controllable environments; which makes it not comparable with models in the wild.

5 Conclusions and Future Work

In this work we introduced MSpecFace, a dataset for facial recognition in the visible, near infrared, far infrared and ultraviolet spectra. We have shown a carefully designed protocol for database acquirement using professional equipment for visual systems. Additionally, we evaluate the model in one of possible classification task, obtaining results which demonstrate that the dataset has enough samples of good quality to test classification and feature extraction architectures. It is also evidenced that the different electromagnetic spectra provide differentiated information that would allow to perform more complex tasks in the machine learning area based on information fusion.

As future work, we will expand our database including more subjects in order to increase variability and amount of samples. Additionally, we expected to develop a new dataset including different facial expressions and continue testing more applications for facial recognition using different spectra information in order to outperform obtained results.

References

1. Su, H.R., Chen, K.Y., Wong, W.J., Lai, S.H.: A deep learning approach towards pore extraction for high-resolution fingerprint recognition. In: 2017 IEEE International Conference on Acoustics, Speech and Signal Processing (ICASSP), pp. 2057–2061. IEEE (2017)
2. Best-Rowden, L., Jain, A.K.: Longitudinal study of automatic face recognition. IEEE Trans. Pattern Anal. Mach. Intell. **PP**(99), 1 (2017)
3. Turk, M., Pentland, A.: Eigenfaces for recognition. J. Cogn. Neurosci. **3**(1), 71–86 (1991)
4. Ghiass, R.S., Arandjelović, O., Bendada, A., Maldague, X.: Infrared face recognition: A comprehensive review of methodologies and databases. Pattern Recogn. **47**(9), 2807–2824 (2014)
5. Arya, S., Pratap, N., Bhatia, K.: Future of face recognition: A review. Procedia Comput. Sci. **58**, 578–585 (2015)
6. Sarfraz, M.S., Stiefelhagen, R.: Deep perceptual mapping for cross-modal face recognition. Int. J. Comput. Vis. **122**(3), 426–438 (2017)
7. Yang, J., Luo, L., Qian, J., Tai, Y., Zhang, F., Xu, Y.: Nuclear norm based matrix regression with applications to face recognition with occlusion and illumination changes. IEEE Trans. Pattern Anal. Mach. Intell. **39**(1), 156–171 (2017)
8. Li, S., Yi, D., Lei, Z., Liao, S.: The CASIA NIR-VIS 2.0 face database. In: Proceedings of the IEEE Conference on Computer Vision and Pattern Recognition Workshops, pp. 348–353 (2013)
9. Dhamecha, T.I., Nigam, A., Singh, R., Vatsa, M.: Disguise detection and face recognition in visible and thermal spectrums. In: 2013 International Conference on Biometrics (ICB), pp. 1–8. IEEE (2013)
10. Espinosa-Duró, V., Faundez-Zanuy, M., Mekyska, J.: A new face database simultaneously acquired in visible, near-infrared and thermal spectrums. Cogn. Comput. **5**(1), 119–135 (2013)
11. Hermosilla, G., Gallardo, F., Farias, G., Martin, C.S.: Fusion of visible and thermal descriptors using genetic algorithms for face recognition systems. Sensors **15**(8), 17944–17962 (2015)
12. Phillips, P.J., Wechsler, H., Huang, J., Rauss, P.J.: The FERET database and evaluation procedure for face-recognition algorithms. Image Vis. Comput. **16**(5), 295–306 (1998)
13. Martinez, A., Benavente, R.: The AR face database, 1998. Computer Vision Center, Technical report, vol. 3, p. 5 (2007)

14. Gao, W., Cao, B., Shan, S., Chen, X., Zhou, D., Zhang, X., Zhao, D.: The CAS-PEAL large-scale chinese face database and baseline evaluations. IEEE Trans. Syst. Man Cybern. Part A: Syst. Hum. **38**(1), 149–161 (2008)
15. Chang, H., Harishwaran, H., Yi, M., Koschan, A., Abidi, B., Abidi, M.: An indoor and outdoor, multimodal, multispectral and multi-illuminant database for face recognition. In: 2006 IEEE Conference on Computer Vision and Pattern Recognition Workshop, CVPRW 2006, p. 54. IEEE (2006)
16. Chang, H., Yi, M., Harishwaran, H., Abidi, B., Koschan, A., Abidi, M.: Multispectral fusion for indoor and outdoor face authentication. In: 2006 Biometrics Symposium: Special Session on Research at the Biometric Consortium Conference, pp. 1–6. IEEE (2006)
17. Jesorsky, O., Kirchberg, K.J., Frischholz, R.W.: Robust face detection using the Hausdorff distance. In: Bigun, J., Smeraldi, F. (eds.) AVBPA 2001. LNCS, vol. 2091, pp. 90–95. Springer, Heidelberg (2001). https://doi.org/10.1007/3-540-45344-X_14
18. Li, S.Z., Chu, R., Liao, S., Zhang, L.: Illumination invariant face recognition using near-infrared images. IEEE Trans. Pattern Anal. Mach. Intell. **29**(4), 627–639 (2007)
19. CASIA-FACEV5: Biometrics Ideal Test (2010). http://biometrics.idealtest.org/dbDetailForUser.do?id=9
20. Bourlai, T., Kalka, N., Ross, A., Cukic, B., Hornak, L.: Cross-spectral face verification in the short wave infrared (SWIR) band. In: 2010 20th International Conference on Pattern Recognition (ICPR), pp. 1343–1347. IEEE (2010)
21. Wang, S., Liu, Z., Lv, S., Lv, Y., Wu, G., Peng, P., Chen, F., Wang, X.: A natural visible and infrared facial expression database for expression recognition and emotion inference. IEEE Trans. Multimed. **12**(7), 682–691 (2010)
22. Maeng, H., Liao, S., Kang, D., Lee, S.-W., Jain, A.K.: Nighttime face recognition at long distance: cross-distance and cross-spectral matching. In: Lee, K.M., Matsushita, Y., Rehg, J.M., Hu, Z. (eds.) ACCV 2012. LNCS, vol. 7725, pp. 708–721. Springer, Heidelberg (2013). https://doi.org/10.1007/978-3-642-37444-9_55
23. Russakovsky, O., Deng, J., Su, H., Krause, J., Satheesh, S., Ma, S., Huang, Z., Karpathy, A., Khosla, A., Bernstein, M., et al.: ImageNet large scale visual recognition challenge. Int. J. Comput. Vis. **115**(3), 211–252 (2015)
24. Kingma, D., Ba, J.: Adam: A method for stochastic optimization (2014). arXiv preprint arXiv:1412.6980

A Proposal for Migrating SOA Applications to Cloud Using Model-Driven Development

Miguel Botto-Tobar[1,2]([⊠])[iD] and Emilio Insfran[3][iD]

[1] Universidad de Guayaquil, Guayaquil, Ecuador
`miguel.bottot@ug.edu.ec`
[2] Eindhoven University of Technology, Eindhoven, The Netherlands
`m.a.botto.tobar@tue.nl`
[3] Universitat Politècnica de València, Valencia, Spain
`einsfran@dsic.upv.es`

Abstract. Software applications are currently considered an element essential and indispensable in all business activities. Nevertheless, for their construction and deployment to use all the resources that are available in remote and accessible locations on the network, which leads to inefficient operations in development and deployment, and enormous costs in the acquisition of IT equipment [6]. This paper aims to contribute proposing SOA2Cloud, a framework to migrate SOA applications to Cloud environments, following a Model-Driven Software Development approach. An example of an application that shows the feasibility of our approach was developed.

Keywords: SOA · Migration · Cloud Computing
Model-Driven Development

1 Introduction

The fast Internet expansion has created an ideal mean for the development of applications that carry out information exchange, such as electronic transactions, product sales, and on-line services, among other functionalities. It has driven organizations to increase their interactions with customers and other companies.

Service-Oriented Architecture (SOA) is based on services development and their reuse, with a clear business and a known functionality, independent and non-coupled, it is offered through a set of intelligent services and coupled interfaces that can provide the same way in other applications [3].

Cloud computing is linked to a novel model of network delivery of different types of IT resources, for instance: basic computing resources, storage, and networking, deploying and running applications, etc., that they are part of a set of resources that can be allocated, provisioned and delivered quickly with minimal interaction between customer and service provider [23].

Cloud Computing expands to SOA adding scalability and GRID Computing. Scalability is required when the software is used as a service, hence the hardware resources are used, and scalability becomes a transcendent requirement.

© Springer International Publishing AG 2018
M. Botto-Tobar et al. (Eds.): CITT 2017, CCIS 798, pp. 171–184, 2018.
https://doi.org/10.1007/978-3-319-72727-1_13

This work was defined taking into account the need for many companies, both public and private, perform inefficient operations in construction and deployment of their applications, and enormous expenses in IT acquisition. With computing available as a service in Cloud Computing, many companies are considering it as a solution for service delivery. Therefore, SOA applications are being migrated to Cloud; and, for this reason, the need to build a framework that allows migrating applications developed in SOA to Cloud environment using Model-Driven Software Development (MDD) [4].

The paper is organized as follows: Sect. 2 discusses related work. Section 3 presents the research method. Section 4 describes an application example, and finally, Sect. 5 presents our conclusions and suggest areas for further investigation.

2   Related Work

Our goal is to develop a framework which allows migration of SOA applications to Cloud Computing environments, using Model-Driven Software Development. In order to fulfill this objective, we first have studied the state-of-art of cloud migration in [5,7], to know which methods and techniques have been implemented, especially those which have used Model-Driven Development.

Babar et al. [2] reported their experiences and observations gained from migrating an Open Source Software, Hackystat, to cloud computing.

Tran et al. [25] proposed a taxonomy of the migration tasks involved, and they showed the costs breakdown among categories of tasks, for a case-study which migrated a .NET n-tier application to Windows Azure.

Guillén et al. [11] proposed a framework MULTICLAPP. The framework follows a three-stage development process where applications can be modeled and coded without developers having to be familiar with the specification of any cloud platform. MDE [22] approaches rely on models as a means of abstracting the development process from the peculiarities of each cloud platform.

Mohagheghi et al. [18] presented a research project (REMICS) to define methodology and tools for model-driven migration of legacy applications to a service-oriented architecture with deployment in the cloud. The main project's objective is to develop a set of model-driven methods and tools that support organizations with legacy systems to modernize them according to the "Service Cloud paradigm".

Nevertheless, they presented either approaches or experiences to migrate applications to Cloud using MDD (applications were not developed using SOA) or legacy systems.

3   Research Method

This section presents a model-based approach defined to generate Cloud applications from SoaML [20] and SLA [21] models deployed in Windows Azure. We established a migration process to carry out this approach, which is based on the SPEM notation [19].

3.1   Metamodels

SoaML. It extends the UML2 metamodel to support explicit service modeling in distributed environments. This extension aims to maintain the different service modeling scenarios such as the description of a single service, service-oriented architecture modeling, or service contract definition [20]. Our SoaML metamodel has been defined based on the specification proposed by OMG, as well as the contributions of Minerva project [9] and Irish Software Engineering Center [1].

Service Level Agreement. SLA stipulates conditions and parameters that commit the service provider (usually supplier) to comply with levels of quality of service against the contractor (usually customer) [21]. Its structure is based on elements presented in an exemplary structure that create in an SLA Fig. 1. It is clear that the description of services, or service level, objectives are the central aspect of each SLA [10].

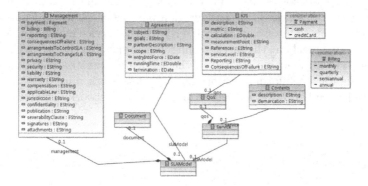

Fig. 1. SLA metamodel.

Cloud Application. SOA is an umbrella that describes any service. A Cloud application is a service. A cloud application metamodel is an SOA model conforming to SOA metamodel. It makes Cloud applications also SOA applications. However, SOA applications are not required in Cloud applications [12]. A Cloud application is an SOA application that runs under a specific environment, which is the cloud computing environment (platform). This context is characterized by horizontal scalability, fast provisioning, ease of access and flexible pricing [12].

Windows Azure. It is a technology set that provides a specific service set to application developers [8]. It also offers a platform where the ISV (independent software vendor) and companies can host their applications and data. It was selected for this research, and a generic metamodel was created. It has characteristics of the development environment and the platform. The Azure metamodel elements are detailed below (it has developed for this research):

- CloudServices. A cloudServices allows creating a solution with the two different types of instances provided by the Windows Azure platform for developers, Web Roles, and Work Roles.
- ServiceWebRole. A WebRole is a role that is customized for programming web
  applications with IIS 7 support, such as ASP.NET, PHP, Windows Communication Foundation and FastCGI. All information in a WebRole is stored in
  a file definition, and its default extension is .csdef [14].
- ServiceWorkRole. A WorkRole is a function that is useful for generalized
  development and can be performed background processing for a web role.
  All information in a WorkRole is stored in a definition file, and its default
  extension is .csdef [17].
- ServiceDefinition. It defines the service model for an application. It also contains the definitions of the functions available in a service, specifies the end
  services, and sets the configuration values for the service. The configuration
  values are found in the service configuration, as described by the Windows
  Azure service configuration schema (.file cscfg) [16].
- ServiceConfiguration. It specifies the number of instances to implement for
  each role in the service, the configuration parameter values and fingerprints
  of all certificates are associated with a role. If the service includes a Windows
  Azure virtual machine, the service configuration specifies the virtual hard disk
  for each virtual machine created. If the service is part of a virtual network,
  the configuration information for the virtual network must be provided in
  the service configuration as well as in the virtual network configuration [15]
  (Fig. 2).

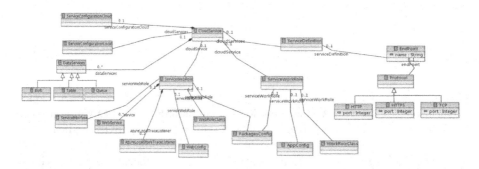

Fig. 2. Azure metamodel.

3.2   Migration

One of the important aspects of this process is the use of two models as input
artifacts, and execution of model transformations: an SOA application model
based on SoaML specification, and a service level agreement model based on
SLA. Unlike other transformation processes, which only use a source model as

input. The migration process is divided into three phases: analysis, transformation, and deployment.

Figure 3 shows migration process. It is entirely independent since it allows developers start migrating from scratch, that is, modeling SOA applications through SoaML specification, or from existing applications modeled in SoaML.

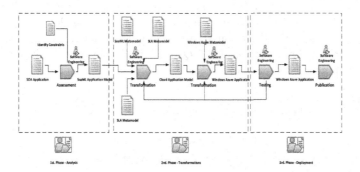

Fig. 3. Migration process.

In the analysis phase, the developer must assess SOA application to be migrated; it will be modeled in SoaML specification, identifying performance and quality restrictions that model may have. It is also important to take account in this first stage that an SOA application may also be source code written in a programming language; therefore, the developer has to use tools that allow obtaining the application model through reverse engineering. Once this phase is completed, a model is ready to be migrated.

The transformation phase is divided into two stages: (1) *transformation*, it uses two models as input artifacts, the first model is SOA application according to SoaML metamodel, and the second model is service level agreement based on SLA metamodel. Then, through model-to-model transformations, a cloud application model is obtained according to its metamodel. This model is transformed (using model-to-model transformations) into a model conforming to Azure metamodel. Finally, we proceed to perform a model-to-text transformation to obtain the source code, for this research, Windows Azure C #. (2) *model validation*, it verifies that all mappings specified in each transformation, from SoaML, SLA to Cloud, and from Cloud to Windows Azure, are matched between corresponding metamodels.

Deployment is the last phase, and the application will be deployed in a Cloud environment, Windows Azure.

3.3 Mappings

The correspondences between SoaML, SLA, and Cloud elements were defined. They specify which elements of source model conforming to source metamodel will be transformed into the target model elements according to target meta-model when the transformations are executed.

Firstly, the correspondences between SoaML and Cloud metamodels are presented in Table 1. *SoaMLModel* element and *ServiceArchitecture* (if it exists in the model) correspond to *CloudApplication* element which includes the rest of model elements. *Participant* and *Agent* elements correspond to *CloudTask* which is where the actions of a cloud application are executed. *Consumer*, *Provider*, and *ServiceInterface* elements correspond to *TaskDefinition* which in the cloud provide the application structure, interface set, and their contracts. *MessageType* element corresponds to *Queue*, which in Cloud is responsible for message exchange coordination.

Table 1. Mappings between SoaML and Cloud.

SoaML (elements)	Cloud (elements)
SoaMLModel	CloudApplication
Participant	CloudTask
Agent	
Consumer	TaskDefinition
Provider	
ServiceInterface	
MessageType	Queue

Secondly, the correspondences between SLA and Cloud metamodels are presented in Table 2. *Agreement* element corresponds to *ConfigurationData* element which is where aspects related to service agreements of the Cloud application are determined. *KPI* element corresponds to *DataInjectionPort* element which is where QoS tasks are modified.

Table 2. Mappings between SLA and Cloud.

SLA (elements)	Cloud (elements)
Agreements	ConfigurationData
KPIs	DataInjectionPort

Finally, the correspondences between Cloud and Azure metamodels are presented in Table 3. *Agreement* element corresponds to *ConfigurationData* element which is where aspects related to service agreements of the Cloud application are determined. *KPI* element corresponds to *DataInjectionPort* element which is where QoS tasks are modified. *CloudApplication* element corresponds to *CloudServices* element which includes all other components of the model. *WebTask*

Table 3. Mappings between SLAs and Cloud.

Cloud (elements)	Azure (elements)
CloudApplication	CloudServices
WebTask + ServiceTask	ServiceWebRole
CloudRotorTask	ServiceWorkerRole
Table	SQL Azure Table
Queue	SQL Azure Queue
Blob	SQL Azure Blob
EndPoint	EndPoint
Protocol	Protocol
ConfigurationData	ServiceConfigurationLocal + ServiceConfigurationCloud

and *ServiceTask* elements correspond to ServiceWebRole which are the application services to be specified. *CloudRotorTask* element corresponds to *ServiceWorkRole* which is in charge of processing web roles in an application on the Azure platform. *Table* element corresponds to *SQL Azure Table* which in Azure is responsible for storing structured information. *Queue* element corresponds to *SQL Azure Queue* which in Azure is responsible for the storage of scalable messages. *Blob* element corresponds to *SQL Azure Blob* which in Azure is responsible for storing unstructured data. *EndPoint* element corresponds to *EndPoint* which in Azure is responsible for the exchange of information between web roles and work roles. *Protocol* element corresponds to *Protocol* which in Azure is the port used by the web roles. *ConfigurationData* element corresponds to *ServiceConfiguration* which in Azure stores configuration data of the web roles and work roles.

3.4   Transformations

Model-to-model transformations were defined through ATL [13], defining the object templates of source domains (SoaML, and SLA) to target domain (Cloud). Since SoaML, SLA, and Cloud metamodels refer to elements of the UML metamodel, UML elements are also included which are accessible from the rules. The defined rules allow ATL transformations to automatically generate the elements of the target Cloud model as defined in the mappings as well as the relationships between the generated elements in the resulting model.

Model-to-model transformations were made between SoaML, SLA to Cloud, and from Cloud to Azure, where all identified key elements of SoaML and key SLA elements corresponded to each key element identified in the Cloud metamodel. Model transformation extract is presented below:

```
-- @nsURI Cloud=http://Cloud.ecore
-- @nsURI SoaML=http://SoaML.ecore
-- @nsURI SLA=http://sla.ecore
```

```
module soaml2cloud;
create OUT: Cloud from IN: SoaML, IN1: SLA;
-- SoaMLModel To CloudApplication
-- In this part was mandatory to include SLA Elements.
rule SoaMLModelToCloudApplication {
from
sm: SoaML!SoaMLModel,
sl: SLA!SLAModel
to
ca: Cloud!CloudApplication (
clientDependency <- sm.clientDependency,
name <- sm.name.toString(),
templateParameter <- sm.templateParameter,
URI <- sm.URI,
visibility <- sm.visibility,
packagedElement <- sm.packagedElement,
packagedElement <- sl.packagedElement
)
}
```

This transformation rule allows a SoaMLModel element to be converted to a CloudApplication. It is also very important to note that the SLAModel element must be included to execute the transformation between SoaML, SLA, and Cloud. A complete list of transformation rules, can be found on: http://www.win.tue.nl/~mbottoto/resources/citt/transformations-rule.pdf.

Finally, model-to-text transformations were made from Azure metamodel to source code. It corresponds to C # programming language used in the Visual Studio tool.

4   Application Example

Our example was a business scenario (see Fig. 4), it is a community of independent distributors, manufacturers, and carriers who want to be able to work together consistently and not re-design business processes or systems when working with other parties of the community. They want to be able to have their business processes, rules, and information. The community has decided to define an architecture oriented to the service of the community to allow this open and agile business environment. This example has been defined to represent the SoaML specification made by the OMG [20].

4.1   Definition

The dealer network is defined as a "collaboration" community that involves three main roles for the participants in this community: dealer, manufacturer, and shipper. In the same way, participants participate in the three "B2B" services, a shopping service, a shipping service and a status service.

Fig. 4. Dealer network community [20].

4.2   Services

The service architecture does not define the service, and it uses the service specification. The service is defined independently and then released into the service architecture so that it can be used and reused.

Fig. 5. Place order service [20].

The place order service is a simple service. The diagram in Fig. 5 diagram identifies the service contract, the terms, and conditions of the service, as well as defining the two roles: order placer and order taker.

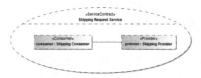

Fig. 6. Shipping request service [20].

The service request service a simple service. The diagram in Fig. 6 identifies the service contract, the terms, and conditions of the service, as well as defining the two roles: shipping consumer and shipping provider.

4.3   Procedure

In IDE Eclipse [24] - SOA2Cloud, SoaML model was created and saved with a format ".soaml". Besides, the model to specify the service agreements between the consumer and SLA service provider was also created in ".sla" format. This environment uses as input for transformations two models ".soaml" (Fig. 7) and ".sla" (Fig. 8), respectively.

Figure 7 depicts the DealersNetwork community modeled through SoaML specification. This model consists of a service architecture, three participants, three service contracts, three consumers, three providers, and three messages types. They interact with each other for forming a service community.

Fig. 7. Dealer network in SoaML.

The model in Fig. 8 represents service level agreements for DealersNetwork community. This model consists of an agreement, a document, a management, a service, a QoS, and a KPI.

Once the models have been created/modeled, model-to-model transformation rules were executed through ATL, and the result is a new model conforming to Cloud metamodel (Fig. 9).

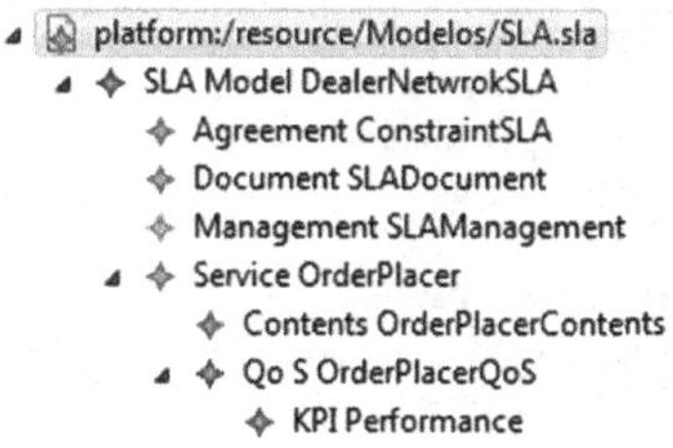

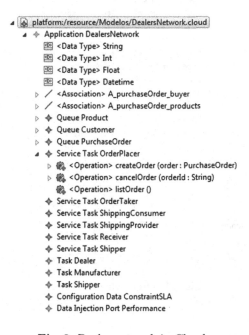

◢ 📄 platform:/resource/Modelos/SLA.sla
  ◢ ✦ SLA Model DealerNetwrokSLA
    ✦ Agreement ConstraintSLA
    ✦ Document SLADocument
    ✦ Management SLAManagement
  ◢ ✦ Service OrderPlacer
    ✦ Contents OrderPlacerContents
    ◢ ✦ Qo S OrderPlacerQoS
      ✦ KPI Performance

Fig. 8. Dealer network in SLA.

◢ 📄 platform:/resource/Modelos/DealersNetwork.cloud
  ◢ ✦ Application DealersNetwork
    ▦ <Data Type> String
    ▦ <Data Type> Int
    ▦ <Data Type> Float
    ▦ <Data Type> Datetime
    ▷ ╱ <Association> A_purchaseOrder_buyer
    ▷ ╱ <Association> A_purchaseOrder_products
    ▷ ✦ Queue Product
    ▷ ✦ Queue Customer
    ▷ ✦ Queue PurchaseOrder
    ◢ ✦ Service Task OrderPlacer
      ▷ ⚙ <Operation> createOrder (order : PurchaseOrder)
      ▷ ⚙ <Operation> cancelOrder (orderId : String)
      ⚙ <Operation> listOrder ()
    ✦ Service Task OrderTaker
    ✦ Service Task ShippingConsumer
    ✦ Service Task ShippingProvider
    ✦ Service Task Receiver
    ✦ Service Task Shipper
    ✦ Task Dealer
    ✦ Task Manufacturer
    ✦ Task Shipper
    ✦ Configuration Data ConstraintSLA
    ✦ Data Injection Port Performance

Fig. 9. Dealer network in Cloud.

After obtaining the Cloud application model, it was necessary to carry out a new model-to-model transformation, however, for this time, the Cloud model was needed as input to obtain the model for Azure (Fig. 10).

Finally, we performed a model-to-text transformation to generate the Windows Azure application, and it was implemented on Visual Studio for its compilation, testing and deployment/publication on Microsoft Windows Azure platform. To see the correct service functioning, we entered to the link provided by the service, which is: http://orderplacer.cloudapp.net/, and it showed the service published (Fig. 11).

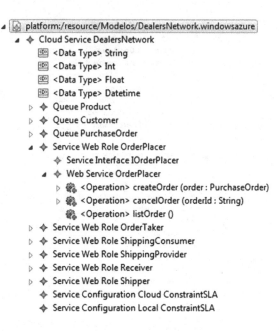

Fig. 10. Dealer network in Azure.

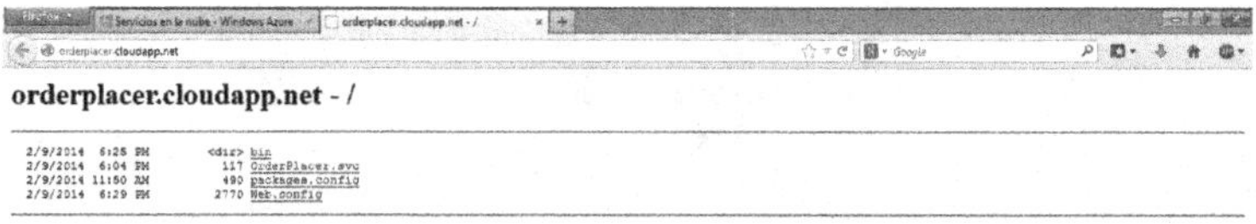

Fig. 11. Order place service.

5   Conclusions

The main motivation of this research is to have a framework to migrate SOA applications to Cloud, following a model-driven approach, since there are proposals that perform this process but do not cover aspects of development model-driven software.

To carry out this work we defined a generic process of model transformations (model-to-model and model-to-text), from SoaML and SLA models, to obtain a target model (Cloud) and its respective source code in Azure.

The final product has been taken into account, which it has been addressed through an application example, and its functionality and performance/deployment in a Cloud service provider have been viewed globally.

6   Future Work

According to our experiences, we can propose for future studies the following:
There is a need for a contribution for migrating SOA applications to other Cloud providers, such as Google App Engine and Amazon Web Services.
Another aspect needed to do is the refinement of the Cloud model by evaluating a wider set of artifacts based on all existing platforms.
Subsequently, an empirical validation of proposed framework will be carried out through controlled experiments, where the framework is evaluated objectively according to its effectiveness and efficiency; and subjectively to its ease of use and satisfaction.

Acknowledgments. This research was supported by the SENESCYT - Ecuador (scholarship program 2011).

References

1. Ali, N., Nellipaiappan, R., Chandran, R., Babar, M.A.: Model driven support for the Service Oriented Architecture modeling language. In: Proceedings of the 2nd International Workshop on Principles of Engineering Service-Oriented Systems - PESOS 2010, September 2009, p. 8. ACM Press, New York (2010). http://portal. acm.org/citation.cfm?doid=1808885.1808888

2. Babar, M.A., Chauhan, M.A.: A tale of migration to cloud computing for sharing experiences and observations. In: Proceedings of the 2nd International Workshop on Software Engineering for Cloud Computing, pp. 50–56. ACM (2011)

3. Barry, D.K.: Service-Oriented Architecture (SOA) Definition. http://www. service-architecture.com/articles/web-services/service-oriented_architecture_soa_ definition.html

4. Beydeda, S., Book, M., Gruhn, V.: Model-Driven Software Development, vol. 1, 464 pages. Springer. Heidelberg (2005). https://doi.org/10.1007/3-540-28554-7_9

5. Botto, M., González-Huerta, J., Insfran, E.: Are model-driven techniques used as a means to migrate SOA applications to cloud computing? In: WEBIST (1), pp. 208–213 (2014). https://doi.org/10.5220/0004963802080213

6. Botto-Tobar, M., Insfrán, E.: Soa2cloud: Un marco de trabajo para la migración de aplicaciones soa a cloud siguiendo una aproximación dirigida por modelos (2014)

7. Botto-Tobar, M., Ramirez-Anormaliza, R., Cevallos-Torres, L.J., Cevallos-Ayon, E.: Migrating SOA applications to cloud: a systematic mapping study. In: Valencia-García, R., Lagos-Ortiz, K., Alcaraz-Mármol, G., Del Cioppo, J., Vera-Lucio, N., Bucaram-Leverone, M. (eds.) CITI 2017. CCIS, vol. 749, pp. 3–16. Springer, Cham (2017). https://doi.org/10.1007/978-3-319-67283-0_1

8. Chappel, D.: Introducing the Windows Azure Platform (2010). http://www. davidchappell.com/writing/white_papers/Introducing_the_Windows_Azure_ Platform,_v1.4--Chappell.pdf

9. Delgado, A., Ruiz, F., García-Rodríguez de Guzmán, I., Piattini, M.: MINERVA: Model drIveN and sErvice oRiented framework for the continuous business process improVement and relAted tools. In: Dan, A., Gittler, F., Toumani, F. (eds.) ICSOC/ServiceWave -2009. LNCS, vol. 6275, pp. 456–466. Springer, Heidelberg (2010). https://doi.org/10.1007/978-3-642-16132-2_43

10. Frey, S., Reich, C., Lüthje, C.: Key performance indicators for cloud computing SLAs. In: EMERGING 2013, The Fifth International Conference on Emerging Network Intelligence (2013). http://www.thinkmind.org/index.php?view=article& articleid=emerging_2013_3_30_40082

11. Guillén, J., Miranda, J., Murillo, J.M., Canal, C.: Developing migratable multi-cloud applications based on mde and adaptation techniques. In: Proceedings of the Second Nordic Symposium on Cloud Computing & Internet Technologies, pp. 30–37. ACM (2013)

12. Hamdaqa, M., Livogiannis, T., Tahvildari, L.: A reference model for developing cloud applications. In: Proceedings of the 1st International Conference on Cloud Computing and Services Science, pp. 98–103 (2011). http://www.scitepress.org/ DigitalLibrary/Link.aspx?doi=10.5220/0003393800980103

13. Jouault, F., Allilaire, F., Bézivin, J., Kurtev, I.: ATL: a model transformation tool. Sci. Comput. Program. **72**(1–2), 31–39 (2008). http://linkinghub.elsevier. com/retrieve/pii/S0167642308000439

14. Microsoft: WebRole   Schema.   http://msdn.microsoft.com/en-us/library/ windowsazure/gg557553.aspx

15. Microsoft: Windows Azure Service Configuration Schema (.cscfg File). http:// msdn.microsoft.com/en-us/library/windowsazure/ee758710.aspx

16. Microsoft: Windows Azure Service Definition Schema (.csdef File). http://msdn. microsoft.com/en-us/library/windowsazure/ee758711.aspx

17. Microsoft: WorkerRole   Schema.   http://msdn.microsoft.com/en-us/library/ windowsazure/gg557552.aspx

18. Mohagheghi, P., Sæther, T.: Software engineering challenges for migration to the service cloud paradigm: ongoing work in the remics project. In: 2011 IEEE World Congress on Services (SERVICES), pp. 507–514. IEEE (2011)

19. OMG: Software & Systems Process Engineering Meta-Model Specification, April 2008

20. OMG: Service oriented architecture Modeling Language (SoaML) Specification. Object Management Group (OMG), May 2012

21. Patel, P., Ranabahu, A.H., Sheth, A.P.: Service level agreement in cloud computing (2009)

22. Schmidt, D.C.: Guest editor's introduction: Model-driven engineering. Computer **39**(2), 25–31 (2006). https://doi.org/10.1109/MC.2006.58

23. SPIRENT: The Ins and Outs of Cloud Computing (2010). http://www.spirent. com/White-Papers/Broadband/PAB/Cloud_Computing_WhitePaper.aspx

24. The Eclipse Foundation: Eclipse Open Source Community. http://www.eclipse. org/

25. Tran, V., Keung, J., Liu, A., Fekete, A.: Application migration to cloud: a taxonomy of critical factors. In: Proceedings of the 2nd International Workshop on Software Engineering for Cloud Computing, pp. 22–28. ACM (2011)

Delimitation and Codification of Hydrographic Units Through the Use of Geographic Information Systems

Freddy Jumbo[(✉)] (iD), Mariuxi Zea (iD), Nancy Loja (iD), Rodrigo Morocho (iD),
Joffre Cartuche (iD), and Edison Loján (iD)

Universidad Técnica de Machala, Km. 5 ½ via Machala Pasaje, Machala, Ecuador
{fjumbo,mzea,nmloja,rmorocho,jcartuche,elojan}@utmachala.edu.ec

Abstract. Geographic Information Systems (GIS) provide new methods and tools for automatic data processing, which are used by organizations to improve process management. The basin is considered as the basic unit of territorial planification, for which the hydrographic units delimitation is the key for water resources administration. The lack of detail in basins geographical information has to be solved, in order to optimize the decision-making process and related tasks. Using the Pfafstetter methodology, the Jubones river basin was subdivided into level 6. For this purpose, we used the level 5 hydrographic units, the SRTM spatial resolution data model of 30 m and GIS software. At level 5, 13943, 13944, 13945, 13947, 13948 and 13949 hydrographic units were identified. In accordance with the selected method guidelines, 9 drainage areas were coded for each hydrographic level 5 unit. 54 hydrographic units at level 6, of which 30 correspond to inter-basins and 24 to basins, thus updating the geographical information. The total subdivided area was 312,223.06 ha. It is important to replicate the research in other basins and publish the results using the Spatial Data Infrastructure (SDI) platforms.

Keywords: Watersheds · Pfafstetter methodology
Geographic information systems (GIS)

1 Introduction

Advances in computer technology contribute with new tools and methods, allowing the strengthening of the different areas of science. Geographic Information systems (GIS) is the field in which various branches of knowledge interact and are responsible for managing specialized information, within which is related to river basins, which historically were delineated through the maps interpretation or topographic charts [1].

In accordance with [2] river basin is a catchment area in which drains the river and its tributaries. It is formed in the highest relief regions delimited by the river basin surface. According to FAO [3], in the catchment area are the natural resources, communities and their different economic activities.

In 1989, the Pfafstetter method emerged as an international standard for hydrographic units' delimitation and codification [4]. In compliance with [5] the method is hierarchical and based on the field topology. which allows to improve the management

© Springer International Publishing AG 2018
M. Botto-Tobar et al. (Eds.): CITT 2017, CCIS 798, pp. 185–198, 2018.
https://doi.org/10.1007/978-3-319-72727-1_14

of river basins and a more control action on those areas. Based on the theoretical foundations, three types of hydrographic units are identified: Basin, inter basin and internal basin [6]. [21] emphasizes that the system is hierarchical and the units are delimited from the junctions of the rivers or from the point of convergence of a drainage system in the ocean.

The GIS implementation for information structuring, storage and retrieval in hydrographical databases was developed by [7]. According to [8], the geo-processing tools use is of great importance for hydrographic water basins delimitation, allowing to optimize time and resources. The delimitation through computational tools requires Digital Elevation Model (DEM) database, which stores the terrain height values.

As claimed by [9] mathematical algorithms and altimetric data can be automatically modeled using a computer, allowing the study and analysis of the Earth's surface in a three-dimensional shape. As stated above, the concept is supported by [10], who placed emphasis on water basin extraction's automated growth using the DEM. Actually, one of the main data models is the Shuttle Radar Topography Mission (SRTM), which in the criteria of [11], was a NASA-led project from which the TOPODATA project was developed through the application of geo-statistical processes.

Several studies have been carried out using GIS, the Pfafstetter methodology and the DEM, among which stand out: [1, 12–15]. In the Jubones demarcation, the main basin is the so-called Jubones River basin, where the geographical information of the sub-basin is important for the activities fulfillment demanded by the integral management of water resources, requiring the sub-basin updated in necessary detail levels, allowing project administration, formulation and planning as well as the correct decision-making and equitable distribution of water resources.

To fulfil the investigation purpose, the following objective was raised: Delimit the Jubones River basin hydrographic units by using GIS software, which allows the correct decision-making and effective water resources management. The following research questions were formulated: what are the methods used for river basins delimitation? What are the hydrographic units to be delimited in the Jubones river basin? What encoding corresponds to each of the delimited hydrographic units?

2   Methodology

2.1   Geographic Location

The Jubones river basin forms part of Jubones hydrographic demarcation. It is located geographically in the southern area of Ecuadorian territory, which can be seen in Fig. 1.

With an area of 431,860.86 ha, the basin covers part of the territory of 3 provinces: El Oro with the cantons Machala, El Guabo, Pasaje, Chilla and Zaruma; Loja with the canton Saraguro; Azuay with Nabón, Girón, San Fernando, Santa Isabel, Oña and Pucará. The metric coordinates WGS84 zone 17 south. The study basin location are detailed in Table 1.

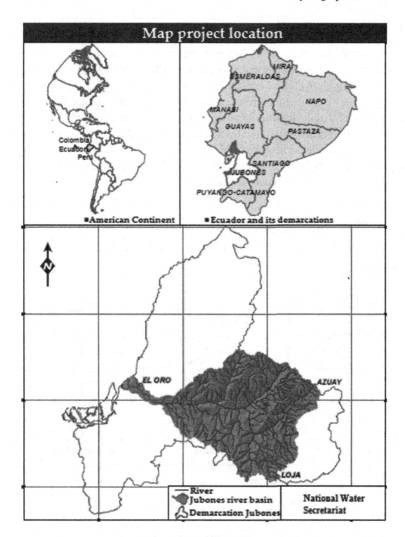

Fig. 1. Project location.

Table 1. Coordinates of the Jubones river basin.

Orientation	X	Y
NORTE	682,099	9,664,777
SUR	686,645	9,588,782
ESTE	730,820	9,638,668
OESTE	612,048	9,643,330

2.2 Base Cartography

The National Water Secretariat officialized through ministerial resolution no. 2011-245, the use of information of basins up to level 5, delimited with the Pfaf-stetter methodology [16]. The basin delineation process had as its main input the HydroSHEDS, which contains the direction and accumulation of water flow.

The cartography of the hydrographic units in level 5, the hydrographic demarcations, and the HydroSHEDS are part of the information bank of the demarcation. Other available maps are those released by the IGM at a scale of 1: 50,000, among which are the subjects of simple rivers, double rivers, limits and reference points, the which are related to the research and its development process.

2.3 Diagram of the Methodology

The methodology to be applied for the delimitation of hydrographic units is shown in the diagram in Fig. 2.

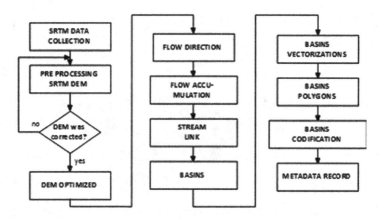

Fig. 2. Diagram of the methodology.

The following describes each of the stages of the methodology:

SRTM Data Collection (NASA): The SRTM data with 30 m resolution were downloaded from the USGS EarthExplorer page (http://earthexplorer.usgs.gov/). The data download viewer graphical interface can be seen Fig. 3.

Fig. 3. SRTM data download page.

In the discharge viewer, the coordinates of the basin to be delimited were defined, which allowed only the required area to be discharged. The geographic coordinates established, are structured in Table 2.

Table 2. Coordinates study area in viewer download.

Order	Latitude	Longitude
1	03°00'00"S	80°00'00"O
2	03°00'00"S	78°54'55"O
3	03°45'00"S	78°54'55"O
4	03°45'00"S	80°00'00"O

Once specifying the coordinates in the viewer, the next step was to select the data type to be downloaded, which was achieved through the Data Sets > Digital Elvation > SRTM > SRTM 1 Arc-Second Global tab. The results displayed in the Results tab, for your download in three formats: BIL, DTED or GeoTIFF.

Pre-processing of DEM: The DEM Pre-processing: The pre-processing phase is determined by two specific tasks which are: Creation of the SRTM image mosaic and the exclusion of incorrect values present in the DEM. With the mosaic images are integrated into a single file, covering the total area of the study basin, the utility in ArcGIS with which this purpose was achieved is: Data Management Tools > Raster > Raster Dataset > Mosaic to New Raster.

According to [17], the topography of the terrain area significantly influences the quality of the elevation model data. That is to say errors on steep or mountainous terrain the incidence can be greater, reason why it is essential to correct the imperfections that contains the DEM. [18] mention that the errors in the DEM derived from SRTM data are called sinks.

Flow direction: This step consists to create a raster map of the flow directions. [8] argue that the direction of flow is determined from the hydrographic relationships between the different points of the basin perimeter and considering the terrain characteristics. According to [19], the flow direction map is calculated based on neighboring cells and indicates the steepest drop direction as a function of slope inclination.

The flow direction in ArcGIS is obtained through the Spatial Analyst > Hydrology > Flow Direction.

Accumulation flow: The flow accumulation map is obtained from the flow direction map. According to [20] flow accumulation refers to the hydrographic network, which provides a new matrix with the specific water accumulation values of each pixel. Flow accumulation is based on the number of cells flowing into each cell, where the resulting value of a pixel are is all the pixels that upstream drain it. The accumulation of flow in ArcGIS is obtained through the Spatial Analyst tool > Hydrology > Flow Accumulation [8].

Calculation of threshold and reclassification of accumulation: According to the [21] criterion, the threshold calculation "[…] is an iterative trial and error procedure; Being the easiest way to determine the appropriate accumulation threshold to obtain the necessary tributaries". The determination of the accumulation threshold, allows to identify the main river course and the four contributors, considering that it is enough that a pixel appears, to be considered as a tributary. The calculation of the threshold is based on the water accumulation. In ArcGIS it is done from the Layer Properties > Symbology > Classified > Classify window.

Calculation of threshold and reclassification of accumulation: According to the [21] criterion, the threshold calculation "[…] is an iterative trial and error procedure; Being the easiest way to determine the appropriate accumulation threshold to obtain the necessary tributaries". The determination of the accumulation threshold, allows to identify the main river course and the four contributors, considering that it is enough that a pixel appears, to be considered as a tributary. The calculation of the threshold is based on the water accumulation. In ArcGIS, task it is done from the Layer Properties > Symbology > Classified > Classify window.

Drainage network: This stage consists in obtaining the categorized drainage network, corresponding to category 1 of the flow accumulation reclassification performed in the previous phase. According to [23], the process related to the generation of the drainage network is essential for the hydrographic units' determination. [22] state that the Stream Link tool, allows assigning the values to each drainage network section. In ArcGIS the procedure is performed from Spatial Analyst Tools > Hydrology > Stream Link.

Generation of basin: [23] mention that the automatic generation of a basin requires the flow direction and the watercourses network obtained from the map of the flow accumulation. According to the criterion of [8], the automatic generation of watersheds in ArcGIS, is obtained through the Spatial > Analyst Tools > Hydrology > resource. As mentioned in the previous paragraph, the flow address files and the drainage network are required for the process.

Basins Vectorization: The basins vectorization is the process of convertion of raster to vector format (points, lines or polygons), with which the polygons final theme of the hydrographic units delimited in shapefile format is obtained. According to [21] the conversion to vector delimited basins format, is a simple technique that is fulfilled applying the following step:

- *Conversion from raster to polygon:* The raster file of basins generation is the input required to perform the conversion to polygon. This procedure in ArcGIS is done with the conversion Tools > From raster > Raster to polygon tool.

Basins codification: Coding is a hierarchical procedure, which consists in assigning unique codes to the basins. It is important that prior to establishing the coding, the main river of each hydrographic unit is identified, to later codify the basins from the river mouth to the origin according to Pfafstetter criterion.

[24] mention that the Pfafstetter codification is based on two principles: The hierarchization of the hydrographic units according to the drainage area and the hydrographic network preliminary recognition of the four main basins, to which the numbers are assigned pairs 2, 4, 6 and 8, while the inter-basins correspond to the odd numbers 1, 3, 5, 7 and 9. If there are internal basins are coded with the number 0.

The allocation of codes in inter-basins and basins, resulting from vectorization should be done clockwise [25].

Metadata record: Metadata record: According to [26], the term metadata refers to the data structured set, which describe other data and its internal structure, whose objective is that the information they represent is understood, shared and exploited effectively by all types of Users who require their use. [27] argue that metadata are becoming a familiar tool for those working with spatial information, so that in order to define a structure that serves to describe the geographic data, exists the ISO 19115 international standard - Geographic Information Metadata [28].

Standard 19115 was used in the definition of the CONAGE PEM document [29]. In the metadata registry, the main sections describing the hydrographic units vector file in level 6 were: Metadata information, identification, restrictions, data quality, maintenance, spatial representation, reference system, content, presentation catalog, distribution, Metadata extension and application model.

3   Results and Discussion

The basin 13943, 13944, 13945, 13947, 13948 and 13949 were divided into 9 hydrographic units in level 6, of which 4 correspond to basin and 5 to inter-basin. The codes assigned to the new delimited units, can be observed in detail in Table 3, 4, 5, 6, 7 and 8.

Table 3. Watershed results 13943.

Level	Name	Type	Area ha.
139431	Hydrographic unit 139431	Inter basin	3,730.32
139432	Hydrographic unit 139432	Basin	3,625.78
139433	Hydrographic unit 139433	Inter basin	1,901.65
139434	Hydrographic unit 139434	Basin	3,467.67
139435	Hydrographic unit 139435	Inter basin	1,808.85
139436	Hydrographic unit 139436	Basin	13,751.07
139437	Hydrographic unit 139437	Inter basin	5,654.89
139438	Hydrographic unit 139438	Basin	18,196.89
139439	Hydrographic unit 139439	Inter basin	9,532.38

The total area of the hydrographic unit 13943 is: 61,669.50 ha.

Table 4. Watershed results 13944.

Level	Name	Type	Area ha.
139441	Hydrographic unit 139441	Inter basin	7,751.22
139442	Hydrographic unit 139442	Basin	5,600.94
139443	Hydrographic unit 139443	Inter basin	2,667.08
139444	Hydrographic unit 139444	Basin	2,368.76
139445	Hydrographic unit 139445	Inter basin	419.71
139446	Hydrographic unit 139446	Basin	2,806.34
139447	Hydrographic unit 139447	Inter basin	2,527.32
139448	Hydrographic unit 139448	Basin	3,793.48
139449	Hydrographic unit 139449	Inter basin	8,213.74

The total area of the hydrographic unit 13944 is: 36,148.59 ha.

Table 5. Watershed results 13945.

Level	Name	Type	Area ha.
139451	Hydrographic unit 139451	Inter basin	1,057.56
139452	Hydrographic unit 139452	Basin	12,623.61
139453	Hydrographic unit 139453	Inter basin	1,934.66
139454	Hydrographic unit 139454	Basin	2,761.88
139455	Hydrographic unit 139455	Inter basin	3,313.56
139456	Hydrographic unit 139456	Basin	10,781.11
139457	Hydrographic unit 139457	Inter basin	13.04
139458	Hydrographic unit 139458	Basin	25,287.38
139459	Hydrographic unit 139459	Inter basin	4,026.49

The total area of the hydrographic unit 13945 is: 61,799.29 ha.

Table 6. Watershed results 13947.

Level	Name	Type	Area ha.
139471	Hydrographic unit 139471	Inter basin	1,349.56
139472	Hydrographic unit 139472	Basin	1,305.92
139473	Hydrographic unit 139473	Inter basin	385.92
139474	Hydrographic unit 139474	Basin	4,858.65
139475	Hydrographic unit 139475	Inter basin	1,776.93
139476	Hydrographic unit 139476	Basin	928.77
139477	Hydrographic unit 139477	Inter basin	3,477.00
139478	Hydrographic unit 139478	Basin	1,815.55
139479	Hydrographic unit 139479	Inter basin	349.58

The total area of the hydrographic unit 13947 is: 16,247.88 ha.

Table 7. Watershed results 13948.

Level	Name	Type	Area ha.
139481	Hydrographic unit 139481	Inter basin	814.97
139482	Hydrographic unit 139482	Basin	26,815.92
139483	Hydrographic unit 139483	Inter basin	2,105.80
139484	Hydrographic unit 139484	Basin	3,483.52
139485	Hydrographic unit 139485	Inter basin	5,011.33
139486	Hydrographic unit 139486	Basin	3,406.86
139487	Hydrographic unit 139487	Inter basin	389.26
139488	Hydrographic unit 139488	Basin	5,821.13
139489	Hydrographic unit 139489	Inter basin	6,425.00

The total area of the hydrographic unit 13948 is: 54,273.79 ha.

Table 8. Watershed results 13949.

Level	Name	Type	Area ha.
139491	Hydrographic unit 139491	Inter basin	10,027.44
139492	Hydrographic unit 139492	Basin	12,319.18
139493	Hydrographic unit 139493	Inter basin	3,118.92
139494	Hydrographic unit 139494	Basin	19,808.00
139495	Hydrographic unit 139495	Inter basin	624.46
139496	Hydrographic unit 139496	Basin	3,404.94
139497	Hydrographic unit 139497	Inter basin	1,343.36
139498	Hydrographic unit 139498	Basin	9,739.23
139499	Hydrographic unit 139499	Inter basin	21,698.48

The total area of the hydrographic unit 13949 is: 82,084.01 ha.

The next map graphically represents the sequence coding established for each delimited hydrographic unit, with based on the detailed in the Tables 3, 4, 5, 6, 7 and 8 (Fig. 4).

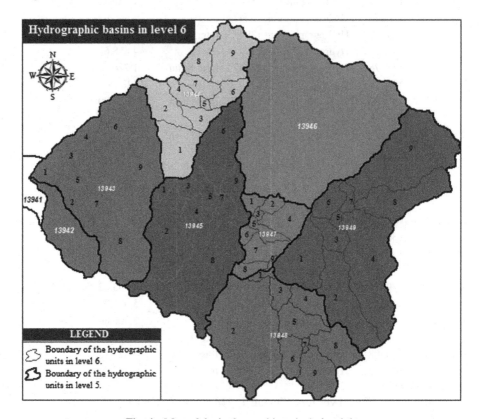

Fig. 4. Map of the hydrographic units in level 6.

With the codification, it is possible to identify the level to which the hydrographic unit corresponds checking the digits number of code, with the which it is fulfilled the fundamental principle of the methodology: The assignment of unique codes to each hydrographic unit. However, the designation of the name of the basin is essential, since its allows to the users of the environment it is become familiar with it quickly.

The hydrographic units coded with the Pfafstetter methodology, allow the continuation of the standard for delimitation established for the South American region [30], as well as at the level of hydrographic divisions of the Water Secretariat. The CNRH proposal [31] defined river basin codes in terms of hydrographic systems, resulting the coding of basins and sub-basins only for Ecuador, while hydrographic units coded at level 6 can be recognized at the level Local and in the countries where the use of the method has been officialized.

In the case of the hydrographic units 13941 and 13946, were not subdivided in this research.

4   Conclusions

Due to its clearly defined methodological approach, the Pfafstetter method was selected and, based on the revision of the theoretical foundations, the stages of the methodology on which the delimitation and codification of the hydrographic units in level 6 of the basin River Jubones. The phases identified were: SRTM data collection, pre-processing of the DEM, flow direction, flow accumulation, threshold calculation and reclassification of the accumulation, drainage network, watershed generation, vectorization, coding and registration of the metadata.

The results of each phase were successful, being elemental the use of the DEM of the SRTM project, which provides significant advantages, compared to the generation of the elevation model, from the information of level contours of the IGM; Also affected by topology errors in its structure. However, in the selected DEM, source errors or "NoData" values were debugged, applying near neighbor interpolation methods. For this purpose we used focused statistics applied to a 10 cell radius, which can change depending on the space or number of pixels that need to be corrected.

The delimited hydrographic units of level 5 were: 13943, 13944, 13945, 13947, 13948 and 13949, the terrain features being an important factor in obtaining the expected results. On the other hand, the 13941 unit, considered to be the mouth of the basin, due to the topographical characteristics of the area, was not defined, since it corresponds to the lower zone of the province of El Oro. Each basin of level 5 delimited resulted in 9 hydrographic units in Level 6, the same ones that are analogous to the denomination of micro-basins.

In total 54 hydrographic units were obtained in level 6, of which 24 correspond to basins and 30 to inter-basins. The coding of the delimited units was established according to the level 5 code. The Pfafstetter code assigned to each hydrographic unit allows the current delimitation level to be determined, by simply counting the number of digits. The code determines the interrelation between the drainage areas of the same level, and allows to establish the spatial relationships with the lower level units.

The subdivision area of the Jubones river basin in level 5 is approximately 312,223.06 ha, corresponding to the inter-basins level 6 an area of 113,450.48 ha, equivalent to 36%, while level 6 basin units comprise A territorial extension of 198,772.58 ha, equivalent to 64%. The delimitation of inter-basins requires particular attention in the calculation of the threshold to obtain the drainage network, due to its characteristics in these units there is no single common drainage point.

The Jubones river basin by its geographical location, territorial extension and caudal, is considered the most important of the demarcation. In this sense the subdivision in level 6, favors the territorial management of the catchment area. The proposed hypothesis is accepted and the results provide drainage areas in greater detail, which contributes to the optimization of the field tasks carried out by the technical staff of the demarcation, facilitating familiarization with the environment, the object of analysis and the Identification of watercourses.

With the hydrographic units in level 6, the geographic information of the basins of the demarcation is updated, allowing the planning and execution of projects oriented to equitably distribute the water resources. Essentially the drainage units obtained strengthen the emblematic project of the demarcation called Participative Inventory of Water Resources (IPRH), executed in the Jubones river basin. The data of the catchment area and code are fundamental for the updating of the bank of the IPRH and for the operative operation of the system of authorizations of use and exploitation of water.

The basins and inter-basins of level 6, allow to identify the communities located in each catchment area, which allows a direct approach with the users, favoring their participation in the training workshops oriented to the care of the flow and water sources. These activities benefit the development of the social water management plan.

The results of this research are related to the National Water Resources Plan, which provides for a diagnosis that allows the conservation of the water resource in the short, medium and long term, considering the micro basin as the minimum unit of analysis. Specifically, the geographical information of hydrographic units at level 6, benefits the elaboration of the plan for the Jubones river basin.

The use of GIS techniques was fundamental, since they allowed to reduce the time required for the generation of the cartography of watersheds. The contribution of this research to cognitive strengthening is related to the management of NASA SRTM data and to the hydrological modeling tools used under the principles of the Pfafstetter methodology. In the shapefile file of the delimited drainage areas, the metadata was registered according to the regulations used by the Water Secretariat, in order to guarantee the access and location of spatial information generated.

5   Recommendations

It is recommended that the demarcation of Jubones officialize and socialize the new level delimited with the GAD, Commonwealth Consortium of the Jubones river basin, other Central Government institutions and users, emphasizing the importance of familiarization and understanding of the code assigned to each unit Area. From its official formalization, it is feasible to plan and execute the delimitation of level 7 of the basin using the Pfafstetter methodology, in order to achieve the permanent improvement of processes related to water resources, as well as to continue the process of delimitation of the level 6 for the other watersheds that make up the demarcation, considering as main input the DEM with 30 m resolution of NASA.

It is also important that the process be replicated for the rest of Ecuador's watersheds, in order to strengthen the National Water Resources Plan of the Water Secretariat, which directly benefits the hydrographic basins. In the new information generated, thematic attributes must be created according to the structure of fields specified in the baseline delimitation levels, as well as to record the metadata of the vector files resulting from the process of delimitation of hydrographic units, considering the standard or ISO standard 19115.

The main institutional management processes of the Jubones demarcation are those related to the water resource of the river basin, where the codification of hydrographic units is fundamental to establish relationships between water sources and drainage areas. New Pfafstetter coding, as well as updating the water use database with the new level 6 codes if necessary.

Taking as reference the study carried out, plans, actions and projects should be undertaken, focused on the conservation of the natural resources that make up the basin, depending on the competencies of each government body, thereby ensuring sustainable development for the community And improvements in the quality of life. The new applications that can be undertaken from the results of the research are: hydrological modeling, water balances, gauging campaigns and determination of water stress.

References

1. Jumbo, F.A.: Delimitación automática de microcuencas utilizando datos SRTM de la NASA. Enfoque UTE **6**(4), 81–97 (2015)
2. Teodoro, V., Teixeira, D., Costa, D., Fuller, B.: Oconceito de bacia hidrográfica e a importância da caracterização morfométrica para o entendimento da dinâmica ambiental local. UNIARA **20**, 137–156 (2007)
3. FAO: Organización de las Naciones Unidas para la Alimentación y la Agricultura. Por qué invertir en ordenación de las cuencas hidrográficas, Roma, p. 40 (2009)
4. Cabral, N.: Criterios técnicos de delimitación y codificacion de cuencas, caso específico región oriental del Paraguay. Secretaría del Ambiente, 36 (2011)
5. Gomes, J., Barros, R.: A importância das Ottobacias para gestão de recursos hídricos. Anais XV Simpósio Brasileiro de Sensoriamento Remoto (SBSR), pp. 1287–1294. INPE, Curitiva (2011)
6. Crespo, A., Van Damme, P., Zapata, M.: Clasificación de Cuencas de Bolivia según la metodología de Pfafstetter. Revista Boliviana de Ecología Ambiental **22**, 69–75 (2013)
7. Verdin, K.L., Verdin, J.P.: A topological system for delineation and codification of the Earth's river basins. J. Hydrol. **218**(1), 1–12 (1999)
8. Amancio, C., Quintao, A., Freire, T., Alvés, C., Dos Santos, E.: Utilização de técnicas de geoprocessamento aplicada a delimitação de bacias hidrográficas. In: Anais XIII Jornada de Ensino, Pesquisa e Extensão (JEPEX), p. 3. UFRPE, Recife (2013)
9. Pérez, A., Mas, J.: Evaluación de los errores de modelos digitales de elevación obtenidos por cuatro métodos de interpolación. Investigaciones Geográficas **69**, 53–67 (2009)
10. Vincent, L., Soille, P.: Watersheds in digital spaces: an efficient algorithm based on immersion simulations. IEEE Trans. Pattern Anal. Mach. Intell. **13**(6), 583–598 (1991)
11. Souza, A., Cruz, M., Aragao, R., Amorim, J.: Delimitação automática de sub-bacias no bacia do rio Japaratuba/Se a partir de modelos digitais de elevação. In: Anais V GeoNordeste, III Seminário de Geotecnologias, Geotecnologias e Interdisciplinarid (2011)
12. Schröder, D., Omran, A.F., Bastidas, R.R.: Automated geoprocessing workflow for watershed delineation and classification for flash flood assessment. Int. J. Geoinf. **11**(4), 31–38 (2015)
13. Gomes, T., Lobão, J.: Delimitação de sub-bacias a partir do uso de imagem SRTM/NASA: um estudo da Bacia do Rio Jacuípe-BA. In: Anais XIV Simpósio Brasileiro de Sensoriamento Remoto (SBSR), pp. 3841–3848. INPE, Natal (2009)
14. Kraemer, C., Panda, S.: Automating arc hydro for watershed delineation. In: Proceedings of the 2009 Georgia Water Resources Conference, Held at the University of Georgia (2009)
15. Ruiz, R., Torres, H.: Manual de procedimientos de delimitación y codificación de unidades hidrográficas: Caso América del Sur. UICN Sur, Quito (2008)
16. Secretaría del Agua: Resolución 2011-245, Quito (2011)
17. Falorni, G., Teles, V., Vivoni, E., Bras, R., Amaratunga, K.: Analysis and characterization of the vertical accuracy of digital elevation models from the Shuttle Radar Topography Mission. J. Geophys. Res. **110**, F02005 (2005)

18. Mendes, C., Cirilo, J.: Geoprocessamento em recursos hídricos: princípios, integração e aplicação, 2da ed. Editorial ABRH, Porto Alegre (2001)
19. Politano, M., Álvares, D., Spinelli, H., Santos, L., Pereira, M.: Delimitação das bacias hidrográficas e de drenagem natural da cidade de Salvador. RIGS 1(1), 107–129 (2012)
20. Walchholz, C., Bazílio, S., Costa, S., Mercante, E., Vilas, M.: Delimitação automática da microbacia hidrográfica do rio das Lontras, através de dados SRTM. In: Anais XVI Simpósio Brasileiro de Sensoriamento Remoto (SBSR), pp. 5515–5522. INPE, Foz do Iguaçu, Brasil (2013)
21. Rosas, L.: Manual de procedimientos de delimitación y codificación de Unidades Hidrográficas, caso Ecuador, p. 34. UICN SUR, Quito, Ecuador (2009)
22. De Godoy, L., Schuh, M., Pereira, R.: Comparação entre a delimitação manual e automática da bacia do arroio Corupá, RS, Brasil. Revista Eletrônica em Gestão, Educação e Tecnologia Ambiental 8(8), 1777–1784 (2013)
23. UICN Sur, Unión Internacional para la Conservación de la Naturaleza; SGCAN, Secretaría General de la Comunidad Andina de Naciones.: Manual de procedimientos de delimitación y codificación de unidades hidrográficas. Ministerio de Medio Ambiente y Agua. La Paz. p. 37 (2010)
24. Pires, C., Faria, S.: Construção da base Otto-codificada em Minas Gerais: implementação da metodologia desenvolvida por Otto Pfafstetter (1989) para escalas 1:100,000 e 1:50,000. In: Anais XVI Simpósio Brasileiro de Sensoriamento Remoto (SBSR), pp. 2455–2462. INPE, Foz do Iguaçu, Brasil (2013)
25. Pacheco, J., Silva, R.: A importância das Ottobacias para gestão de recursos hídricos. In: Anais XV Simpósio Brasileiro de Sensoriamento Remoto (SBSR), pp. 1287–1294. INPE, Curitiba, Brasil (2011)
26. Callejo, M., Poveda, M.: Metadatos implícitos de la información geográfica: caracterización del coste temporal y de los tipos y tasas de errores en la compilación manual. GeoFocus 9, 317–336 (2009)
27. Maganto, A.S., Iso, J.N., Ballari, D.: Normas sobre Metadatos (ISO 19115, ISO 19115-2, ISO 19139, ISO 15836). Mapping 123, 48–57 (2008)
28. ISO, International Organization for Standardization: ISO 19115 Geographic information - Metadata. Recuperado el 02 de 07 de 2015, de http://www.iso.org/iso/catalogue_detail.htm?csnumber=26020 (2003)
29. CONAGE, Consejo Nacional de Geoinformación: Perfil Ecuatoriano de Metadatos (PEM) según norma ISO 19115:2003 e ISO 19115-2:2009, Quito, Ecuador, p. 72 (2010)
30. UICN, Unión Internacional para la Conservación de la Naturaleza; CAN, Comunidad Andina de Naciones. Informe de delimitación y codificación de unidades hidrográficas de Sudamérica - nivel 3 a escala 1:1000,000, Lima, Perú, p. 61 (2008)
31. CNRH; Consejo Nacional de Recursos Hídricos. Memoria técnica: División hidrográfica del Ecuador, propuesta del CNRH y el grupo interinstitucional para oficializar en el Ministerio de Relaciones Exteriores, Quito, Ecuador, p. 29 (2002)

A Diagnosis of Threat Vulnerability and Risk as It Relates to the Use of Social Media Sites When Utilized by Adolescent Students Enrolled at the Urban Center of Canton Cañar

Cristhian Flores[1]([✉])(iD), Cristina Flores[1](iD), Tito Guasco[1](iD),
and Joffre León-Acurio[2](iD)

[1] Universidad Católica de Cuenca, Antonio Ávila Clavijo, Cañar, Ecuador
{chfloresu,cmflores,tsguascog}@ucacue.edu.ec
[2] Universidad Técnica de Babahoyo, Babahoyo, Ecuador
jvleon@utb.edu.ec
http://www.ucacue.edu.ec
http://www.utb.edu.ec/

Abstract. The present article is the result of a research project executed by the Catholic University of Cuenca of Cañar Computer Engineering program: "Proposed Controls For Minimizing The Risks Arising From The Internet And Social Networks On High School Students In The Urban Center of Canton Cañar". A Diagnosis of the internet and social networks use was performed as a means to determine digital vulnerabilities. Through a theoretical study it was determined which threats are most commonly inherent in utilizing the internet and social networks. Surveys were applied to 40% of enrolled students. Given surveys then indicated the common uses of the internet, social networks, and potential vulnerabilities that could be exploited by malicious people. Results determined that threats with higher risks are related to violations of privacy, which are visible to behavioral tendencies in the adolescents placing them in vulnerable situations susceptible to privacy violations.

Keywords: Informatic risk · Digital vulnerabilities · Threats
Social network · Information security

1 Introduction

In the last 10 years the number of Internet users have grown exponentially, as well the improvements that ease access to it. In certain ways, thanks to the improvement of the mobile networks worldwide, of the 7.476 billion [11] inhabitants there are now 3.773 billion [11] Internet users. In addition there are 8.047 billion [11] mobile subscriptions, 2.549 are active mobile social users. This large amount of mobile connections has created the need for new connection protocols such as IP v6, and at the same time has allowed certain mobile applications and web pages to grow in number of users; largely because of the ease of access

© Springer International Publishing AG 2018
M. Botto-Tobar et al. (Eds.): CITT 2017, CCIS 798, pp. 199–214, 2018.
https://doi.org/10.1007/978-3-319-72727-1_15

provided by the mobile devices. Such is the case of social networks as: Facebook 1.871 million [11], YouTube 1000 millions [11]. At the regional level, the trend does not change since 1.006 billion [11] inhabitants are in the Americas. Of the 718 million [11] Internet users, 1.069 billion [11] Mobile subscriptions, and the most commonly used websites, social networks are Facebook and YouTube.

In Ecuador for 16.51 millions inhabitants there are 13.47 millions [11] internet users while there are 14.36 millions [11] mobile subscriptions. In terms of social net-works and websites the most used is Facebook with 10 million users [11].

In the Canar province the populations is 205,643 [12], approximately 50% of the population have access to internet.

What the data reveals is that there are practically more telephone lines than inhabitants. To some extent, this can be explained by the reduction of costs of mobile voice and data connections, and the improvement of the networks by the providers, as well as the increasing demand of Users to be permanently connected to the internet.

The ease of access to the Internet and therefore its services, especially social networks, which create virtual worlds in which a person can interact with different people around the world, have also created new vulnerabilities and risks derived from its use. In some cases the users will face these vulnerabilities and risks without knowledge. The purpose of this research is to make a diagnosis about trends of the use of the internet, as well as the computer vulnerabilities presented to secondary school students in the urban center of Cañar, Cañar province, Ecuador.

Based on the results obtained from surveys applied to a statistically obtained sample, the writers of this article intend to determine which are the greatest computer vulnerabilities inherent to the use of the internet and social networks. An attempt will also be made to associate these vulnerabilities with the greater computer risks, many of which are considered computer crimes, such as phishing, grooming, malware, etc.

2   Literature Review

2.1   Computer Risk and Information Security

Information risks are present when two elements influence: threats and vulnerabilities. Risks and vulnerabilities are closely linked, and there can be no consequences without their association with each other. Threats must take advantage of vulnerabilities and can come from anywhere, internal or external sources, as they relate to the organization environment [8].

Vulnerabilities are a weakness within technology or in a processes related to the information, and as such, are considered characteristics of the information systems or the infrastructure that contains it. As an example, a vulnerability allowed an attacker to embed advertisements in the form of pop-ups on the accounts of certain users. If the user accepted the alleged update, it downloaded a program that infected the operating system [9].

A vulnerability is also defined basically, by factors or parameters that must identify it.

1. **Target**
   To define a vulnerability, the first step is to know which app, web page, desktop program, hardware it affects. It could be caused by errors (that belong to the program or hardware in use) or human errors such as: lack of knowledge of the correct use or misguidance by other people that act deceitfully in order to lead the user to make mistakes that can be exploited [10].

2. **Vulnerabilities**
   The starting point is the incorrect use of the target (app, web page, desktop program) that could be, the user is not using the latest update of the OS, antivirus or lack of common sense whilst using technology such as sharing passwords, publishing private information, accepting unknown requests. All of the before mentioned are known Informatics vulnerabilities [10].

3. **Informatic Risk**
   The Informatic Risk is a measure of the magnitude of damages facing a potential threat. The risk is measured assuming each threat that could take advantage of said vulnerability [10].

4. **Risk Analysis**
   The measure of the risk depends on the likelihood of taking advantage of the vulnerability associated to the magnitude of damage it can originate. The impact largely defines the severity of the vulnerability [10].
   One way to represent Risk Analysis graphically is by using a Risk Matrix, that is a two-dimensional representation of Risk, the first dimension depicts the likelihood and the dimension depicts the magnitude of damage it can provoke. The two-dimension values can be qualified as insignificant, low, medium, high, and in turn quantified in values between one and four. The risk is calculated by multiplying the quantitative value of the likelihood by magnitude of the damage, for values between 1 and 6 its considered low risk, for values between eight and nine are considered medium risk, and for values between 12 and 16 considered high risk [10] Fig. 1.

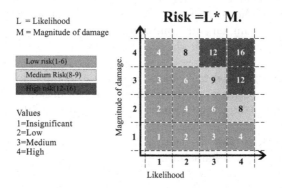

Fig. 1. Risk analysis matrix

2.2 Threats

A threat can be defined as any element or action capable of undermining the security of information or information security. Threats arise from the existence of vulnerabilities. A threat can only exist if there is a vulnerability that can be exploited, regardless of whether or not the security of the information system is compromised.

Various situations, such as the increase and improvement of social engineering techniques, the lack of training and awareness of users in the use of technology, and above all the increasing profitability of attacks, have led to the increase of organized threats in recent years.

2.3 Types of Threats

Unintentional. Where actions or oversights of actions occur that, while not seeking to exploit a vulnerability, endanger information assets and can cause harm (for example, threats related to natural phenomena).

Intentional. If deliberate damage is attempted (for example, theft of information using the technique of trashing, propagation of malicious code and social engineering techniques). The following explains the most common:

- **Malware**
  Also known as badware, malicious code, or malicious software, is a type of software that aims to infiltrate or damage a computer or information system without the consent of the owner [1].
- **Sextortion**
  It is sexual exploitation in which a person is blackmailed with a naked image or video of herself or performing sexual acts, which has generally been previously shared through sexting [2].
  In most cases it is performed by an ex-partner of the victim.
- **Cyber bullying**
  Cyberbullying includes sending (repeated) threats or false accusations by e-mail or mobile phone, posting them on websites, stealing a person's identity or data, or spying on and monitoring the computer or using the internet. Sometimes threats can reach physical spaces [3].
- **Grooming**
  It is a practice of sexual harassment and abuse against children and young people that, in most cases, happens through social networks [4].
  The most frequent modality is that the adult creates a false profile in social networks, pretending to be younger than he is, to achieve fraternization with as many children as possible, seeking later to get encounters or appointments that will lead to sexual harassment or abuse.

- **Children pornography through digital media**
  It is a disturbing and alarming social phenomenon that children and young people are going through in this digital age. They have also described the legal consequences of their actions that can trigger a series of crimes [5].
- **Espionage through electronic media**
  Is the procedure of gathering information, which involves the execution of different tasks that necessarily entails the use of technical resources, in order to obtain a collection of data subject to rights [6].
- **Unauthorized access to computer systems and services**
  The computer phenomenon is an unquestionable and irreversible reality; Definitely, computing has settled amongst us to never leave. This is a consequence of the continuous and progressive development in the field of applied informatics at present to all aspects of daily life; For example, the use of computers in industry, commerce, public administration, banking and financial institutions [7].
- **Cyber Addiction**
  Its the use without boundaries or surveillance of electronic devices or services provided by Internet which causes compulsive behavior that interferes with a normal life style. Interfering in the persons social life and Work environment.
- **Privacy violation**
  It consists of publishing of private affairs, disclose private information, personal data without the consent or permission of the involved party.

3 Methods and Materials

3.1 Design

The subjects of research are high school students from the urban center of Canton Cañar, with 3586 students in attendance. This information was given by the Education District D0302.

The information collection was made using a survey, including a list of variables that were established and measured.

Variables:

- Place and modality of access to Internet
- Daily internet connection time.
- Activities performed using internet
- Favorite Social network
- Behavior on Internet and more specifically on social networks
- Parental control over the activities on Internet specifically on social networks

3.2 Population and Sample

A random sampling was used from a population of 3586 with an Estimation error of 2.5, and statistical confidence of 98.5%. A distribution of 50% was recorded and the sample obtained was 1426 applied surveys.

4   Results

4.1   Analysis of Data

The results are displayed graphically, only the questions relevant to this research will be displayed:

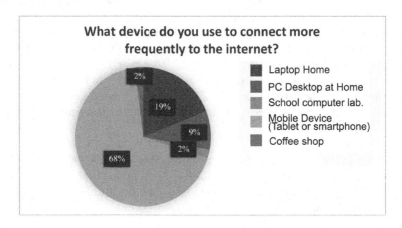

Fig. 2. The graph shows the devices used by students to connect to the internet

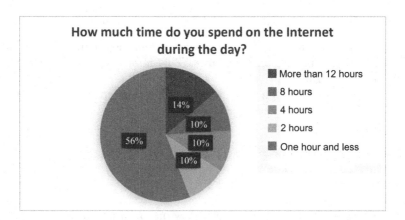

Fig. 3. The graph shows time spent by the students connected to the internet

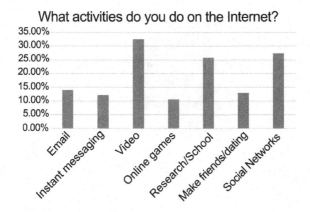

Fig. 4. The graph shows activities in which students use the internet

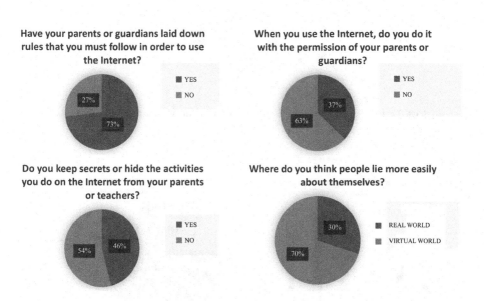

Fig. 5. The graph shows the behavior and the conception that the students have with regards to the internet and its users

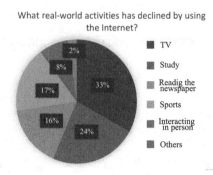

Fig. 6. The graph shows some activities that have declined due to the use of the internet and social networks

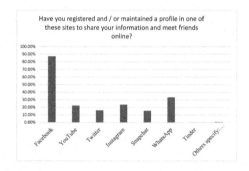

Fig. 7. The graph shows preference of social networks of the students

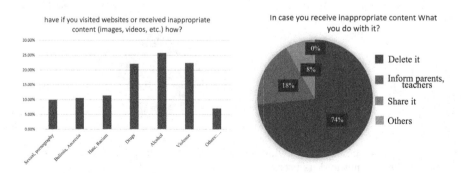

Fig. 8. The graph shows what students do when they receive inappropriate content

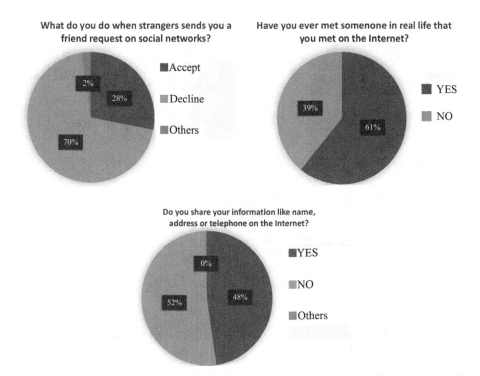

Fig. 9. The graph shows the students behavior when interacting with other users

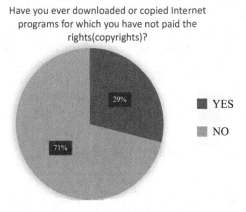

Fig. 10. the graph shows the students awareness of copyright laws

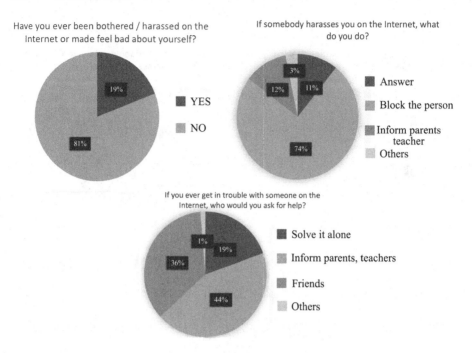

Fig. 11. The graph shows the students attitude towards harassment

5   Discussion

From the indicated results derived from Internet and Social Network usage by the high school students of the urban center of Canton Cañar, the possible inherent vulnerabilities will be deducted.

At the same time, said vulnerabilities were associated to potential threats that those who were surveyed face while using the internet or social networks. Also, it was determined that the risk was based on the likelihood and the magnitude of damage it could provoke as shown in the next table:

After the performing the risks analysis the following diagnosis is obtained, that the threats with greater risk of incidence are: Sextortion, Cyber bullying, Grooming, Children pornography through digital media, Cyber Addiction, Privacy violation.

Table 1. Risk analysis

Th.	Vulnerabilities	L	M	R
Malware	– 34% Is connected more than 4 h Fig. 3	Medium	Low	Low
	– 30% have downloaded or copied programs from the internet Fig. 10			

(continued)

Table 1. (*continued*)

Th.	Vulnerabilities	L	M	R
Sextortion	– 68% uses mobile Internet connection Fig. 2	High	High	High
	– 27% have no parental controls Fig. 5			
	– 63% use the internet without permission Fig. 5			
	– 46% hide their activity on the internet Fig. 5			
	– 30% are nave to the intentions of other users on the internet Fig. 5			
	– Approximately 90% maintain Facebook accounts Fig. 7			
	– 28% accept friend requests from unknown users Fig. 9			
	– 61% have met up with a person they only met on the internet Fig. 9			
	– 48% share personal information Fig. 9			
	– 55% attempt to solve their problems with someone on the internet, while refusing to consult an adult caregiver or authority Fig. 11			
	– 8% shares inappropriate content Fig. 8			
	– at least one out of every ten surveyed have received sexual content or pornography Fig. 8			
Cyber bullying	–68% uses mobile Internet connection Fig. 2	High	High	High
	– 27% have not parental control Fig. 5			
	– 63% use internet without permission Fig. 5			
	– 46% hides their activity on the internet Fig. 5			
	– Approximately 90% maintain Facebook accounts Fig. 7			
	– 28% accept friend request from unknown users Fig. 9			
	– 48% share personal information with users they only met online Fig. 9			
	– 11% are provoked and respond on the internet Fig. 11			
	– 55% attempt to solve their problems with someone on the internet, while refusing to consult an adult caregiver or authority Fig. 11			
	– At least three out of ten surveyed have willingly received violent content Fig. 8			

(*continued*)

Table 1. (*continued*)

Th.	Vulnerabilities	L	M	R
	– At least one out of ten surveyed have received racist content Fig. 8			
	– 8% share inappropriate content Fig. 8			
Grooming	– 68% uses mobile Internet connection Fig. 2	Medium	High	High
	– 27% have not parental control Fig. 5			
	– 63% use internet without permission Fig. 5			
	– 46% hide their activity on the internet Fig. 5			
	– 30% are nave to the intentions of other users on the internet Fig. 5			
	– Approximately 90% maintain Facebook accounts Fig. 7			
	– 28% Accept friend requests from unknown users Fig. 9			
	– 61% have met up with a person they only met on the internet Fig. 9			
	– 48% share personal information Fig. 9			
	– 55% attempt to solve their problems with someone on the internet, while refusing to consult an adult caregiver or authority Fig. 11			
	– 8% share inappropriate content Fig. 8			
Children pornography through digital media	– 68% use mobile Internet connection Fig. 2	Medium	High	High
	– 34% are online more than four hours per day Fig. 3			
	– 27% have not parental control Fig. 5			
	– 63% use internet without permission Fig. 5			
	– 46% hide their activity on the internet Fig. 5			
	– 30% are nave to the intentions of other users on the internet Fig. 5			
	– 28% Accept friend requests from unknown users Fig. 9			
	– 55% attempt to solve their problems with someone on the internet, while refusing to consult an adult caregiver or authority Fig. 11			
	– at least one out of ten surveyed have received Sexual content or Pornography Fig. 8			
	– 8% share inappropriate content Fig. 8			

(*continued*)

Table 1. (*continued*)

Th.	Vulnerabilities	L	M	R
Cyber Addiction	– 68% use mobile Internet connection Fig. 2	Medium	High	High
	– 34% are online more than four hours per day. 3			
	– 98% spend less time in real world activities, than previous generations Fig. 6			
	– 27% have not parental control Fig. 5			
	– 63% use internet without permission Fig. 5			
	– 55% attempt to solve their problems with someone on the internet, while refusing to consult an adult caregiver or authority Fig. 11			
Unauthorized access to computer systems, services	– 34% are online more than four hours per day Fig. 3	Low	Medium	Low
	– 30% are nave towards the intention of the people on the internet Fig. 5			
	– Approximately 90% maintain Facebook accounts Fig. 7			
	– 28% Accept friend requests from unknown users Fig. 9			
	– 48% share personal information Fig. 9			
	– 55% attempt to solve their problems with someone on the internet, while refusing to consult an adult caregiver or authority Fig. 11			
Espionage through electronic media	– 68% use mobile Internet connection Fig. 2	Low	Medium	Low
	– 34% are online more than four hours per day Fig. 3			
	– 30% are nave to the intentions of other users on the internet Fig. 5			
	– Approximately 90% maintain Facebook accounts Fig. 7			
	– 28% Accept friend requests from unknown users Fig. 9			
	– 48% share personal information Fig. 9			
Privacy violation	– 68% use mobile Internet connection Fig. 2	High	High	High
	– 27% have not parental control Fig. 5			

(*continued*)

Table 1. (*continued*)

Th.	Vulnerabilities	L	M	R
	– 63% use internet without permission Fig. 5			
	– 46% Hide their activity on the internet Fig. 5			
	– 30% are nave to the intentions of other users on the internet Fig. 5			
	– approximately 90% maintain Facebook accounts Fig. 7			
	– 28% accept friend requests from unknown users Fig. 9			
	– 61% have met up with a person they only met on the internet. Figure 9			
	– 48% share personal information Fig. 9			
	– 55% attempt to solve their problems with someone on the internet, while refusing to consult an adult caregiver or authority Fig. 11			
	– at least one out of every ten surveyed have received sexual content or pornography Fig. 8			
	– 8% share inappropriate content Fig. 8			

Th = Threat, **L** = Likelihood, **M** = Magnitude of damage, **R** = Risk Fig. 1.

6 Conclusions

Based on the theoretical research, and the calculated results of applied surveys in relation to the high school students of Canton Cañar as well as the analysis of the risk based on the likelihood and the magnitude of the damage, the following conclusions have been reached:

– The threats that pose the biggest risk are the ones related with privacy violations, such as Sextortion, Grooming, Child Pornography through digital media, and including privacy violation. At least one of every ten surveyed have received sexual content or inappropriate content and 8% will share the content. Some activities that seem normal or common make the user more vulnerable to threats. Approximately 30% accept friend requests from unknown people, 61% have met up with a person they only met online, but did not know prior to meeting them online. Forty-eight percent share personal information. The aforementioned data assists us in understanding the severity of the situation as these kind of naive individuals can be used by people with malicious intent, and in some cases predators. The institutions that govern the Education System should become involved and educate the students from an early age with guidelines of how to behave on, and use the internet as well as social networks. The parents should have a working knowledge of how to implement parental controls.

- At least one of every ten surveyed people have been exposed to sexual content or pornography.
- Eight percent share inappropriate content.
- Another threat that must be taken seriously is Cyber Bullying. This includes a variation of common bullying that the students have always faced. In recent years, the schools and states have launched campaigns seeking to eliminate bullying, however, this has proven to be a difficult task, due to adapting to the new technologies. Around 90% of the surveyed maintain Facebook accounts. Twenty-eight percent of those with Facebook accounts accept friend requests from unknown people. Forty-six percent hide their activity on the internet and make the situation worse.
- Cyber Addiction is a threat that most teenagers face, and even some adults are victims to this threat. Thirty-four percent are connected more than four hours, and 98% spend less time in real world activities compared to previous generations. This indicates that measures should be taken to minimize the risk.
- Espionage through electronic media and unauthorized access to computer systems, malware presents minor risk of incidence, but it should not be dismissed because through them more dangerous threats can be achieved.

The current worldwide trend is moving towards mobile connectivity, and this is confirmed by the data in the research, 68% of the surveyed individuals use a mobile internet connection. This presents advantages to internet users such as ease of access to mobile apps or web pages, including Facebook. Ninety percent of the surveyed have an account along with new vulnerabilities. Twenty-seven percent have no parental controls. Sixty-three percent use the internet without permission which places the student in an even more vulnerable position with regard to threats. These include: sextortion, cyber bullying, grooming, child pornography via digital media, cyber addiction, and privacy violation.

For all the cases aforementioned, the best way to solve the problem is to seek adult help from parents, teachers, etc. The situation is only provoked when 55% attempt to solve their problems by denying adult supervision.

References

1. Análisis de caraterísticas estáticas e ficheros ejecutables para la clasificación de malware. In: Guevara, R., Paúl, R. (eds.) 2014 España/Universidad Politécnica de Madrid/2014
2. Aprendemos para el buen trato o para la violencia? Actas del VIII seminario estatal isonomia contra la violencia de género. In: Gil, G.E., Ortí Porcar, M.J., Boix, S. (eds.) Ann 2013 Fundación Isonomía. Universitat Jaume I
3. Ciberacoso y violencia de género en redes sociales: análisis y herramientas de prevención Verdejo Espinosa, María Ángeles 2015 Universidad Internacional de Andalucía
4. Delito de grooming? Necesidad de tipificación en la legislación penal ecuatoriana? In: Quinteros, C., Márcell, W., et al. (eds.) Universidad Andina Simón Bolívar, Sede Ecuador (2015)

5. En TIC Confio. http://www.enticconfio.gov.co/en-que-casos-existe-pornografia-infantil
6. Ciberespionaje y derecho internacional. In: Raggio, M.L., Alfranca, L., del Valle, M. (eds.) Retos del derecho ante las nuevas amenazas, pp. 139–160, Dykinson (2015)
7. Enrique Yupanqui Informatica Forense (2009)
8. Brauch, H.G., Spring, Ú.O., Mesjasz, C., Grin, J., Kameri-Mbote, P., Chourou, B., Dunay, P., Birkmann, J. (eds.): Coping with Global Environmental Change, Disasters and Security: Threats, Challenges, Vulnerabilities and Risks. Springer, Berlin (2011). https://doi.org/10.1007/978-3-642-17776-7
9. Internet Security Threat report, vol. 21. Symantec, California, USA, April 2016
10. Sp 800-30. Risk management guide for information technology systems. In: Stoneburner, G., Goguen, A.Y., Feringa, A. (eds.) Falls Church, Virginia, USA (2002)
11. We are social. https://wearesocial.com/
12. Instituto nacional de estadistica y censos. http://www.ecuadorencifras.gob.ec/institucional/home/

Moving Towards a Methodology Employing Knowledge Discovery in Databases to Assist in Decision Making Regarding Academic Placement and Student Admissions for Universities

María Isabel Uvidia Fassler[1,3(✉)] 🆔, Andrés Santiago Cisneros Barahona[2,3] 🆔,
Diego Fernando Ávila-Pesántez[1,2] 🆔, and Ivonne Elizabeth Rodríguez Flores[2] 🆔

[1] Pontificia Universidad Católica del Ecuador, Sede Ambato, Ambato, Ecuador
[2] Escuela Superior Politécnica de Chimborazo, Riobamba, Ecuador
[3] Universidad Nacional de Chimborazo, Riobamba, Ecuador
muvidia@unach.edu.ec

Abstract. At institutions of higher education, data is generated daily. This massive amount of information is stored in different repositories, and it is increasingly difficult to locate specific data on which decisions can be made because universities are unaware of processes that allow for the extraction of valuable and reliable information. In this paper, we present a methodology that includes the Knowledge Discovery in Databases (KDD) coupled with the HEFESTO version 2.0 methodology for the construction of Data Warehouses and the use of Data Mining (DM) techniques. By implementing the proposed methodology, problems stemming from a lack of information relating to student placement and admissions in the UNAE and New Student Orientation (NSO) departments at the Polytechnic School of Chimborazo (ESPOCH) may be resolved. To accomplish this established goal, a Data Warehouse (DW) was implemented based on the requirements of the UNAE to find reliable information through cleaning and data integration techniques while respecting the Extraction, Transformation, and Load (ETL) process. In addition, several methods of DM were analyzed, culminating in the discovery of the pertinent information to ascertain the classification of students by areas of study, gender analysis, as well as to know the projection of the number of students who will commence university careers offered by ESPOCH in upcoming years.

Keywords: Data warehouse · HEFESTO methodology
Knowledge discovery in databases

1 Introduction

Veridical information must be the cornerstone of all managerial action. Therefore, it is essential to have relevant and timely information in order to make decisions that allow institutions to achieve objectives, implement improvements, and take definitive action. The Knowledge Discovery in Databases (KDD) has the task of distinguishing accurate and sound information from data. However, the quality of these models is closely related

© Springer International Publishing AG 2018
M. Botto-Tobar et al. (Eds.): CITT 2017, CCIS 798, pp. 215–229, 2018.
https://doi.org/10.1007/978-3-319-72727-1_16

to the stored data and depends on factors such as the existence of erroneous data or the large size of the databases [1]. Currently, public and private universities generate a substantial amount of data, which is stored in different repositories and from which few results can be obtained because they are unaware of the process to extract valuable and reliable information [1]. For this reason, the importance of successful data analysis and the extraction of information is clear. Through the application of the KDD process to identify valid, useful, and comprehensible patterns, as well as structures that convert the data into usable information, institutions can make appropriate decisions, organize workflow, and implement relevant actions [2].

The importance of the analysis of information and the precise extraction of knowledge to ensure proper decision-making cannot be overstressed. The real value of data lies in the information that can be extracted from it. Information helps to improve our understanding of phenomena that surround us. Today, advanced analytical methods are a fundamental element for many successful businesses because they proffer an opportunity to increase profits, maximize operational efficiency, reduce costs, and improve customer satisfaction [3]. Consequently, this paper proposes a methodology that uses the main features of KDD and the HEFESTO v.2.0 methodology. It focuses mainly on two processes: Data Warehouse (DW) and Data Mining (DM) applied at UNAE – ESPOCH.

2   Knowledge Discovery in Databases - KDD

KDD is an automated exploratory modeling software utilized in the analysis of large data repositories. Fayyad [4] states: "The discovery of knowledge in databases is the non-trivial process of identifying patterns in data that are valid, novel, potentially useful, and ultimately understandable." Appending this definition, authors Maimon and Rokach [5] define KDD as a valid, novel, useful, and organized identification process that generates recognizable patterns from large and complex data sets that an institution of higher education manages. Additionally, KDD is an iterative and interactive process that can be defined in nine steps.

Figure 1 presents a description of the KDD process. The initial phases, 1, 2, 3 and 4 on the graph, constitute the principal component of the analysis. For the KDD process to be successful, it is necessary to identify the area of business where the process will be implemented. The objective of the analysis (application domain) must be identified through the cleaning, pre-processing, and transformation of data sources. The predictable result of this process is the implementation of a data repository or DW (phases 5, 6, 7 and 8 on the graph). Additionally, it is necessary to analyze and choose DM algorithms and obtain patterns that are then evaluated and applied and produce relevant and timely information in order to make decisions as can be seen in the last step, step 9 of the diagram.

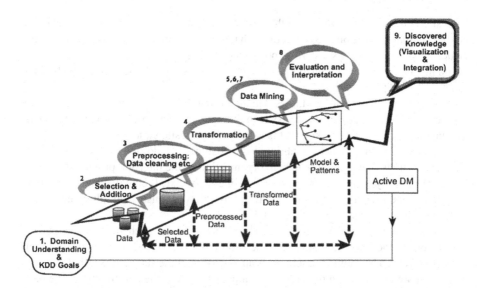

Fig. 1. The process of knowledge discovery in databases (Maimon and Rokach 2010).

Within the phases of analysis, DM is one of the most significant, since it is a working demonstration of the aptitude of these techniques to solve business problems. Also, it contributes to the resolution of scientific quandaries that include handling large amounts of data [6]. In conclusion, it could be said that DM is a process that integrates the data from various sources to later extract an important piece of knowledge, in other words, to identify meaningful, valuable, and useful information, from which the institutions will be able to make a significant decision [7].

The works of Moine et al. [8] propose KDD models or methodologies such as CRISP-DM, SEMMA, and Catalyst respectively. These methodologies present a sequence of actions that must be performed within each phase. CRISP-DM is the methodology most employed but is not considered as the simplest to implement. The SEMMA methodology involves a more technical approach but excludes business analyses, which might be considered the most important component in determining a sample of data to be managed. Finally, Catalyst (P3TQ) fails to explain in detail the tasks to be performed during the process of knowledge discovery. Reflecting on the above analysis and recognizing the generic phases of the KDD process indicates the need for which this research paper was developed.

3   Methodology HEFESTO Version 2.0

HEFESTO version 2.0 by Bernabeu is a GNU (General Public License). The result of executing the HEFESTO is a DataWarehouse. Inmon [9] declared that "a data warehouse is a subject-oriented, integrated, time-variant, nonvolatile collection of data in support of management's decision-making process." Kimball [10], states more succinctly that "a data warehouse is a copy of transaction data specifically structured for query and analysis." Likewise, with regard to the design of a DW, Kimball's vision [11] is based on the fact that it is the business processes that must indicate the way in which it should be designed. It suggests as a starting point recognizing that data already exists in Data-Marts in a more-or-less organized fashion and that these should be used as the basis of future DWs [11].

A DW is composed of fact tables which contain the elements that will be used by business analysts to support the decision-making process and contain quantitative data. The fact table has a primary key that is usually a composite structure that is a subset of the primary keys supplied by additional dimensions. In addition, a DW consists of dimension tables that define the logical organization of the data and provide the means by which to analyze the information in a business context. It contains qualitative data and renders the aspects of specified interest, through which users can filter and manipulate the information stored in the fact table [12].

There are several schemata for DWs. The favored is the star schema that is organized with a central fact table and several dimension tables related to it, connected to their respective keys. The snowflake schema is an extension of the star model with dimension tables that are organized in hierarchies of dimensions. And the constellation schema is composed of a series of interconnected star schemata, each representing summaries of the principal. These tables lie at the center of the model and each is related to its respective dimension tables [12].

The HEFESTO version 2.0 methodology has been developed for the construction of DW. It begins by collecting the information needs of the users and listing the

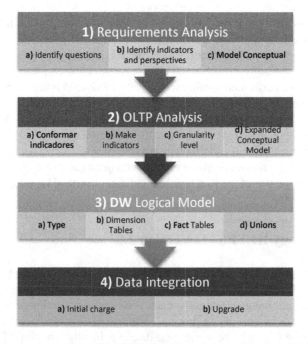

Fig. 2. Steps of the HEFESTO v2.0 Methodology (Bernabeu 2010)

fundamental business questions. Then, it identifies the indicators resulting from the interrogatives and their respective perspectives of analysis, and subsequently, a conceptual model of DW is constructed. Next, On-Line Transaction Processing (OLTP) is analyzed to determine how the indicators must be constructed and to identify which data corresponds with the source data. That allows for the selection of the areas of study from each perspective. Once this is finished, a logical model of the reservoir is constructed, which defines the type of schema to be implemented. Subsequently, the dimension tables and fact tables are created, and then their respective unions are created. Finally, using data cleaning and quality techniques, ETL processes, and other processes, policies and strategies are defined for the DW Initial Load and its corresponding update [12]. In Fig. 2, you can see the steps of the HEFESTO version 2.0 Methodology employed to create a DW.

4   Proposal of Knowledge Discovery in Database - KDD ESPOCH

For this work, the HEFESTO v.2.0 methodology was combined with to the nine phases of the KDD process. The first four phases, learning the application domain, gathering and integrating a set of data on which discovery can be based, cleaning and pre-processing, and data transformation, are included in the DW subprocess and produce a DW constructed by HEFESTO V.2.0 consisting of validated and consistent data. The following 3 steps fall within the DM subprocess and are choosing the appropriate DM task, choosing the DM algorithm, and using the DM algorithm by generating patterns of interest. The penultimate step, evaluation, and interpretation of the discovered knowledge lead seamlessly to the final step, using the knowledge to make decisions appropriate for an academic user at an institution of higher education. Additionally, it is important to note that specific tools must be used to ensure compliance with each phase, thus successfully developing the KDD process, as described in Fig. 3.

The first and one of the most important steps, "learning the application domain," defines all the information requirements to be developed. It entails having a clear knowledge the area of application and of the basis on which decisions will be made while considering the objective and characteristics of each information requirement, source, and data attribute. To do this, we propose a matrix that compiles the necessary data as shown in Table 1, for example, the requirements and description of the information (for example information about the students, teachers, etc.) In the additional columns, the source and the columns source are identified. They describe the information available from the OLTP files. Also, it is important to know that for each information process within the classified business there is a unique matrix.

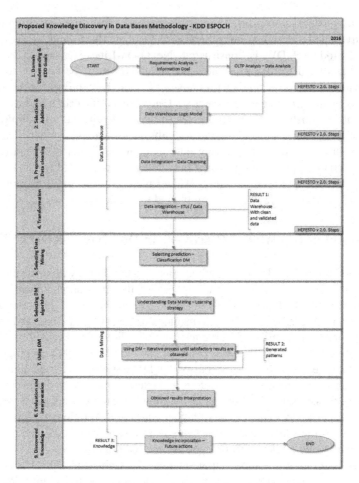

Fig. 3. Phases of the proposed KDD methodology.

Table 1. Matrix learn the domain of the application

PROCESS NAME:					
N°	Request	Description	Characteristic	Source	Attributes

Once the information objectives and available sources of OLTP data have been ascertained, the second phase "gathering and integrating a set of data on which discovery can be based," may begin. All additional required information must be identified and work on the design of the DW can be formulated, derived from a knowledge base. In this step, the Logical Model of DW is defined, starting with its type of schema, its dimensions, fact tables, and how they relate to one another. This compliments the matrix Learning the knowledge domain, and allows for the determination of all the characteristics of the data source: attributes, data types, columns, and main keys of the tables, as seen in Table 2. As a result, work on the design and the conceptual model may continue.

Table 2. DW selection and creation matrix

PROCESS NAME:								
N° Request	Description	Characteristic	Dimensions	Attributes	Keys	Type	Source	Attributes

"Cleaning and pre-processing" is the third phase and aims to ensure the consistency and reliability of the information stored in the DW. Exclusive software for data cleaning is used to collect, validate, and analyze data which may be atypical and missing. It is vital to ensure that the data is correct and reliable since it would not be beneficial for a company to work with data that is not veridical or that produces inconsistent on unreliable information on which decisions will be made.

The fourth and last phase of the DW subprocess is "Data Transformation". A functioning DW appears during this step. The technique of Information Integration, ETL (Extract, Transfer and Load), relocates the information from the sources into a DW and ensures data accuracy and suitable data types (transformation). Because of the preceding phases, the DW will have a design suitable for providing information with acceptable response times and according to information objectives.

The fifth phase, "choosing the appropriate DM task", begins the DM subprocess. Accordingly, it is time to decide on the type of DM algorithm to be applied, such as classification, regression, or grouping algorithms. The chosen algorithm depends principally on the KDD goals and on the previous steps that ensure consistent and reliable information. Within KDD, there are two main objectives in DM, prediction and description. Prediction refers to DM that has been overseen (proven techniques) while descriptive DM includes unsupervised aspects (untested and validated techniques) and visualization of DM [5].

Once the DM target is defined, the sixth phase "choosing the DM algorithm", focuses on selecting the algorithm that is applied to the data to obtain patterns. For this process, the accuracy or percentage of reliability of the algorithm must be compared against the comprehensibility of the graphical results of this procedure. Nonetheless, algorithms should be estimated from the simplest to the most complex, i.e. decision trees, Bayesian networks, linear regressions, minimal sequence optimization, etc. Doing so allows for the introduction of the analyst in the DM world, yet also allowing for the analysis of patterns with greater probability of reliability and with greater knowledge to interpret.

In the seventh phase, "using the DM algorithm", it is necessary to use a DM tool. Some of the most frequently utilized tools are R, WEKA, RapidMiner, Knime, among others. These use algorithms that generate patterns and produce results and can be executed several times, as an iterative process, until achieving satisfactory results that match the requirements. Additionally, the second outcome is obtained and the patterns are evaluated.

In the eighth phase, "evaluation", the obtained standards (rules, reliability, etc.) are considered and interpreted with respect to the defined objectives. In this step, the results of DM are considered, that is, the comprehensibility and utility of the induced model against the discovered knowledge. The information base and the extracted patterns are always kept for further analysis.

In the last phase "Using the discovered knowledge," it is time to appropriate the knowledge for future action. Seeing how the knowledge is used and how its understanding influences decisions and solutions determine the success of the KDD process. Once finished this process, the final product, that is to say, the knowledge generated, is analyzed, it becomes an important resource for the improvement of plans, guides, projects, etc. Its implementation makes productive decision-making possible.

5   Case Study Results

In the case study of the UÑAE department at ESPOCH, all nine phases were utilized. The first four corresponded to the DW subprocess, thus ensuring consistent data stored in an integrated DW repository, "where its primary purpose is dependable storage, its use being paramount in supporting decisions" [13]. The next five steps are part of the DM subprocess where patterns could be observed that generate knowledge and allowed the administrators of this academic unit to make decisions.

In the first phase, "learning the application domain," the data for the scenario where KDD would be implemented was obtained. There were approximately 1270 flat Excel files that represented the source file of the UNAE. It encompassed the information of the students in each of the different careers and were grouped in areas of knowledge as shown below (Table 3):

During this first phase, the data sources of the study scenario were collected. The information was grouped based on student admissions, placement, and levels in each area of study through analyzing related source documents and existing information against other data types, and resulted in the "selection and creation of a set of data on which the discovery could be made." Figure 4 shows graphically the process that resulted in the discovery of matrices that function as support tools for information gathering (Table 4).

Table 3. University careers and areas of knowledge - ESPOCH

ID	Area of knowledge	University careers
CING	Engineering	Mechanical Engineering
		System Engineering
		Electronics Engineering
		Electronics and Telecommunications Engineering
		Automotive Engineering
		Maintenance Engineering
		Industrial Engineering
		Chemistry Engineering
		Chemistry
		Computer Science Statistics
		Environmental Biotechnology Engineering
SRV	Services	Gastronomy
		Ecotourism
		Transportation Engineering
AGR	Agriculture	Forest Engineering
		Agronomic Engineering
		Zootechnical Engineering
		Engineering Animal Science
COM	Commercial	Business Administration
		Finance Engineering
		Marketing Engineering
		Accounting and Auditing Engineering
		Commercial Engineering
SLD	Health	Medicine
		Promotion and Health Care
		Nutrition and Diet
		Biochemistry and Pharmacy
ART	Arts	Graphic Design

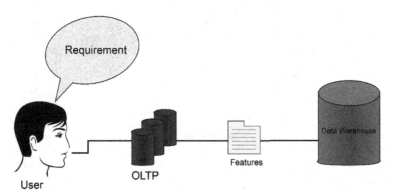

Fig. 4. Steps to generate the UNAE – ESPOCH matrix.

Table 4. Matrix domain understanding and KDD Goals – process: income of students with a quota at ESPOCH

Process: Income of students with a quota at ESPOCH					
N°	Requirement	Description	Feature	Source	Source columns
1	Students information	Students information from SENESCYT	Cod_Estudiante	MTN_ESTUDIANT ES	Campo Incremental
			Nombres		Nombres
			Apellidos		Apellidos
			Id		Identifier
			Etnia		
			Género Discapacidad…		Género Discapacidad
2	Academic location information ESPOCH Areas SENESCYT information	Academic location information ESPOCH – areas SENESCYT	Id_Ubicacion_Aca demica	Ubicación Academica ESPOCH	Campo Incremental
			Sede		Sede
			Cod_Facultad		Cod_Facultad
			Cod_Escuela		Cod_Escuela
			Cod_Carrera		Cod_Carrera
			Area…		Area
3	Academic period information	Academic period information: 2012-2S, 2013-1S, 2013-2S, 2014-1S, 2014-2S, 2015-1S…	Id_Periodo	Periodo	Campo Incremental
			Cod_Periodo		Cod_Periodo
			Año…		Anio
			Fecha de inicio		Fecha_Inicio
			Fecha fin		Fecha_Fin
4	Type of leveling information	Type of leveling information, of careers, general and special	Id_Tipo_Nivelacio n	Tipos Nivelacion	Campo Incremental
			Nivelacion…		Nivelacion
					Fecha_actual
					"I" Insert
5	Geography location information	Ecuadorian geography location information	Id_Ubicacion_Geo grafica	Ubicación Geográfica	Campo Incremental
			Cod_Ubicacion_G eografica…		Cod_Ubicacion_G eografica
6	Status students information	Status students information. exonerated, assigned, enrolled, approved, disapproved	Id_Estado_Estudia nte	Estados Estudiantes	Campo Incremental
			Cod_Estado_Estud iante		Cod_Tipo_Nivelac ion
			Estado		Nivelacion
					Fecha_actual
					"I" Insert
7	Admission and leveling information	Admission and leveling information about their income to ESPOCH	Id_Estudiante		Campo Incremental
			Id_Ubicacion_Aca demica		Id_Docente_Habili tado
			Id_Periodo…		Id_Ubicacion_Aca demica

In addition, in this second phase, the DW Constellation Scheme with nine Dimensions (DIM) and Aggregate Facts and Fact tables were determined by implementing ROLAP and it is a part of a conceptual model (Fig. 5).

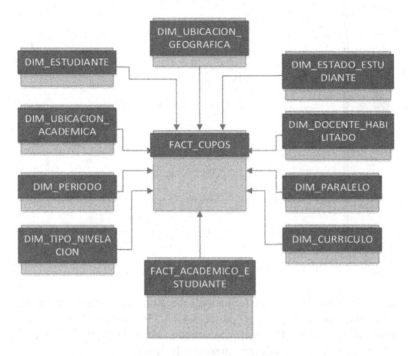

Fig. 5. DW conceptual model.

In the third phase "cleaning and pre-processing", the analysis of the source data was obtained with the Data Cleaner 4.5.3 tool and it was possible to identify inconsistencies in the data and clean them to guarantee quality information would be available when making decisions. Figure 6 shows where the most frequent inconsistencies from the performed analysis were: duplicity of students, id (identifier) with less than ten digits, names and surnames with special characters, and same id with different names and surnames. There was an average level of inconsistencies found in the data analyzed.

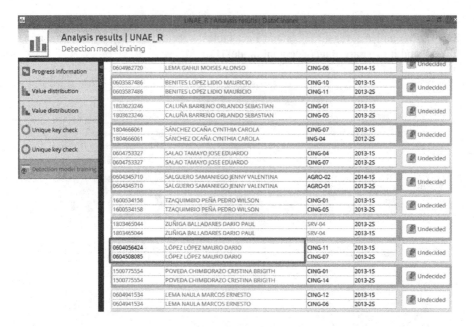

Fig. 6. Student data analysis results

In the fourth phase, "Data Transformation", the source data was loaded using ETLs created in Pentaho Data Integration - pdi-ce-5.4.0.1-130. Spoon[1]. The outcome was a DW, the first product of KDD, which was stored in PostgreSQL 9.3[2]. Figure 7 shows one of the programmed ETL was used to secure the information in the DW.

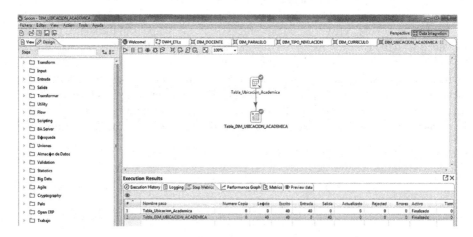

Fig. 7. Academic location dimension

---

[1] http://community.pentaho.com/projects/data-integration/.
[2] http://www.postgresql.org.es/.

The fifth, sixth, and seventh phases choosing the appropriate DM task, choosing the DM algorithm, and Using the DM algorithm, fall under the DM subprocess. The following classification algorithms: Decision Trees and Bayesian Networks were chosen because they generate rules for the classification and hierarchy of a set of data that can easily be translated into business rules and possible events when identifying knowledge sources, such as the new study areas of knowledge with strong female selection, the majority of students per year. Linear Regression and Sequential minimal optimization were used to make predictions based on random data and to obtain patterns from the information from the study areas of the careers chosen by male and female students, being the most important the preferences of careers over the next few years. In Fig. 8, one of the patterns obtained during these phases is shown using WEKA Developer 3.7.13[3].

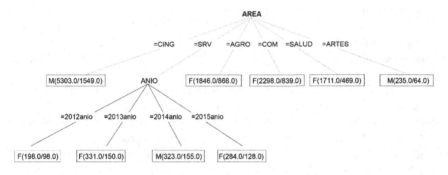

Fig. 8. DM - decision trees - areas of study and gender of students

The generated patterns were evaluated in the eighth phase, "Evaluation", so that in the ninth and last phase "Using the discovered knowledge", knowledge could be generated within the academic area of the UNAE - ESPOCH.

The most valuable knowledge extracted from the analysis was information related to the number of students in each area and their gender. The greatest number of students of ESPOCH in the years 2012, 2013, 2014 and 2015 were students in the area of Engineering, with a total of 5303 students. 29% of the students were of the feminine gender and 71% the masculine gender. Also, in the last four years, the second most popular area is Sales and Marketing, which has generated a total of 2298 students, 37% men and 63% women. The area in third place in the number of students is Agriculture with a total of 1846 students. 47% of these students are men. In the area of Arts, which only includes the career of Graphic Design, the majority of students were men. In the area of Services, 2014 had the most students, 323, and 48% of the students were women.

The number of male students represents 53% of the total number of students. Although slightly higher, it shows that the difference between the two genders is almost equal. The final year investigated, 2015, was the year in which there was the highest number of women students.

---

[3] http://www.cs.waikato.ac.nz/ml/weka/.

ESPOCH is projected to increase in students over the next 3 years. We anticipate having 7576 students for the 2018 semesters. Engineering has the highest number of male and female students. For female students, the second largest area is the Sales & Marketing and for male students, it is Agriculture.

Finally, there was a growth in the total number of students between 2012 and 2013 of 33%, a decrease between 2013 and 2014 of 3%, and a 52% increase between 2014 and 2015 in students who entered ESPOCH.

6   Conclusions

Through this experimental research, it has been possible to create a proposal of KDD methodology appropriate to the requirements of the placement and admissions units of Ecuadorian public universities using ESPOCH as a reference. This schema proposes nine stages of development. The first four are within the Data Warehouse subprocess and coupled with the HEFESTO version 2.0 methodology. The five remaining phases fall under the Data Mining subprocess and allow us to investigate useful algorithms for knowledge discovery. The results of applying all the phases resulted in three final outcomes. The first was a DW utilizing the constellation schema hosted in PostgreSQL 9.3 which consists of nine dimensions and three fact tables that contained reliable information. The data passed through cleaning phases and ETLs, ensuring the reliability of the information. The second result included DM patterns that produced the identification of academic information of the students by careers, and also boasted high percentages of reliability. Finally, the third outcome was the generation of knowledge for making decisions relating to student admissions in the different areas of knowledge and identification of the career preferences of different genders in ESPOCH. The information can be considered correct, consistent, and adequate for the academic processes in this department.

Perhaps the most significant piece of knowledge generated was identifying that the area of study of Engineering is the career choice that attracts the most students. That is appropriate considering that, in a Polytechnic School, the greatest number of vocations offered are technical. Noteworthy, too, is that, in this area of study, only about 30% of students are female. The Sales and Marketing area ranks second with the largest number of female students. In the area of Agriculture, in spite of the fact that it is a career whose distinction is land and countryside, more than 50% of students are women.

The final outcome of this generated knowledge allows ESPOCH to point to a projection of an increase in students to 7576 for the 2018 semesters, which suggests the need for planning and construction of more infrastructure and laboratories. Likewise, it intimates the implementation of strategies for postulation of potential applicants who want to choose ESPOCH as their option to develop professionally. With the knowledge of the tendencies of each gender when applying in the different careers, it is possible to present a more attractive offer that combines distinct social, political, economic, environmental, and cultural dimensions.

References

1. Fernández, T., Duarte, A., Hernández, R., Sánchez, Á.: GRASP aplicado al problema de la selección de instancias en KDD (2010)
2. Juan, I., Moine, M., Gordillo, D.S., Ana, D., Haedo, S.: Proyectos de minería de datos, pp. 931–938 (2011)
3. Asencios, V.V.: Data Mining y el descubrimiento del conocimiento. Ind. Data **7**(2), 83–86 (2004)
4. Fayyad, U., Piatetsky-Shapiro, G., Smyth, P.: From data mining to knowledge discovery in databases. AI Magazine **17**(3), 37 (1996)
5. Maimon, O., Rokach, L.: Data Mining and Knowledge Discovery Handbook, pp. 22–38. Springer, Boston (2010). https://doi.org/10.1007/978-0-387-09823-4
6. Aluja, T.: La Minería de Datos, entre la Estadística y la Inteligencia Artificial. Qüestiió **25**(3), 479–498 (2001)
7. Daza Vergaraym, A.: Data Mining, Minería de Datos, Primera. Editorial Macro, Lima (2016)
8. Moine, M., Haedo, S., Gordillo, D.S.: Estudio comparativo de metodologías para minería de datos. XVII Congreso Argentino de Ciencias de la Computación, CACIC 2011 (2011). http://sedici.unlp.edu.ar/bitstream/handle/10915/20034/Documento_completo.pdf?sequence=1. Accessed 03 Dec 2015
9. Inmon, B.: Building the Datawarehouse. Wiley Computer Publishing, New York (1998)
10. Kimball, R.: The Datawarehouse Toolkit. Wiley Computer Publishing, New York (1996)
11. Inmon, B.: Data warehousing 2.0 modeling and metadata strategies for next generation architectures. In: Architecture, p. 13 (2010)
12. Bernabeu, R.: Hefesto, p. 146 (2010)
13. Bradley, P., Fayyad, U.M., Mangasarian, O.: Data mining: overview and optimization opportunities. INFORMS J. Comput. **11**, 217–238 (1999)

Author Index

Printed in the United States
By Bookmasters